journey

journey

FROM POLITICAL ACTIVISM TO THE WORK

⌒

JANET ROSE

HOHM PRESS
PRESCOTT, ARIZONA

COVER DESIGN:

Kim Johansen, San Francisco, California

LAYOUT AND DESIGN:

Celina Taganas-Duffy, Tustin, California

www.taglineinc.com

LIBRARY OF CONGRESS CATALOGING-IN-PUBLICATION DATA

Rose, Janet, 1949-
   Journey : from political activism to the work / Janet Rose.
      p. cm.
   Includes bibliographical references.
   ISBN 1-890772-09-7 (alk. paper)
      1. Rose, Janet, 1949- 2. Hohm community—Biography. 3. Spiritual biography—
      United States 4. Psychotherapists—United States—Biography. 5. Spiritual life.
      I. Title.

BP605.H58 R67 2001
299'.93—dc21
[B]
                                                                00-054212

HOHM PRESS
P.O. Box 2501
Prescott, AZ 86302
800-381-2700
http://www.hohmpress.com

This book was printed in the U.S.A. on acid-free paper using soy ink.
   04   03   02   01   5   4   3   2   1

TO MY TEACHER

To my Teacher
  and my Teacher's Teacher
    and to the lineage of the Teaching
      from which they flower and which they serve.

CONTENTS

~

PREFACE

*I*n our age, and in our Western society, the life of a devotee committed to a spiritual path defined and oriented around relationship to a guru is not common. Why would a radical feminist, peace activist, liberally educated psychotherapist, intellectual, and member of Phi Beta Kappa raised on political analysis and political solutions choose the path of participation in a spiritual community based on principles of renunciation, individual and communal transformation, and obedience to the guidance of a guru? To answer that question is to throw the light of inquiry onto the very foundation of our Western humanist society. It is to point toward a matrix of divine reality in which I believe the human animal develops and finally emerges, as a butterfly from the chrysalis, into a possibility that is beyond the imaginings of those whose vision is limited to dimensions we can see.

Yet, the American ideal of independence and freedom originally held its meaning within a matrix of spiritual understanding. The Founding Fathers voiced their commitment to the right of each person (at the time, of each man) to pursue spiritual growth in his own way. Stripped over time of its spiritual matrix, the principle of individual freedom has come perilously close to a crass justification for personal license and depravity. As a culture, we have been taught a kind of separative independence which is really dependence on doing things stubbornly and, perhaps fatally, our own way. In the United States we allow gross avarice and aggrandizement by individuals while we refuse, as a political body, to finance even the most minimal provision of food and shelter not only for adults but even for children. Many of the political arguments of our day and the considerations about cults and the risks of trusting spiritual authority are thin cloaks intended to disguise our resistance to living with nobility and compassion in relation either to the citizens of our own country or to the world community.

Simultaneously, the planet itself is struggling to survive under the impact of the barren fruits of American consumption and individual and collective irresponsibility. Yet, that essential commitment of the Founding Fathers to freedom to pursue one's spiritual path within the protections of political democracy still has a beneficial effect. In the United States we are guaranteed the freedom to explore spiritual paths to a degree that has allowed our country to become a focal point for the meeting of the spiritual traditions of East and West. We have the chance to integrate the true creative, intelligent independence of the West with the capacity for devotion, obedience, and adherence to a lineage of the East—to participate in grounded education and growth through relationship to a living spiritual community and teacher.

This book tells the story of apprenticeship to a master, in the old-fashioned sense of learning a craft. It is a story of apprenticeship to the deepest craft—to the practical work through which the human can carry out service to the divine. It is an account of work with a teacher in one small spiritual school centered on an ashram in the high desert plateaus of Arizona.

Throughout the ages, human beings have gathered in small spiritual schools under the instruction of a teacher or master. The names of some of these teachers, such as Jesus and Buddha, are widely known in our Western culture. Others, such as Pythagoras in ancient times or G. I. Gurdjieff in our contemporary era, may be vaguely familiar. In some cases we know only what a school produced, such as the mystical poetry to the divine Beloved written by Jalal al-Din Rumi.

In earlier periods, apprenticeship to a master was a typical method by which young people learned arts and crafts, from woodworking to sculpture. Even in our own time, we don't consider it strange for a person to apprentice to a master sculptor or a film director or a computer whiz. Yet apprenticeship in the field of spiritual work has always remained a challenge embraced by relatively few.

In apprenticeship in a physical craft, it is generally well understood that the apprentice begins with learning what appear to be small and even unimportant skills: how to carve shavings to kindle a wood fire, for example. These basic skills are the foundation for the much more complex and demanding skills that finally refine and transform the apprentice into a skilled artisan, perhaps even a master.

Similarly, in a spiritual school the work begins with small tasks and demands for simple kindness and generosity in relationships with others, obedience and precision in handling basic responsibilities, and growing awareness that can begin to shift the deeply rooted self-reference in which most of us live. As we demonstrate reliability in these foundational areas, we show our readiness to gradually assume larger responsibilities. The process can seem at times excruciatingly slow, as we work with the refinement not of a physical craft but of our own being. At other times the same process can move with a speed and intensity of demand that hurls us into a raging river of confrontation with our deeply-held fantasies and illusions.

Some spiritual communities combine inner attention with a major focus on outer social service. Liberation theologians in the Catholic faith, the Peacemakers in the Zen tradition led by Bernie Glassman, and the nuns of Mother Teresa working in the streets of India offer inspiring examples of that path. Yet, although I come from a background of social activism and idealistic political vision, I find myself in a school that works not through political action or social service but through the arts—music, theater, and writing—and through a basically renunciate lifestyle that focuses attention on the mystical reality of the divine expressed through ordinary life.

Beyond the focus of individual work, as we mature the possibility develops for participation in work as a bonded, unified group. This kind of work generally takes place within the framework of a spiritual community. Within that larger body, smaller groups can serve as organs or centers of energy, which contribute to the community's functioning and service. Just as a more complex body in an animal species makes possible a greater range of sensitivity and creativity, so the development of a more complex group body made up of individual units enables the group organism to work in a wider and deeper range of awareness and action.

In building such a body, it is essential that we continually align ourselves more deeply with our real purposes. It is in this process of deepening alignment that the help of the teacher is particularly important as a safeguard both for ourselves and for society. If we as humans build a group body that invites energies of cruelty or selfishness to inhabit it, we give those energies a door to take deeper root in the body of humanity. Greed, for example, can manifest more powerfully and destructively through a group body than through an individual. On our planet we now have massive multinational corporations such as weapons manufacturers, pharmaceutical drug companies, and even huge clothing companies that exemplify a level of greed that leads to mass social irresponsibility and dehumanization. On the other hand, if we build a group body that invites energies of kindness, wisdom, and compassion to inhabit it, we open a door to a deeper rooting of those energies within our human realm. In the former case, we open the door to energies, or entities, that can destroy us. In the latter, we open the door, through our shared group work, to energies that can lift us beyond our individual capacities into a life of unified creativity, inspiration, and service.

In Part One I have focused on my initial introduction to and integration into the body of the *sangha* (spiritual community)*—and into work with the master, Lee Lozowick, who guides and teaches this particular group body. Part Two describes the setting of roots and a progressively refined engagement of and entry into subtler forms of demand and responsibility within the Work and the Hohm community. In Part Three I have focused in particular on the teaching that is communicated through daily life with the teacher and on the extraordinary gift of my visit to India, to the feet of my master's master, the Indian saint, Yogi Ramsuratkumar, and to the cradle of ancient spiritual traditions which deeply inform our contemporary work. Stories and events are reported roughly chronologically, with commentary on the teaching lessons they engendered.

The book is written from memory, largely without the benefit of notes taken during the course of these inner and outer events. As a result, quotations are in general approximate, based in my best memory and understanding of what was said. I hope that this account, if not precisely accurate in the journalistic sense in every detail, is true to the spirit, the core reality, of these events and this life engaged in the company of the teacher.

Most of us begin spiritual work with a set of characteristics, habits, and dynamics that make us almost totally predictable to any astute observer. It is this mechanicality that makes us so easily manipulated by those who wish to use others for their own abuses of power. Our fear of such manipulation is part of what fuels our fear of authority, our fear of being duped by spiritual cults. In fact, it is that in ourselves which manipulates us, our own attachment to egoic power and autonomy, that fears the real teacher and fights this process of deepening self-knowledge. Yet real spiritual work,

---

* *Most italicized words and many terms specific to this Teaching are defined in the Glossary.*

and real spiritual authority, take us in the direction of penetrating self-observation which begins to free us from our mechanical activity. We become able to choose based not on predictable and entrenched desires and prejudicial attachments and opinions, but from the basis of real clarity. As we begin to experience moments of clarity and self-observation without judgment, we experience also an inherent desire to penetrate more deeply into the realms of the Real. A teacher who can help us do this ceases to appear as a fearsome threat and becomes a guiding light for which we are profoundly grateful. We begin to experience the teacher—the master—as the spiritual Friend.

At the beginning of the spiritual path we are worked with as largely unconscious objects, responding as separate individuals to the guiding pressures and direction which we inchoately sense. As our work progresses, we engage increasingly conscious participation in the evolutionary process which is guiding both our individual development and our integration into a group, a larger body of work, as part of a yet larger pattern in which many spiritual schools and paths participate.

My point of view is unabashedly theistic. This is my experience: that a Supreme Being exists and informs this entire created universe; that this Being, while never fully known, is One with whom we come into deepening relationship, a relationship in which we discover both the personal and the impersonal nature of Love. At the same time, in considerations and shared work with friends and co-workers in non-theistic traditions such as Buddhism, I find no essential conflict in our practices or our purposes. It may seem that such a fundamental difference in perception must by nature divide us from each other in the directions of our work; yet I find that regardless of how we perceive this great question of spiritual reality, the varied spiritual traditions on our planet support and complement each other as we grow toward realization of a reality beyond our mental comprehension. It is my hope that this book may speak to those of the non-theistic traditions as their offerings have spoken to me and inspired me in my work. My intent is simply to speak clearly what I have experienced and to feed this experience into a common process of spiritual growth in which we can support each other regardless of differences and similarities in our traditions.

A society that shuts out the numinous, the world of spirit, the practical and subtle influence of a larger reality, and vests its trust instead in the cold and finally fatal comfort of unlimited material consumption, or even in the humanist-based power of psychological maturity, is a society that divorces itself from the roots of life itself—from the source of creation and evolution. The ancient term for this pride of the human that trusts itself as the final authority is "hubris." Our society has gone far in this direction of the rejection of the gods.

This is a story about life based in the choice of faith—faith in larger realities which encompass and guide and nourish our human evolution and which demand from us in return our growth in self-knowledge, in compassion for others, and in service to a greater process of evolution in which we are tiny and yet perhaps pivotal participants. This particular story, which happens to be my own, is simply one facet of the human story.

PART I

THE CALL

"When we are ready, the teacher will call us."
—Lee Lozowick, Mexico seminar, spring 1999

CHAPTER I

A NEW DIRECTION

~

M y story begins with a question. When did the interweaving first begin? When did the hand of the Great Process of Divine Evolution first pick up this strand that "I" am and begin to add it to the living design that is this particular path of spiritual life—life in the Hohm community in the company of the tantric master Lee Lozowick?

Did this interweaving begin when I was born? Or in ancient lifetimes, vast aeons before this age of the millennium with its computers and technology, its ecological crisis, and its spiritual angst? Or in the dream where I first met Lee, years before I met him in a physical body; a dream in which he began to give me healing for wounds I did not yet know I had? Did it begin with my own private spiritual experiences as a child and young teenager, experiences for which I could find no contemporary religious form that seemed to fit?

Perhaps it does not matter. Yet beginnings influence direction. Where and how we begin directly affects the path along which we will walk and the goals we will reach. For me, some moments on this path have felt full of compassion and gentle guidance; others have fiercely confronted and challenged my entire worldview.

I have come to believe that relationship is a deeper good than individual liberation; and that relationship with the teacher is the central and focalizing relationship which opens the way not only to all human relationships but even to my relationship with God Himself, with the ultimate Divine. As we mature, relationship opens the possibility of achieving among a bonded group an enlightened state that has the potential for catalytic and alchemical effects in our world beyond our imagination. Unreachable as this goal may seem, even the work toward it releases transformative energies with a psychic power comparable, on the physical level, to that of nuclear fusion.

The process of bonding may begin even before we have any conscious relationship with the teacher and the group with whom we will work. Two years before I physically met Lee, I experienced an unexpected and profound shift in my relationship to the realm of the divine. It was, in retrospect, the first hint of the path that was beginning to open before me. The moment of that shift is beyond the sequential processes of time and space. Though my contact with it ebbs and flows, it remains a present moment.

It is the spring of 1985: a lovely afternoon in the green and flowering suburbs of Atlanta, Georgia. (I later learned that at about this time Lee was visiting Atlanta for the first time, at the invitation of one of his students. But at the time I had never heard of Lee Lozowick, nor of the Way of Longing on which he walks.) I am spring-cleaning in the backyard of the house where I live alone—except for my dog, a Siberian husky as stubborn as myself—at the edge of a shady wood. For almost seven years I have been deeply involved in a small spiritual group, working closely with the teacher and a few other long-term students. In that time I have had a variety of spiritual experiences: deep personal confrontations, ecstatic meditative

states, and participation in the consistent daily work that is at the founda-
tion of spiritual life.

    Yet now an experience begins to open that is different from any I have
had before. Suddenly, without warning, the entire space in which I am
standing begins to change. The air around me, my mind, my feelings, and
my own body are suffused with a Presence whose orientation to life over-
takes and—for a moment—totally shifts my small human perspective. I have
known divine Presence many times before, in meditation and in daily life,
in overwhelming moments that I can remember even back into earliest
childhood. But the Presence on this rare afternoon carries an entirely dif-
ferent mood from anything I have yet experienced. It is the first hint of the
lineage toward which I am inwardly, if not yet consciously, turning.

    I have previously experienced God as Love. Now I experience God as
Lover. I am held and embraced by a personal tenderness, an infinite
acceptance, and a mysterious, indefinable sweetness. For the first time it
dawns on me that not just the great impersonal love of agape but the deeply
personal, intimate love of Eros which we find with a human lover is actu-
ally a reflection of a pervading quality of divine Love.

This was my first glimpse of the divine as Beloved, a mystical
relationship exemplified in the shattering relationship of Rumi to
his teacher, the beggar Shams; in the meeting of bride and
Bridegroom in the poems of St. John of the Cross; and in the
dance of the gopis with Krishna under the autumn full moon in
the poetry of Indian scriptures. At the time, however, I knew little
of any of the classic traditions from which these mystical relationships arose. What I was experiencing was something quite new in
my own relationship to the divine.

    I was steeped in spiritual work as a deeply practical process of
self-observation, of bonding within a working group, and of commitment to service. I had never encountered a divine Beloved who
held me with greater tenderness than any human lover. Years later

I heard Mother Tessa Bielecki, leader of a Carmelite community in Colorado, speak about spousal prayer. Her description of the relationship of some celibates to the divine as one of sacred marriage fit remarkably closely with what I experienced that spring day in Atlanta.

I had a copy of the *Bhagavad Gita*, given to me by a Hare Krishna devotee in an airport years earlier, which tells the story of Krishna as a king and a warrior, but I had read little of it. I had yet to discover the *Bhagavata Purana*, in which a wise teacher instructs King Pariksit, helping him to understand relationship to Krishna as the consummate embodiment of the divine as Lover. Only years later would I find that the translation of this text by Father James Redington serves as a central focus of study in the Hohm community. In the introduction to his work, *Vallabhacarya on the Love Games of Krshna*, Father Redington explains that a devotee may approach Krishna through one of several major moods of relationship, including that of friendship, of parental love, and of Lover. This last, relationship with the Beloved, is the mood of the *gopis*, the women who meet Krishna in the forest by the Yamuna River under the autumn full moon.

According to Father Redington, there is a further stage to this relationship of lover to Beloved into which the *gopis* are thrown: that of "love-in-separation," in which the *gopis* discover that after the consummate play of love, their Lover has left them; he has apparently abandoned them in the forest. At that moment, they enter into the relationship to the divine at which Lee has hinted in *The Only Grace Is Loving God* (Prescott, Ariz.: Hohm Press, 1982): the relationship of Longing, the specific human possibility of relationship to God as Beloved.

> Loving God . . . is the only true Gift of God to
> Mankind . . . The ancient Vedic scriptures say

that God grants Mukti or freedom to beings
quite easily but that He grants Bhakti or Love,
very selectively and rarely. Mukti or freedom
frees one from the binds of Earthly or human
concerns, while Bhakti or Love binds one to the
Earthly or human expression of the Beloved's
Whimsical possibility. And God is bound to the
Lover and free of the Mukti. Loving God is the
only Grace there is, and the possibility of Loving
God is a Grace to God from Mankind as well as
a Grace from God. Loving God is truly a
human, earthly Grace. (pp. 44-45)

This to me is the seminal presentation of Lee's teaching—the
aspect of Lee's school that is his unique contribution to the spiritual path.

On that spring afternoon I had my first taste of the possibility of that grace that Lee refers to as "Loving God." I glimpsed
depths of real feeling. I knew that I was accepted in my humanness,
in my emotionality, in my sexuality, in my physicality, in my
imperfectness, in my incarnate reality. All those emotions that
were forbidden to me as a child—deep anger and rage, sorrow, even
joy—all those emotions had space to breathe in the great embrace I
experienced. I knew that they have a place in the universe, and I
could enter that place without fear. Even fear itself could be
embraced and known and entered as an aspect of the Heart of God.

It was my first taste of the tantric path in which all dimensions of ordinary life are embraced as fields in which the most
esoteric work can take place: reality, or the divine, found within
the mundane planes of human existence. In this field of meeting,
all aspects of humanness are embraced, even honored—met with a
depth of caring and compassion that can allow these crass ele-

ments of the unrefined human to shift and melt in the crucible of divine passion—divine embrace—into a transformed and transformative possibility of true being. Many popular texts discuss and pretend to represent the tantric path, focusing on the use of sexual energy as a titillating and fascinating attraction for the Western mind. What I experienced that day included sexual aspects of the human as simultaneously ordinary and potentially transformative currents within *the unified whole* of the human as expression of the divine. It was the experience of embrace of all things *as they are* that made possible the opening of these ordinary elements into something extraordinary.

Perhaps what I felt was the paradoxical opposite to the human adoration of the divine. It was the divine's adoration of the human—adoration in the sense of an energy that awakens the quintessential reality at the core of a human being. Adoration as a mother adores her child in the moment of birth. Adoration of divine innocence revealed within the awakening heart of a child as the representative of divine incarnation. Adoration of the lover, which is again—but from a different point of view—the adoration of the divine discovered whole and inherent within the human.

It seems paradoxical and indeed inexplicable that the animal nature and the divine capacity of the human should have the potential to express through the same external form: in the meeting of masculine and feminine in the fire of sexual encounter. Yet this is perhaps what creates the intensity of the edge of possibility that can open through sexual energy—an energy that can take us to both the depths and the heights of human experience.

To use this energy does not necessitate, though it can sometimes involve, physical sexual engagement. St. John of the Cross wrote some of the most beautiful mystical poetry in human history, poetry that uses the metaphor and currents of sexual passion to express the meeting of human and divine that takes place beyond any physical form or encounter. St. Teresa of Avila spoke passionately of the marriage in Christ—to God as the Beloved—which the celibate nun or monk engages.

I had always believed that I saw human marital and sexual relationships as potential building blocks in spiritual life. On that spring afternoon I realized that I had seen the relationship of human couples as being somehow a "lesser" level of spiritual work. Yet in this experience of the divine as Lover, I glimpsed a possibility for sexual energy, in both celibacy and in the physical relationship between couples, to directly serve fields of divine work that I had never glimpsed before. For the first time I knew that divine Presence embraced me not just as a celibate practitioner but as a woman—as someone to be loved and cherished at every level, from the most subtly energetic to the most intimately physical. And in the field of this cherishing, I became able to open areas of myself that had been locked away from my conscious knowledge, areas that held tremendous power and possibility for my spiritual work.

E. J. Gold, a powerful and enigmatic American teacher, teaches that to unlock secrets and potentialities for work that are locked within the feminine, a man must approach a woman with adoration. The effect of the quality of adoration that I experienced that afternoon was to unlock hidden areas within myself that I did not know existed.

Vallabhacarya comments on this possibility:

> Therefore the Joy of worshipping Kṛṣṇa through love becomes established perfectly in women. Men will come to experience it through them, and in no other way . . . For women alone can taste this Joy, and then a man can taste it in women. This is why the Blessed Lord Kṛṣṇa delighted in love with

women day and night. This He did in two ways—
internally and externally—but the internal is the
supreme reward. (Redington, J. *Vallabhcarya's
Commentaries on the Love Games of Kṛṣṇa*, New
Delhi: Motilal Benarsidass, 1983, p. 49)

When I heard Mother Tessa Bielecki speak at the Conference
on Crazy Wisdom years later, she seemed to indicate the possibility of this internal relationship in the sacred marriage between the
celibate nun and Christ. Not just her description but her entire
way of being communicated an embrace of Christ or God as Lover;
a relationship in which sexual and physical energies of the human
are neither carelessly indulged nor rigidly repressed and rejected
but are fully lived and lifted into a meeting with the divine.

The divine Presence that suffused my world on that spring
afternoon had no name; if anything, I felt simply the divine reality I call God.

Looking back, I would say that over a year before my first
physical meeting with Lee the interweaving of this strand that is
myself into the pattern of this school began to make itself visible in
practical changes in my life. In the same year as my spring
epiphany, a few weeks before Christmas the teacher of the group I
was involved with at the time came to me and asked me to leave the
group temporarily. I was devastated. The group was my entire life.
To leave it, even for six months as he recommended, was worse
than a divorce; for me it was death. It was only much later that I
could remember a moment in November, a month earlier, when I
had made an inner decision: "I will act in such a way—rejecting and
angry and rebellious—that my teacher will have to ask me to leave. I
will keep doing this for however long is necessary."

It took one month from this point of decision, made and
then buried in my unconscious, to the evening my teacher came to

my house and recommended a leave of absence from the group. In retrospect, I would say that something in me knew that my direction was no longer with that group, but to reject and separate from my first teacher was something I could not find it in myself to do except by making him reject me. If there was any fault in the situation, it would be mine and not his. I was the one who had been unworkable. It was unconsciously the way I found to leave with honor; honor for him. (Ironically, it was during this same month, in December of 1985, that the Hohm Community was publishing an issue of its quarterly journal, *Divine Slave Gita*, entitled "How to Leave a School.")

After my teacher left the house that December evening I meditated with utmost intention on what I was to do. I knew that I was responsible to persevere in an inner obligation, even if it meant I was totally alone. I was responsible to an essential spiritual path, even if I did not know how to carry out this responsibility. Yet I knew no one to whom I could turn for help; no one who might have the slightest understanding of the work I was trying to do. I knew almost nothing of other spiritual groups. I knew only the group in which I had worked, which was not connected to a specific tradition.

My inner sense said very clearly: "*Go somewhere where you know no one. Make no contact with friends and family. You are making a leap over a gap, and in order to complete it you must have no distractions. Even the bonds of ordinary human relationship are a distraction at this point. You must have the space to see and act with absolute clarity.*"

At the time, of course, I had no idea what this gap might be, except the inner gap between my essential commitment to spiritual work and my ability or willingness to act on that commitment. I never imagined that I might be required to cross a physical gap of thousands of miles, as part of a leap into a different spiritual school. Looking back, I can see how easily I could have turned to family and friends on the East Coast, found a good job as a psychotherapist through my personal connections, and quickly been saddled with the baggage of responsibilities to my job, my clients, my family and friends. Ordinary life could have swallowed me up as easily as a pond swallows a sinking stone, leaving no trace of the stone's movement. It would have become difficult—almost impossible—to make my way for no external reason to a small cowboy town in Arizona or to a study group hidden in the foothills of the Rockies in Boulder, Colorado.

I turned again to my inner sense and asked for specific instruction about where to go. "*Go to Boulder, Colorado,*" was the clear message. I could not believe I was hearing correctly. "This must be the first attempt at distraction," I thought to myself. Though I had never been to Boulder, I had the impression from others' reports that it was a yuppie town that had lost touch with a spiritual energy that had been present in the early '70s. And my brother lived near there. (As it turned out he lived over an hour away, but at the time I was unfamiliar with the wide distances of the West.)

This could not be the "place where I knew no one" that my first sense indicated. It must be my resistance interfering with the communication. I turned inward again for the specific name of a place to move. Again I registered Boulder, Colorado, but convinced that this was my resistance, I waited for a different destination.

"*Go to Durham, North Carolina,*" I was told (since I was obviously not going to accept Boulder as my destination).

My sense was to leave Atlanta for my new location almost immediately, to complete my physical move as a way of building momentum toward the inner leap that was required. For years I had been living on a minimal income so I could devote my energy to spiritual work. I had just enough money to pay essential bills and drive east toward North Carolina with one hundred twenty dollars cash in my wallet. I had no credit cards; no contact with family or friends who would gladly have given me whatever money I needed. I was working within exact and absolute limitation.

I arrived in North Carolina and found a motel that would give me a weekly rate of one hundred dollars. That meant I had one week and twenty dollars with which to settle myself in Durham. I made calls to temporary agencies for work, but it was the week before Christmas and no one was hiring. I had no money to offer prospective landlords, and no prospect of getting any for at least two weeks. I had a roof for only one week. Yet I did not feel hopeless. I was in a state of faith. Perhaps by the action of risk and commitment that I made when I drove out of Atlanta with my one hundred twenty dollars I opened the door to this flow of an energy whose presence I could not command but only welcome. I felt buoyed by this energy, carried by a stream of trust and faith in divine Presence.

In retrospect, I realize I was living—spontaneously, as a result of simple obedience—as a beggar. It was an opportunity to align with the lineage toward which I was moving, the lineage of the Beggar Saint, Yogi Ramsuratkumar, and his spiritual son, Lee Lozowick (he of the sweatpants with holes, worn every day for weeks at a time, who begged for rice at the inception of his French ashram). This was not a passive faith, however; it demanded my continuing action, my response to its movement. I was not simply to wait for the universe to move and care for me. I had to reach out and beg. I kept calling agencies (which typically do not offer work in advance) and, uncharacteristically, one promised me a job starting January 2.

In the meantime a newspaper ad described exactly the place I wanted, but it seemed totally outside the realm of possibility. It was a small house in the country just outside of Durham, by a forest, with space for me to engage my inner work and for my dog to run.

Not to be daunted, I went to look at it, even though the landlord already had about twenty-five other people interested, all of whom undoubtedly had more than twenty dollars to offer. Unbelievably, he agreed to rent the house to me. He said he knew what it was like to get started in a new place; I had a guaranteed job, and he could wait for my first paycheck. So I had a home, a job, and the space to pursue the inner work that was demanded of me. I had given up all my human relationships for an indeterminate amount of time; yet in the midst of what could have been unutterable loneliness and despair, I was given instead the experience of the utmost abundance and limitless generosity of the divine, working through the ordinary humans around me. I was given the reminder and the affirmation that I was still a part of the human family, the human community, welcomed by these strangers and given by them the same trust that I had given to God.

During the next six months in Durham, I found a job doing word processing in the psychiatric department of the University of North Carolina Hospital. For the first three months I did my job and came home to confront a series of inner hells. I saw in myself the competitor, the aggressor, even the murderer. I saw the depths of hatred and deception hidden within my ordinary human relationships with those I loved. I saw that love was truly present, but it was twisted and even made impotent by these hidden currents. I looked into levels of my personal underworld, the collective unconscious, and the larger underworld, which feeds off of and reinforces our personal negativity. I saw depths of the human psyche that I could not possibly have faced if I had been in contact with anyone I professed to love or whose love I craved.

I was brought up to try to make things nice, and while the truth of God is more than nice and includes blissful harmony and union, it also includes fierce realities that we may experience as hell. To try to make Reality "nice" leads to pretense and deception.

The fact is that short of divine Reality there is the reality of the present human condition, which is one of profound woundedness. To try to deny that wounded nature in the human being—in myself and others—that lives not in divine harmony but in a separative state of violence and cruelty is unconsciously to allow those negative states to rule, while covering and even excusing them with a pretense that things are "nice."

In the safety and sanctuary of my solitary home in the woods I did not have to maintain these lifelong pretenses. I was free to look reality in the face as deeply as I could allow myself. (Deep as this was, I would discover years later that there were still deeper levels which I could not penetrate alone; that I could explore only through the confrontation and support of group work within community.) In that face I saw both hells and heavens. Much of what I confronted in those months was not pleasant—was in fact even agonizing—but it was profoundly liberating. I felt tremendously alive and grateful for this opportunity that was given me to live so closely with God.

At the end of six months in Durham I was beginning to build a counseling practice and was working four jobs to make enough money to pay the costs of opening an office. I left the house before dawn to deliver newspapers along suburban streets. I worked at U.N.C. during the day. After work I would take counseling appointments. On weekends I waited tables at a local family restaurant. Meanwhile I was also going through an interviewing process for an interesting and lucrative job as counselor for a weight loss clinic run by a doctor highly respected throughout the region. If I got this job I would be assured not only a stable income from the job itself but a burgeoning private practice, as many of the patients at the clinic would become my private clients as well, to engage more intensive psychotherapeutic work. My guaranteed annual income, at a minimum, would be three times as much as I had ever made in my life. I was on the third round of interviews with the clinic director, and it was clear that I would most likely be offered the job at the end of the week.

It was at this point, as I planted marigolds on a Sunday afternoon during a few free hours before waiting tables for Sunday dinner, that I received a sudden, shocking inner instruction to drop everything and make another move. *"Go to the Rocky Mountains outside Boulder, Colorado, for a three-month retreat. It is time to set something right in your relationship with Me."*

At the time I felt this communication simply as divine demand from that great Presence which I call God. Now I realize that Presence was more specific than I could then understand. It was perhaps the second major experience of Lee's presence in my inner world. The one with whom I needed to set things right was the one who was calling me, from across the plains and deserts of both inner and outer worlds, telling me, "the time has come." I sat down, motionless, under the tall pines. I was in total shock, yet I had no question about the validity of the communication. It was an experience of intense, inescapable guiding presence. I could deny it only at the peril of my inner life.

Although I was achieving a lot externally, I had nothing to lose by acting on faith. My clients could be responsibly referred to other counselors in the area. I was in touch with no friends or family who would be embarrassed or frightened or deeply hurt by my sudden move or my crazy behavior. The only risk was for myself; and I was willing to take that risk, trusting this inner guidance as I had trusted it before. Because I had obeyed the instruction in December to have no contact with personal friends or family, I had no emotional entanglements, which for me would have been far harder to escape than the financial and professional temptations. I had disobeyed the instruction to go to Boulder in December out of distrust of myself; nevertheless, I had acted with sufficient obedience that I was now free to obey this new instruction.

As I sat on the ground under the pines in shock, registering clearly that I was to leave for Colorado, the inner instruction continued with exacting and specific details. I was to begin breaking my ties to North Carolina immediately. "*Leave in two weeks,*" was the clear instruction. "*If you wait longer, you will lose momentum. If you wait six weeks, you will not go.*"

I knew that while this inner communication held power for me in the moment, if I did not act on it with immediacy I would lose touch with the realm where it was founded. Ordinary life would grasp me in its claws and sear my consciousness with outraged accusations about the gullibility and idiocy that were prompting me to consider giving up all I was building for some voice in my head (or heart). I had to choose in that moment, and I had to act on my choice. Otherwise, inaction would kill what was, in that instant, alive.

In the Quaker faith in which I grew up, stories abound of those who heard the call of an inner voice that demanded radical actions that would seem inexplicable and even crazy to conventional minds. This inner instruction calls us and directs us in many small ways throughout every day; yet there are, for most of us, particular points where dramatic transitions are required. If we listen in those moments, our lives jump to a higher level of possibility. We may skip huge detours and find ourselves synchronized with a larger movement that carries us like the current of a river rolling boisterously and irresistibly toward the ocean. This for me was one of those moments. I had heard the call of a flute, and I had the chance to leave everything and answer it.

Unfortunately, I did not leave quite everything. While I sold most of my belongings at a yard sale when I left Georgia and divested myself of belongings again before leaving Durham, at both

17

times I kept just a little more than I could fit in my Datsun. My addiction to the collections of a packrat ruled over common sense and my inner sense, and in each case I rented a small storage locker for the few treasures I could not take with me. When I left Atlanta I expected to return in six months; when I left Durham I expected to return in three months. Twenty-five dollars a month for a small storage locker seemed an inconsequential sum, adding up to a total of less than a hundred dollars for my entire prospective retreat. I did not see how it could possibly cause a problem. I did not foresee that it could be years before I would return to close those lockers. These tiny acts of disobedience would eventually cost me close to a thousand dollars.

Again I was facing a move for which I did not have the money. And this was a bigger move: more than halfway across the country, traveling alone in an old Datsun that did not inspire confidence in driving long distances. A month before, in fact, the Datsun had been about to die; its transmission was making throaty rattling noises.

In the endless serendipity of those months I briefly took a weekend job at a Waffle House where an elderly African-American man came each evening for coffee. He had a quiet kindness that was in marked contrast to many of the late-night devotees of the Waffle House, and on deserted shifts we struck up conversation—mainly me listening to the fascinating stories of his life. One night he heard the Datsun's death rattles as I pulled into the parking lot for work. He told me he could fix the transmission in his shop with the help of his sons. Two days later the Datsun was healed, the beneficiary of the laying on of hands of this old mechanic. In a sense, that car had been raised from the dead, resurrected or reborn. Little did I know that with the little Datsun as my chariot I myself was about to enter a process of rebirth that would come to its culmination in exactly nine months, when I would physically meet the man who would become my teacher.

So my Japanese chariot was ready and waiting. Yet, after only six months in a new place, I did not have enough money even for necessary repairs, new tires, and gas to drive to Colorado—let alone for renting a cabin in the mountains for my retreat. I could not possibly make enough money in two weeks for this level of expense—especially as I was being told to quit my jobs immediately except for the work at U.N.C. The chances of my getting a bank loan appeared to rest at zero. I had never had a credit card; I owned nothing for collateral, not even a television or computer; and I had lived in North Carolina only six months. Yet I had no other options. I met with the loan officer at my bank and answered her questions. I could not fully meet even one of the bank's requirements, but I did have positive references. The bank officer said she would consider the loan. I was to call back in a week. What I had not told her was that I also planned to leave town in a week.

Once again I was buoyed by a faith that might appear inexplicable to any rational person. I did not have enough money to reach Colorado, and the chances of being approved for the loan were less than slim. I had no other option for gathering the money in the remaining week. Yet I went ahead with my plans, systematically burning bridges behind me according to my inner instructions. I gave notice to my landlord, and he immediately found a family to move in the day I moved out. I worked the last day at my job and received my last paycheck. I told my clients I would be out of town for three months.

The morning I was to leave, I called the bank. The loan had been approved. I had one thousand dollars (and a credit card) with which to make the trip to Colorado and establish my three-month retreat.

ON THE ROAD

Ecstatic, replete with faith and cash, I headed west toward the lush blue-green heights of the Carolina hills, the Blue Ridge Mountains. I reached the mountains about sundown. As the night deepened, I drove through the darkened hills, up over the crests and down the other side, finding no motel with a vacancy, no light of human habitation in the protected forest area. Finally, in the early hours of the morning, in a forested valley, I saw a dim sign for a campground. To reach it I drove across a rickety bridge over a chortling river. The office was closed, but I found a campsite and immediately fell asleep.

The next morning I woke to the chatter of children mingling with the chuckling of the river. Looking out into the morning sunshine, I saw that the campground was filled with Native American families fishing by the river, washing clothes, and preparing breakfast. Mine was the only white face in sight. Having stumbled into the summer home of these tribespeople, I was treated with disinterested acceptance. Although some of the men fishing by the riverbank gave me coldly hostile stares, curiosity prompted several of the children to approach me. The women in the next campsites gave me warm smiles and went on with their cooking; when it was done they offered me breakfast.

There was an essential communion extending throughout this Native American community and the world of earth and spirit with which they lived harmoniously, fishing in the river in silence or sharing a relaxed camaraderie in the morning sunlight. Having blundered over the bridge that marked their territory during the night, I was accepted as part of their world. Once again it was clear that while I was asked to make choices that seemed to take me deeper into aloneness, these choices, however paradoxically, took me deeper into the center of the human community.

After breakfast I drove west again. Each day after that I drove through the changing worlds of the American South and Midwest. I would drive on the freeways for a while and then, unable to endure their endless monotony, I would take smaller roads, constantly traveling west. In Arkansas I drove past some of the poorest shacks I had ever seen—the dwellings of the legendary "white trash" of the South. The pale, pinched faces of obviously beaten children; the lifeless faces of the men who beat them, at the tiny gas stations— the existence of these humans appeared no better than that of their scrawny dogs. Worse, in fact, since somewhere in these human hearts rested the instinctual knowledge that their heritage, by birthright, is that of the divine. The dogs had the blessing of unconsciousness. In these humans consciousness might be buried, stillborn, or tortured, but the pain of its twisted denial contorted their faces. These lives were more poor, in spirit, than those of the Carolina tobacco pickers whose tarpaper shacks line the edges of the fields as one drives south toward the great sand dunes of the Atlantic Ocean, where man first learned to fly. In those tarpaper shacks live African-American descendants of slaves who are still enslaved to the production of wealth for huge corporations and their white bosses. Yet in those North Carolina shacks there was still some dim sense of tribal life and human community; in these Arkansas huts there was a sense of total loss of hope—a hopelessness that breeds hatred, a despair that is at the root of cruelty. The listlessness that hung in the air was unbearable. After a few miles I found this living death worse even than the dead sameness of the four-lane highways cut through the living earth, and I returned to the scenic drive across our "great America."

Death and life, ugliness and beauty, poverty and riches, the yin and the yang often lie so close together that we find one hidden within the other. Also in Arkansas I discovered one of the most beautiful, brilliantly alive places that I visited during the entire trip west. It was a state park in the Ozark Mountains, where trees hundreds of years old towered over lakes and rivers, and the spirits of the trees still dwelt with living presence among the hills. God is not lost or absent in the roads lined with shacks. He is only forgotten, so that despair blocks the door through which He could enter our hearts.

As I drove on I felt strongly that inner presence, the guiding force that was leading me into the unknown, that accompanied me in this outwardly lonely journey across the vastness of American spaces and the unknown territories of my own inner terrain. At night, a single woman camping alone with only my dog (who was too friendly to serve as much of a guardian), I often felt fear and, not infrequently, terror, even though I carefully chose national campgrounds with rangers and a sense of safety about them. During the day I felt mostly excitement, a sense of adventure, and even an ecstatic joy that I have found emerges repeatedly in the act of obedience to a direction larger than my own. In fact, the joy is often proportionate precisely to the degree of sacrifice required to engage that act of obedience.

I would have said before this that I already knew guiding love: knew it intimately, having deeply loved and learned from family and friends, and having felt loved and wisely guided through years of my life. Yet now I experienced something different. I felt a power of Love acting directly upon me that began to teach me, through experience, dimensions that simultaneously revealed and dissolved some of the very motivations—such as fear and guilt—that had carried me this far in my work. It began to teach me about other, deeper motivations, such as the simple power of caring—of kindness, generosity, and compassion, which are central teachings in Lee's work.

Having opened to this shift in my inner direction but being far from able to hold it steady, I had set myself up to enact resistance to it. We humans are so mechanically and frustratingly pre-dictable, at least until we engage a level of self-observation that begins to take us down into the swampy roots from which our unconscious motivations drive us. In the external physical world, physicists have observed that every action breeds reaction. In the inner world, the same principle applies—at least as long as we are acting based in the mechanical dynamics of the untransformed human. Watching the teachers, I sense that it is possible to radical-ly shift the ground from which one acts to a field of subtle substance that behaves differently from the dense substance of human psychology and dynamics to which we are accustomed. In those higher planes, action feeds further action, so that synergy grows and momentum builds to possibilities we do not yet imagine. But I was definitely moving within the planes of typical human dynamics, where the mechanicality of the human machine creates predictable reaction to any action. I had acted, and now reaction was waiting in the wings. Its power of opposition would occupy center stage often in the days and months to come.

But for the moment I drove on across plains that felt as wide as the arms of God. As the land changed, I stopped here and there to swim in clear lakes, to climb a mountain where hawks flew over-head, or to eat in a roadside cafe where the lives of a whole community intersected and lay visibly outlined to the observing stranger. In small towns I would look for a spiritual bookstore and browse, perhaps striking up a conversation with the owner. I had never had much interest in Eastern spiritual paths, but in one small store I found a book on Krishna and Christ which captured my attention. I knew nothing about Krishna, and had never before wanted to know anything, but I bought the book and drove on. Always I had the sensation that I was driving deeper into the Heart that was calling me; that whatever was to be "set right" in my rela-tionship to God, the process had already begun as I drove west in

obedience to that call. Neither my terrors in the night nor the difficulties caused by my own resistance could truly interrupt the flow
of movement that had begun and that deepened ineluctably with
each day's drive west.

As I drove through New Mexico—through the strange, haunting shapes of rock and mountain plateaus shaped by wind and sand,
inhabited by the wounded yet still living spirits of early Native
American tribes—I began to feel a compelling impulse to continue
driving west for a few more days rather than turning north in
Albuquerque toward Colorado. I could drive west for a day or so
and then turn north to go through Utah, bringing me into the
heart of the Rockies on my way to Boulder. This impulse grew
stronger as the hours passed. I took out a map, perused it carefully, and folded it so that it showed the route I might take. Yet,
parallel to this magnetic attraction to something farther west, the
voice of fear began to arise again. My car was old and had just traveled over two thousand miles without a breakdown. How much
farther could it go? Wasn't I hearing an ominous sound from
somewhere in its entrails? If I turned north at Albuquerque, I
could visit this strange and attractive area of New Mexico and
Arizona at any time, with a newly repaired car and a home base to
which to return. And that noise—wasn't it getting louder?

To have a lesson demonstrated in action, in our lives, is what
Lee calls an "object lesson." At this opportunity to choose between
the habit of fear and the unknown possibility offered by that guiding sense, I once again chose fear. I turned north at Albuquerque.
The noise in the Datsun's intestines began to sound so loud that I
stopped at a garage to have the car checked out. The mechanic
found nothing wrong, and when I drove on again, the noise had
disappeared.

I drove toward Boulder, leaving the folded map in the glove
compartment. A year later, as I prepared to drive from Colorado

for my first visit to Lee's ashram in Prescott, Arizona, I pulled out this map, still folded from the summer before. It was folded to show the route west from Albuquerque to Prescott. The folded map perfectly defined Prescott as the endpoint of my westward journey. At the time, I had never heard of Prescott and did not even notice the name of the town that delimited my potential route.

BOULDER

So I drove north that day of choice, and by afternoon I reached Boulder. From what I had heard, I had been expecting a small town, but Boulder had grown. I drove past malls and condominiums with a sinking heart. This did not look like a place for spiritual retreat and renewal. Although I was heading for the mountains above Boulder, the look of the city did not offer confirmation that my inner sense to relocate there was correct. My reading in December—that this was a dead yuppie town—looked much more accurate.

I passed a park with a wide grassy hill and a stunning view of the Rockies rising into the endless Western sky. It was a warm August afternoon. I sat down and meditated for a few minutes while children scampered around me and kites flew from the hill. Then I looked up toward the mountains where I was to center for three months. They were lovely, living energies rising out of the solid earth: the nourishing breasts of the Mother and the stern, narrow-edged principles of the Father. I knew with a wide, embracing sense of the unity of all things that I had not made a mistake in coming. "All things are connected," in the words of the Ocmulgee tribe in Georgia. Whatever connections I was supposed to make, within myself and with divine purpose in my life, were in process as I turned from the grassy hillside toward these sheer peaks.

When I was done meditating I went to a phone booth at the edge of the park. In the yellow pages I found a message service, which I called to arrange for a phone number where people could leave me messages. I called the local paper and put an ad in the classifieds, to run the next day, advertising my Datsun. If I could sell it, I could use the money for a down payment on a newer car. Then I headed out of town looking for a campground.

On the way through town I passed a large brick building whose energy somehow drew my attention. A sign in front read, Naropa Institute. Facing the Institute, almost hidden behind flowering vines and bushes, was a lovely old Victorian house with an adjoining cottage. A sign said: Briar Rose Bed and Breakfast. I slowed down as I passed it. I felt as if I knew this place, or the people in it. That voice in my heart said clearly, "*This is the place to stay tonight.*" But I was intent on finding a campground, where I could stay for free or for much less than the cost of an elegant and pricey bed and breakfast establishment. It was the rational thing to do, of course, since even with the bank's generous loan, I had a limited amount of money with which to carry out the purpose for which I had been sent.

Outside Boulder, heading up into the mountains, I found a group of wooded campsites by a motel next to a dancing river; however, the motel was deserted and so were the sites, and a large sign forbade camping. I didn't relish the idea of sleeping in a deserted place alone, especially with the sense of some kind of disturbed energy that vaguely haunted the place. (Later I learned that the family who owned the motel had been forced out by a bank trying to foreclose on the property so it could be used to build condominiums.) There was, in fact, a lot of psychic disturbance permeating the place, and that voice in my heart was becoming a stronger pressure, a weight urging me to obey its direction and return to the Briar Rose.

I went back into town and looked for a cheaper place than this obviously upscale option. But the voice would not be still. The inner pressure increased and became a sense of urgency. *"This is the place to stay. Only this place,"* it said. I could not ignore it without facing that uncomfortable experience of inner disobedience, so I let go my miserly grip on my wallet and walked into the Briar Rose. As it happened, there was a small room available that night, not nearly so expensive as their usual rooms. I spent the night, and in the morning I came to the dining room for breakfast.

A tall, vibrant woman with eyes that were both penetrating and receptive met me as she came out of the kitchen. She was the manager and part-owner of the Briar Rose, and she was busy with a thousand details, from a wedding party in the afternoon to a piano concert in the living room scheduled for the next night. Yet there was an energetic connection between us that she seemed to recognize as instantaneously as I did. She sat down with me and we drank tea together and talked. She told me that she and the other co-owners of the Briar Rose were members of Chögyam Trungpa Rinpoche's Buddhist community; she had been with her teacher for about thirteen years. She was to become a friend—a kindred spirit—with whom I shared our distinct yet not unrelated passages during the next months; the only human being with whom I maintained a personal relationship during my mountain retreat.

I called the message service. There had been only one response to my ad for the car. Apparently a dowager Datsun was not a hot item on the upscale Boulder market. I returned the call. A man told me that he was interested in checking out the car, but he could not drive to meet me as he was with his small son at home and his ex-wife had his car. I drove to his house and he took the Datsun out for a test drive.

He smiled at me ruefully. "I'm looking for a car for my ex-wife, to replace the rattletrap she's driving now," he explained.

"But this car is no better than the one she has." He obviously felt chagrin that he had put me to the trouble of driving to his home only to find that there was no chance of a sale. "The least I can do is invite you in for tea, if you'd like," he added and, to my own surprise, I accepted his invitation. It was the only time I had accepted such an invitation except for a Christmas dinner at my neighbor's farmhouse in Durham half a year ago.

As the teakettle began to steam, the man's three-year-old son came into the kitchen and opened the refrigerator door with lively self-assurance, finding himself a snack. We began to talk, over tea. He told me he was part of a spiritual community led by a teacher named Lee Lozowick, with an ashram in Arizona. As he talked about his community, I realized that many of the principles of this community's work correlated with the principles I had learned and lived by. He even spoke of "the Work." I had never met anyone other than the few members of my original spiritual group who even knew this term, let alone understood some of its implications. (At the time I assumed that I understood more of its implications than this unknown community could possibly know. So much for assumptions!)

To my own utter astonishment, I found myself telling this total stranger, whom I had met just half an hour earlier, about my own spiritual group; about having been asked to leave and about my intention to engage a spiritual retreat in the mountains. I had never given the least hint of information about my spiritual group or my personal life to anyone during the six months in North Carolina. I had assumed there was no one outside my group who could possibly understand; and I had felt that the principle of conservation of energy around esoteric work demanded my silence. Now I was telling this man my entire story, and I had the astonishing sensation that it was feeding rather than dissipating work energy! I had an inexplicable sensation that a healing was beginning to take place for me as I spoke to him. I had no conscious idea that this man's teacher might be related to a dream I had had two years earlier in which an unknown master had healed me at the brink of death. When the conversation ended, I made another assumption. I assumed that this encounter, beneficial as it was, was complete, and that I was now to return to my focus on my solitary retreat. I thanked him and drove away.

I found a small cabin in the foothills where I could stay temporarily while I looked for the log cabin in the mountains that was to be the center for my retreat. I had seen this cabin clearly, through inner vision, when I had received the message about going to the Rockies. I knew that it existed and that I had only to find it. I studied the classifieds and made exploratory ventures along dirt roads among the peaks and high canyons.

Just when it seemed I had fruitlessly exhausted all possible avenues, an ad appeared in the Boulder paper: "Log cabin near Continental Divide." I called immediately and drove up a dirt road that wound past all other habitations to the edge of national forest looking out over the ranges of the Rockies. It was the cabin I was seeking. It was rustic, barely finished, with wood heat, no drinking water, and no electricity. The residents of the lush mountain homes with Jacuzzis and indoor greenhouses might have considered it unlivable, but for me it was perfect.

The night before I planned to move to my solitary retreat, my phone service gave me a message. I had not checked in with the service for days, having no reason to imagine I would have any messages now that my rental was handled. Yet there was a series of messages, all from the man I had met when I tried to sell my Datsun. I called him. He said diffidently that what he had to say might be hard for me to understand, but he felt compelled to say it. Bluntly, he went on, after our talk he had felt that it was demanded of him to maintain contact with me, not to let that one conversation be the end of any interaction.

To most Western women this might have been a total turn-off. Any woman with a hard-won sense of self-esteem developed through years of psychotherapy might have responded with outraged rejection of his personally intrusive message; however, it was the one possible approach that might have interested me in maintaining contact. I felt clearly the validity and truth of his communication as he spoke; that he was in fact asked to do this, and that it was neither an insult nor a come-on nor a compliment to me, but simply what he was asked to do.

However, I did not find in myself the same compelling instruction to maintain some contact with him (and through him with his community) that he obviously felt in relation to me. I hung up after a terse acknowledgment. After careful consideration, I called him back and told him that my focus for now was my solitary retreat; when that was complete, I would consider contacting him. I thanked him again for what he had given me the afternoon we met: for the work integrity he had communicated and nourished in our conversation. He said to me that if at any point I wanted to attend, there was a study group his community had formed that was open to anyone who might want to share with them a consideration of work principles.

His offer about the study group stayed with me, again to my surprise. I didn't have the least interest in sitting around with a bunch of people talking about work ideas that in all likelihood most of them would never carry into action in their own lives. The demand of the Work as I knew it was so high that I had lost most of my friends in the attempt to pursue it. Most people were not even interested in trying to meet this demand, and of those who did try, the majority I had known sooner or later chose an easier path. I knew for myself that I fell far short of its true possibility in my life.

The chances that these people would do more than talk were so slim that (rationally, once again) I saw little point in attending their meetings. In addition, based on considerations in my previous group, I was highly concerned about contamination by energies of distraction and distortion. I told myself that the chances of picking up negative emotional energies and entanglements were even higher than the chances of pointless and boring discussions. I was in Colorado for a solitary retreat, a meeting with God, not with other human beings. The man I had met certainly had an uncommon work integrity, but to imagine that the group would be full of others like him seemed a totally unrealistic expectation.

I packed my Datsun and moved up to my cabin in the mountains, making no further contact with the man and his community.

Both in this decision about attending the study group and in the decision whether to drive west to Prescott from Albuquerque, I was offered possibility but was left free to make my own decision. There was no inner sense in either case, such as the strong instruction to leave North Carolina within two weeks. It is only now, more than a decade later, that I am coming to understand the pattern that was evolving. The magnetic field of Lee's influence was drawing me toward him and his community, drawing me across the country and out of another life. The energy needed to break out of the matrix of my old life required dramatic confrontation, specific instructions that shattered the old forms, and my conscious obedience to these commands. Yet once I had stepped free of the old and was moving toward the field of the new, I was no longer commanded. I was left free to choose for myself when and how to step into Lee's actual physical company, when and how to meet him and begin to engage the work he held.

Of course, I did not know that this was the choice I was facing; nevertheless, it was a choice that had to be freely made. I didn't have the chance for that free choice if I was trapped in outer circumstances at a great distance from him. So I was given help to move out of those circumstances—help that was made available through the choice of obedience to inner instruction. The closer I moved toward Lee's physical presence, the less pressure or guidance was offered me from my inner voices. Even though I did not know what I was moving toward, I had to make the choice to move forward on faith, so that I became responsible for introduction into his company at a level different even from that of radical inner obedience. In fact, when I finally did make permanent contact with Lee's community four months later, it was only because, having exhausted all my stubborn ideas about what I was doing and having reached an apparent total dead end, I asked deeply for help.

These I would say are the two requirements that emerged after the initial requirement of obedience: the requirement of responsibility, and that of willingness to ask for and accept help. Although these two requirements may sound mutually exclusive, they are, in fact, intimately linked. To the degree that I accept responsibility, I put myself in a position in which I am capable of using help, because I am already moving and the help can be added to that motion. To offer help when a car is stalled and the driver doesn't even have the key is a totally different matter than to give a push when the car is rolling, the driver is at the wheel, and all that is needed is a little extra momentum to achieve a jumpstart.

At the same time, to ask for help with real intention is itself an act of responsibility—responsibility to the purposes one serves. A person who works within a spiritual lineage receives and uses the help of that lineage as a structural fact. It is responsibility to the lineage that opens the door to the help of the lineage; and the help of the lineage enables us to take deeper responsibility. I had been brought to the edges of the field of this lineage. To enter the field required my own choice and action.

As I packed my belongings in my cabin in the foothills, I noticed in a corner of my bedroom a box that I had never unpacked. On top was a small publication that the man with the work knowledge had given me. It offered an introduction to his community, with several articles and pictures. It had sat on top of the box for the two weeks I had lived there, and during that whole time, though I had not noticed it previously, a face had been looking out at me. It was the face of the man's teacher, Lee Lozowick.

This was a good face. The man I had met had a good teacher, a teacher with something real, something living, in his eyes.

I opened the publication. An article about life in Lee's community caught my attention, and I sat among the fragments of my life—the half-packed belongings—and read it. The article seemed tremendously idealistic. It spoke about principles of spiritual practice in community life, and the principles were exemplary.

The writer spoke as if the people in this community were actually living these principles. I knew enough about community living from my own experience to know that no group of humans on earth, at least no group of Western humans, lived together without currents of greed, selfishness, jealousy, competition, and abuses of power manifesting. Perhaps these people truly believed they were living these principles without contamination by common human vices, but if so they were in deep denial. Yet regardless of how unrealistic their idealism might be, the level of their commitment to their principles was inspiring. The article might be flawed by a devotion to the community that blinded the writer to some of its inevitable failings, but it nevertheless communicated powerfully a commitment to living these principles. Such commitment would continue to bear fruit. The community might not yet be what its members believed it to be, but they were clearly building a momentum that could create a level of shared work and communion in human life that was not common.

I settled into my cabin in the mountains and stayed there until the snows began to fall. By that time I needed to find work again to pay rent and essential bills. Once again I got work through an agency for temporary office help, this time working for a law firm that provided legal services for the Who. I worked at the office each day with a minimum of personal interaction and then returned home to my meditations and walking contemplation on the snowy trails along the heights of the Continental Divide. My life was also moving along a slow divide, and the waters were about to start pouring down the other side of the mountain. Totally unaware of the changes awaiting me, I continued with my inner focus.

The snows were falling more deeply now. Driving home from Denver, I would stop at the bottom of the dirt road that led two miles up into the peaks to my isolated cabin. I would lie under the car in my office dress and winter coat and put snow chains on the tires so the car could make it up the steep drive, fishtailing through the last winding half-mile. Many of the mountain dwellers drove Subarus with four-wheel drive, which plowed straight up the steep slopes without hesitation.

Once more I decided to sell my car, this time to buy a Subaru, so that I could complete my time in my mountain cabin. I drove down the mountain roads into Boulder and went straight to Alfalfa's, a gourmet natural foods grocery where the "hip people" shopped. There was an ad board at the front door where people posted signs about cars to sell, houses for rent, and political and spiritual meetings to attend. If there was a Subaru in town that I could afford (which would certainly not be at a used car lot, given my meager financial status), this board was the place to find it.

There was only one Subaru advertised on the board, but there was a poster that reminded me of the man I had met and his community—something about a public talk offered by the Hohm

Community. I was still in retreat, and I ignored the poster. I called the number for the Subaru.

The woman who had posted the ad said I could come right over. When I arrived at her house, she was walking out of the door with her small son. It was the day before Halloween. He was dressed in a raccoon costume, complete with bushy tail—a costume obviously made at home with skill and love. Something about him seemed familiar. The woman offered me a test drive in her car, and we drove it up into the Flat Irons, along a precipitous mountain road that could test the car's response to the challenges of my own steep road home.

Once on the mountain curves, it was obvious that this Subaru was no better than my old Datsun. It did not have four-wheel drive, and it rattled and growled in the same crotchety language as the Datsun's. Nevertheless, the journey into the heights had given us time to talk. Somehow, within minutes I was telling her that I was spending a time of spiritual retreat in the mountains, and she was telling me that she was a member of a spiritual community. In fact, her teacher was coming to town the next week; I would be welcome to attend his public talk and some other events if I was interested. She mentioned also that she was trying to sell the Subaru because her ex-husband wanted to buy her a better car.

Something clicked. "I think I've met your husband," I exclaimed. "He looked at my Datsun to see about buying it for you! That's why your little boy looks so familiar. I met him that day! I've heard about your community from your ex-husband . . . but I don't think I'm ready to come to any meetings."

We said goodbye, and I went back up into the mountains. She told me later that I was the only one who called in response to her ad for the car, just as her ex-husband had been the only one who called about my car. It reminded me of stories of spiritual magic like those of Carlos Castenada, where perfectly ordinary physical elements remain somehow invisible except to those who are supposed to see them. Apparently those ads were meant only to anchor strands of connection between us, and no one else even registered the ads as existing.

Finally the snows got too deep for me to furrow my way up to my cabin. Knowing I had to move out and sensing that my period of retreat had been completed, I felt that I was ready both literally and symbolically to enter the valley again: to reenter relationship with other human beings and to begin to discover what came next. The man I had met in August had told me that he lived in a house with a group of people. I wondered if they might have a room available to rent. (While I was familiar with group living and with spiritual community, I was not familiar with the idea of a community household as a kind of satellite ashram, in which members share a common commitment to foundational practices and membership in the community. I didn't realize that I was asking to enter something more than a circumstance of group living.) I didn't remember his address or his phone number but, amazingly, when I reached into a box of unsorted papers I pulled out his number like the boy pulling the plum out of the plumcake.

I called the house, and a woman answered. Her manner was cold and brusque, as if she felt it a great inconvenience just to have to answer the phone. It was a totally different energy from the energy I had encountered in the two community members I had met previously. As it turned out, she left the community a few months later, and that movement was already dominating her inner process. But I did not question her authority or use of power in my position as a stranger asking for alms. She said that the man I had met and another man who was in charge of the house were both at the ashram in Arizona. She didn't know when they'd be back; she didn't think there was a room available; and even if there were, she herself didn't know me and couldn't help me.

Finding that door apparently shut, I turned elsewhere. I looked for an apartment in Boulder, but coming up with the first and last month's rent plus a deposit, which was commonly demanded, was far beyond my means. Since the community house was not available, I answered an ad for a more conventional group house. As soon as I walked in, I knew it would be disastrous to live there. I had not realized how intensely vulnerable I still was after my months in retreat. To work on a computer in my own small office in a law firm was a totally different thing than to live day and night in the unconscious, fragmented, distracted field of emotional compulsion which these people took for granted. It was for me equivalent to trying to breathe the air emanating from a toxic waste dump. It was not a possibility. The next group house was no better. This polluted psychic environment was what people accepted as normal.

I had nowhere to live. For the next few weeks I wandered. I camped briefly in Rocky Mountain National Park, amidst the December snows of Colorado. When the need to get warm became overpowering, I paid for a motel room for a few nights. I did temporary work in offices when I could get it. After almost a year of intense inner direction and obedience to that direction, it was vastly unsettling to find no clear direction emerging within me. Finally, in my meditations I received a recommendation to go to a retreat center at the Snowmass Monastery, high in the Rockies, for a few days. My friend at the Briar Rose knew the monks at this monastery as well as the abbot, Father Thomas Keating. I called and made a reservation for an individual retreat.

When I arrived at the monastery, I was taken to a small suite at one end of a barn. I could hear the sheep and lambs bleating on the other side of the wall. The energy in the space was like a deep, strong river current; it had obviously been fed by the intention of many serious retreatants and by the committed life of the monks who offered this hospitality. I went to mass and sat in the visitors' section listening to the monks chant. Coming out, I heard the monastery bells pealing across the snow-packed fields. This was definitely a place of healing, a place with a profound heartbeat that drew even the visitor into its deep rhythms.

In that space of healing meditation, in a barn reminiscent of the barn with the lowing sheep where the Christ Child was born into the heart of this world, I felt a healing of relationship born in my own heart. Whatever transition I was making, whatever bridge I was building, I no longer needed isolation from family and friends to complete it. I drove into the town of Snowmass, found a public phone, and called my parents to tell them I was coming home for Christmas.

At the time I saw this reopening of relationship as simply my own movement on my individual path. In retrospect, however, I would say that this was one of the gifts that Lee's influence was already creating in my world, even before I had physically met him or accepted the invitation to contact with his community. Lee's teaching includes an emphasis on right relationship with family and friends, ordinary work in the world, and acceptance of the practical responsibilities of human life as foundation for work in more subtle and esoteric realms. His entire teaching is predicated on the fact that our experience of separation is an illusion. He calls his way the path of "enlightened duality"—the path of realizing the unity in all things and, beyond that realization, being able to live in the world in its manifestation of duality. It was this context that underlay the shift in relationship to my family that opened that day.

My retreat in Snowmass complete, I drove back into the valley—this time straight to Boulder. I wanted to call the man I had met in August and ask again about a room in his community house, but in my wanderings I had lost his phone number and I could not remember where he lived. I took a room at the Briar Rose once again. My friends there told me that someone had left a number of messages for me during the past month, but the messages had been thrown away by mistake. I assumed they were from one of the temporary agencies checking to see if I was available for work, and I thought no more about it.

Years later I discovered that these messages were from the man I had met in August. He had been trying to reopen contact with me, and when I disappeared so completely he was perplexed. He had been quite sure upon meeting me that I was destined to join the community, which was why he had freely given me community publications that were not normally distributed to the public. As a study group leader, he was accustomed to letting people approach at their own pace, so he was not surprised when I did not jump into participation immediately. But when I apparently disappeared completely, he wondered if he could have been mistaken in his perceptions or whether he had made a mistake in not pursuing contact with me more actively.

"You didn't make a mistake," I told him in this conversation years later. "I was just busy running."

Gurdjieff taught that there are three major currents operating in the created world: the affirming force, the denying force, and the reconciling force. The loss of the phone number on my part and the loss of the phone messages on the part of others are examples of this denying force exerting itself strongly in response to the tidal wave of the affirming force that had brought me to Colorado and into immediate contact with Lee's community members. Yet, eventually the denying force itself can draw into action the power of our determination to move forward. It can evoke in us muscles for work and commitment to responsibility that we do not even know we have.

I found work in Denver until the time for my trip east to visit my family. Although they would gladly have given me whatever I needed, I did not tell my parents that I was almost completely out of money. I knew without question that I still had to complete whatever transition was happening in my life using my own resources, without outer dependence on friends or family. As soon as I returned from my trip east, I moved out of the Briar Rose, telling my friend there that I had found an apartment, so she would not feel responsible for providing housing for which I could not pay.

Once again it was clear to me that I was facing some inner passage that was informing the outer events, but I had no idea what this passage was. It was simply clear to me that it was required that I make this passage through my own efforts and resources. I could not ask my parents for money. I could not ask my friend for lodging beyond the weeks she had already given me at a reduced rate during her busiest season. I could not even ask her about renting a room from someone in her Buddhist community, although I was well aware that in a community that large there would likely be someone who could provide a place for me to stay. Trungpa Rinpoche's Buddhist community, through my friend and the Briar Rose, had given me a sanctuary I deeply needed during a time of transition. They had given me a bridge to wherever I was going. That bridging function was complete, and now I had to take the next step on my own. Although I had no idea what that step might be, I knew it was not deeper into that community, much as I respected what I had seen. To move forward I had to move out of that sheltering field.

The only direction I could imagine taking at that point was east—returning to renew contact with my original spiritual group; but I did not seem to be able to gather the money to do so. If I had been able to accept financial help, I would have used it to drive east. Fortunately, I obeyed the sense that such help was not lawful. Chögyam Trungpa Rinpoche once said, "Sometimes help is no help." Financial help at this time, which would have expanded my options, would only have short-circuited the field that was holding me. I would have used it to drive as far as I could out of the field of Lee's influence, without knowing I was doing so. I would have been moving in the opposite direction from the destination that was calling— almost corralling—me. Although the influence and energy of the teacher and of the Work is not defined by geographical boundaries, the immediate opportunity for making physical contact with this community resided in remaining in the geographical field of Boulder.

Knowing that I could not accept financial help, I planned to work until I had saved enough money for the trip east. Yet for the first time in the years I had taken temporary office work, I could find no work whatsoever. I was alone, homeless, and penniless, but I could not turn for help in directions that I recognized as inwardly unlawful.

In *Rudi: Fourteen Years with My Teacher*, John Mann's story of work with Swami Rudrananda, Rudi gives an explanation for why we must sometimes, because of a felt inner necessity, make outer choices that make our lives much more difficult and inconvenient than might seem necessary.

> When I was in college . . . I stayed for the summer with a very rich family in Oregon. It was wonderful. I loved them. They loved me. They wanted to adopt me, but I couldn't stay. It would have undermined my whole development. In the end, I had to force myself to return to an uncertain, brutal existence. I did it for the sake of my own growth . . . I can't afford

to take the easy way out. It will catch up with me later when I really need the strength. At this point, it may not be necessary, but I am not just living for today. I am living for what may be required ten years from today. (Mann, J. *Rudi: Fourteen Years with My Teacher*, Portland, Ore.: Rudra Press, 1987, p. 117)

As students, it is easy to assume that it is only the teachers who must make such radical gestures of commitment to their work. Yet the fact is that each of us is faced with the choice of how deeply we will make ourselves available to the process of this work. Although I did not then know it, doubt and my own self-distrust had already cost me a year of Lee's physical company and instruction. Attachment to comfort and convenience could have cost me another year or more. Perhaps there was something particularly lawful in my choice to forego that attachment, which meant that I would approach this school of Baul beggars as a beggar myself—begging for the warmth of a room in which to stay as I was also, unconsciously, begging for the warmth of an inner room in which the heart could open and find a way to serve.

It did not occur to me, as I faced the lonely prospect of moving out of the Briar Rose into homelessness, that the direction I was to go had already been given to me, and that what was blocking my progress forward was such a minor resistance as one lost phone number coupled with an unwillingness to brook some unknown woman's cold rejection once again.

Although it was January in the Rockies, I drove back up into the mountains and found a campground by a frozen lake above Boulder. There I slept in the car with my ancient down quilt and my dog. In the mornings the snow was sometimes above my knees.

After a few days of camping, I found a temporary office job again. But the agency did not pay until a week after the week worked, so it would be two weeks before I had a paycheck. I dressed in office suits and dresses in the early dawn in my car by the lake and drove down to Denver to work. In the evenings I returned to the lovely alpenglow of sunset on the Rockies, and the coldest nights I had ever known.

One night as I left Boulder to drive up into the mountains the radio predicted a low of fifteen degrees. Fifteen degrees in Boulder meant below zero up at my mountain campground. I pulled over to the side of the road and stopped. In utter loneliness and despair, I thought, "I can't do this. I can't do this another night."

There was a shelter for the homeless in Boulder, but I knew I could not stay there. The suffocating energy of the group houses I had visited would be like pristine mountain air compared to the energetic weight and suffering that would permeate the homeless shelter. Still fresh from my mountain retreat, I had not yet reestablished normal psychic boundaries. Sometimes I could hardly distinguish others' suffering from my own. I could not face the weight of gathered pain at the shelter.

I meditated by the side of the road, praying deeply for some guidance out of the dead end that had followed my radiant period of retreat. The response was once again unexpected, clear, and shocking. *"Go to the house of the woman who showed you the Subaru. Ask her if you can stay there for the night."*

Again I was confronted with an instruction which demanded action that from a conventional view would appear irrational, even crazy. It was already pitch dark, nine o'clock on a winter night, past the hour that reasonable people visited even their friends. And I was going to knock on the door of someone I had met only once when she showed me her car for sale? It seemed impossible for me to do this—in contradiction to my entire childhood training in basic courtesies, let alone social conventions. As I hesitated, knowing that this inner guidance had asked difficult things of me before, a vision passed through my mind of applying to rent the house in Durham when I had no money and leaving North Carolina at this same inner direction.

I drove to the woman's house and knocked. No one answered. Disappointed and relieved at the same time, I started to drive back up into the mountains. I got as far as the same spot at the side of the road, and something stopped me. I had asked for help and I had received an instruction in response. Just because I had knocked once did not mean I had completed my obligation to use the help for which I had asked.

By then it was almost ten o'clock. The woman was a single mother with a small child. I was concerned that she would be frightened by the knock of a stranger at the door at that hour; and certainly to appear with my unconventional request was not calculated to inspire her confidence in my sanity or enhance her receptivity to my presence in her home for the night. Nevertheless, the instruction was unchanging. I turned around, drove back into Boulder, and knocked at her door again.

This time she answered the door. She did not appear frightened or even particularly surprised at my presence. She was unbelievably accepting. I made my request, and she responded with welcoming graciousness.

"A friend of mine has been sleeping on the living room floor, and she just left this morning. You're welcome to stay overnight."

I slept that night with Lee's books just above my head. The bookshelf was full of community publications and his picture looked out from their pages as I glanced through them.

The next morning I explained my entire situation to Elaine, my hostess. She invited me to stay for a week, and that week stretched on into another, and another. I was able to share in the rent, which was a welcome addition to her finances, and she and her son embraced me in their lives. The next night her ex-husband, Greg, the man I had met when I tried to sell my Datsun the day after I arrived in Boulder and who had made repeated overtures to me, came to dinner. He invited me again to the study group, and this time I accepted the invitation.

From that day until the day I met Lee several months later, I never missed a study group. Far from my projections about a group lost in idle talk about unlived ideals, this was a group that grappled with the daily confrontations of relationship with both other humans and with the divine. It was a food so strong and a nourishment for which I was so hungry that each meeting was a feast met with profound gratitude.

Before dinner, my new friends spoke a blessing. The poetry of this blessing, like no grace I had ever heard, pierced my heart with its bare longing for right relationship to the divine in our daily lives. Only months later did I discover that it was a blessing written by Lee, which was spoken before each meal at the ashram and in many households. It was for me one example of the way Lee's school brought the most ineffable longing and mystery into daily life, permeating the ordinary with the extraordinary.

After dinner, I talked late into the night with Greg. At our first meeting his receptivity and understanding of work principles had drawn me into confidences about my spiritual work and world view that I had never shared with anyone outside my original group. This second conversation took a dramatically different turn. Feedback, or accepting the observations and help of others to see into our own blind spots, is an important aspect of practice in the school I was approaching. This conversation was my first experience of receiving "feedback" in the Hohm Community.

As I spoke about my retreat during the fall and the work of the group from which I had come, Greg responded with a clarity which I could not deny, yet his commentary confronted some of my foundational perceptions and the choices I had made based upon them. He said that it seemed it was time for me to turn away from solitary spiritual work and toward the work of relationship with others. I said that my school had focused on group work, and he answered that although that was undoubtedly true, it seemed to him my earlier teacher did not have what was needed to guide me in whatever work involving human relationships I was being called to do. It seemed to him that I was ready to go on from that school. The implication, if not spoken outright, was that his and Elaine's teacher, Lee Lozowick, did have what I needed to progress further; that he would be able to guide me in the direction toward which I was unconsciously reaching.

It was clear as Greg spoke that he had no personal investment in what he was saying. There was no emotional charge; it was as if the space itself was speaking to me, simply using him as its voice, and that voice was objective in a way that I could not pretend to miss. Yet I was outraged almost beyond bearing at the suggestion that there was any weakness or incompleteness in my original group, and especially in its teacher. I knew I had to listen until the communication was complete, but as soon as it was done, I left the apartment and drove into the mountains in a state of fierce reaction.

It was that purest time of night, the early hours just after midnight, and the stars above the mountain peaks shone as sharply as truth in the black emptiness. In the isolated safety of my car I shouted my outrage and then my pain, howling in this crisis of faith in the path I had known until then. Although I did not believe that my first teacher was perfect, I could not bear the observation that he might have a fault that limited the work in which he could guide me. I could not bear the agonizing idea that the path in front of me might mean leaving that group completely. I did not essentially object to the feedback that had just been given to me for myself: that it was time for me to engage human relationship at a deeper level. This, in fact, fit with my own knowledge that it was time to come down out of the mountains into the valley where people lived.

There had been other observations that were not so easy to stomach—that penetrated into protected areas in my psyche with all the comfort of a surgical knife. Yet uncomfortable as they were, I recognized their truth; and the same vulnerability that had made it impossible to live as a housemate with Boulder yuppies allowed these observations to enter me without normal defense. But the observations about my group and my teacher—these I could not accept. I felt that Greg could not possibly know what was true about a school and teacher he had never met, and he now appeared to me as perhaps the most penetrating and insidious contaminant I had encountered since leaving Atlanta a year ago. Perhaps all this contact with an unknown spiritual community and its members who had seemed to meet me everywhere was just the biggest seduction I had to refuse before finding my way back to where I belonged.

As I drove higher into the mountains, I considered the possibility that it was best to end all contact with these people at that instant. I could leave whatever belongings were in that living room; I had left more than belongings many times already. I could drive on into the mountains and never return. I could begin driving east at that moment and drive until I ran out of money for gas somewhere in Oklahoma, then wait tables at some truck stop to make enough money to drive the rest of the way to Atlanta.

I turned inward with utmost intention, ready to make whatever dramatic break or movement was required. The response was again unexpected. "*Go back to the apartment,*" my inner voice said. "*You have something to learn from this man and his community.*" I drove back to the apartment and quietly slipped into sleep in the hour before dawn.

When I saw Greg the next day, he said to me, "I had the feeling you might leave and never return." So, here he was, tuned into one more truth.

"I wanted to," I said, "but somehow I couldn't turn from the truth."

When I told him some of the content of my reaction, he assured me that he was in fact making no comment about my first teacher's weaknesses or strengths, which he did not feel were up to him to evaluate; rather, his observations had been about my own path—that it seemed I was ready to move on from that group and that I was reaching for a sphere of work in which he felt Lee could guide me. My reactions had involved a misinterpretation based in the desire to discredit observations and feedback that were essentially directed toward myself rather than toward my earlier teacher.

So I had stepped into the door of relationship: relationship to these new friends, relationship with the study group, relationship with a teacher I had never met whose voice I heard on tapes alternately cajoling, shouting, joking, and tenderly teaching intimate truths about the possibility of communion in human life. Yet still, unbeknownst to my new friends, even as I walked deeper and deeper into this new world I was stubbornly planning to return east as soon as I could save money for the trip. I kept getting enough work to pay the rent, but not quite enough to save what I needed. I couldn't understand what was wrong. I was sure I was supposed to return to my original group; that all the food I was receiving in this new environment was to be fed into the ability to work again in the environment I already knew.

Weeks stretched into months and I was still in Boulder, still attending the study group, and about to participate in my first Hohm Community Celebration. I was about to meet Lee.

CHAPTER 2

MEETING THE TEACHER

❧

*I*n April of 1987, the day before I met Lee for the first time in physical form, reverberations of that transforming Presence I had experienced on a spring afternoon in Georgia two years earlier again broke through the standard parameters of my human existence. I was walking through the woods in the Colorado mountains when this One seemed to break into my world, calling and shouting, yet approaching me with the utmost, pristine gentleness. I felt again the energy of the divine as Lover; but this time the energy had a more specific form. Drunk on the energy of this Presence, I found myself leaping and dancing through the woods like a whirling dervish set loose in the midst of the Colorado pines and mountain meadows. I felt that I was racing across time and space to meet someone whom, paradoxically, I had always known. Fortunately, no humans in an ordinary state of consciousness passed me on the trail. They would never have understood a dancing hiker under the intoxicating effects of a crazy wisdom master who could not be seen!

My first physical meeting with Lee the next day, at the home of the leader of the Boulder study group, could not have been more different. It was outwardly absolutely ordinary and uneventful. If I had told him about my behavior in the woods the day before, he would undoubtedly have laughed. I remember no words associated with our meeting. Perhaps someone introduced us; perhaps he said, "I'm Lee," or I said my name. All I remember is looking into his eyes. I barely saw his physical form. I saw only his eyes. There was no end to them. They opened into a space of infinity, a space beyond the human. In their light, even his own shape and form dimmed into vague shadows, as when one looks at a light too bright to bear. I looked down. One glance was enough. Even greed dissolved in this light. I knew in that instant that I could trust him as a teacher. I could trust him because he stood rooted in the land of the Real.

I did not, however, see him as *my* teacher. Regardless of the intensity of the energetic experience the day before, or the experience of physically meeting him—or the mystical experience of two years prior, which I did not yet connect to Lee—I saw him simply as a teacher I could trust to help me find my way to my own true path. I did not believe that path lay with him. I told him this up front, from the beginning. I asked him if it was possible to accept his help, to bond with the *sangha* through working together, and yet to receive this help as a temporary boon on the way to my own path, which I believed to be in another school. He said this was not a problem; I could work in this school for now and let things unfold.

Although it was his eyes that held the focus of my attention, there was one other thing about Lee that registered strongly, almost subliminally. This was a man who was not hiding anything. Gurdjieff once said, "All my sins are on the surface." In meeting Lee I felt that in this man there were no hidden agendas. There were none of the entangled currents in the emotional body which muddy the energetic field around most of the humans I have known. This man might do outrageous things, but he would do them out front, in full view of anyone who wanted to observe and evaluate his actions. Another new student later expressed a similar experience of Lee's energy by saying that in this man there were "no lies."

Having looked into Lee's eyes—into the unfathomable dimensions into which they opened—having sat in his presence in the mysterious and magical evening gathering where I had shyly observed him from a darkened corner, I returned the next morning to ordinary life. I spent the morning helping other members of the Boulder *sangha* prepare for a potluck picnic with Lee, community members, and guests that had been planned for that afternoon.

Carrying our contributions to the feast, we walked up the hill of Chautauqua Park, a lovely green expanse of grass leading toward the sheer cliffs and high peaks of the Flat Irons and the Rocky Mountains beyond. Lee and a number of his students were spread out across the grass like brightly strewn flowers. Their "brightness" was not an outer manifestation. They looked to normal eyes perfectly ordinary: casually and even sloppily dressed in the ubiquitous jeans and T-shirts of our time, relaxing and half-reclining like any picnickers, without a hint of the formal posture of meditation practitioners. Yet I was seeing with a newly-opened inner eye—with the intensified awareness and vulnerability to impression of a newborn baby surveying the outside world for the first time. With this inner vision, these human beings scattered across the spring grass appeared to me as bright jewels, radiating through their ordinary exterior forms an energy that was wholly extraordinary. These beings were not perfect, but they had been changed. There was a coal burning at the center of each heart that illuminated the space and charged it with what Carl Jung called "numinosity." The energy of these burning hearts formed a magnet that was tugging irresistibly at my own.

Looking back, I am amazed that in the face of such a deep heart recognition of this man and his community I nevertheless held to my mental construct that this was not *my* community but simply a teacher and a community with whom I could share work for a temporary period until I returned to my own root school. Walking into a field of meeting so bright that sparks seemed to dance from the hair and eyes of those gathered on the hill, I remained adamant in my attachment to my mental understanding of the world. The instant I saw him again, I was aware of Lee as a spring of nourishment from which I was deeply drinking—from which I had been drinking since the moment the night before when I had discovered his eyes and the world into which they led.

After a lovely picnic of which I remember nothing—I was consuming such a rich inner food that the outer food did not even register in my field of attention—we gathered around Lee for an impromptu consideration of questions about practice and the teaching. Having met Lee for only a few minutes the night before, and inwardly aghast at my own temerity, I found myself asking him a question. I couldn't help it. I had no choice about opening my mouth or about what I said. I asked him something like, "How do I know if I can trust the experience of love? How do I know if I can trust someone as a lover? How do I know whether to trust what feels like love in a group, a community? How do I know whether to open my heart?"

After seven years of celibacy, I had recently re-engaged the world of relationship with a human partner. It might have appeared that I was asking a question at least in part about my personal relationship, but what I was really asking Lee was, "How do I know if I can trust *you*?"

The actual meaning of my question was to me so obvious that I was flushed and embarrassed asking it, but I did not have the luxury of silence. And I could not phrase it in some less vulnerable or provocative way. What business did I have asking if I could trust him? He had not offered me anything. I had not asked if I could be a student. I had met him less than twenty-four hours earlier, and I did not intend to become his student, only to learn from him for a time till I could return to my original teacher. I was not interested in devotion, let alone love; I was interested in the Work. The school and the teacher were clearly doing some good work; that was enough for me at the moment. Yet here I was asking him about love, and about the heart. Even if I had wanted to be his student, he had made no indication that he would accept me as such; and to suggest that my relationship with him as a student would involve this thing I knew of as love seemed the height of hubris. These were all the mental considerations chattering within me as I steadfastly allowed my heart to form words that came out of my mouth, leaving my face aflame.

"How do I know if I can trust someone as a Lover?"

Lee answered me in the same coin in which I had phrased the question, as if he were speaking about my personal relationship with a man. Yet everything he said applied directly to my real question. In his answer he spoke about the heart. He said that for a time, as we develop relationship, we test ourselves and each other; we observe and discriminate about whether and how a person is trustworthy. At some point, however, we must face the choice of commitment. Once we have observed and engaged each other to a degree that gives us a reasonable sense of whether a relationship is trustworthy, we must make the choice to commit ourselves to the other person and to the relationship itself. In this choice, and in the choice to bear that which is less than perfect, we enter a realm of possibility in love that can never be glimpsed or opened so long as we guard ourselves and withhold our trust.

To throw ourselves into this level of trust and commitment without initial observation and discrimination is foolhardy, Lee said. Not everyone is worthy of such trust or able to engage such a level of relationship. But when we find a person or a group that is capable of such engagement, then the only way to enter the deeper possibility, the real possibility into which love can open, is to risk vulnerablity in spite of the fact that we will at times get hurt. In commitment and vulnerability lies a realm that is rarely entered, a realm infused with, informed by, and invocative of the love of the divine.

The next day Lee held *darshan* in a local ecumenical church. This was the first *darshan* I had ever attended. My new friends explained to me the basic protocols. Men sat on the right; women sat on the left. The guru sat at the front of the hall, and we could each approach him in turn to offer a piece of fruit or a flower as *prasad*, and to receive from him some candy or other *prasad* as blessing. There would be chanting of traditional Indian chants in Sanskrit at the beginning, followed by a discourse by Lee, usually including the chance to ask him questions.

The usual protocol in giving *prasad* to the guru was to bow— to kneel—in front of him, and then offer and receive *prasad*. The idea of exchanging *prasad* was unfamiliar to me but quite acceptable. The idea of bowing in front of any other human was not. I told the friends who had invited me that I would not bow to Lee; I would never bow to another human being, only to God. That was fine, they said. I could walk up and stand before him and give the *prasad*. The choice to give *prasad*, to bow, to find our right relationship to him, was up to each of us.

When the afternoon of *darshan* arrived and I walked up to give my *prasad* to Lee, I found my knees bending, and I kneeled and bowed before him. That moment revealed to me the truth of the relationship between devotee and spiritual master. I bow before another human being not because he is human, and not because he is more than human, but because he is an open doorway into the Source of all things. I bow to the One he has become, and the fact that he is still in the process of becoming that One only makes his service to me, to us, the deeper. In this process, the teacher clears a way, a path, for those who follow.

For *prasad* I gave Lee a long tapered candle. Shortly after, another woman gave him the same kind of candle. He sat in his formal Indian dress, surrounded by flowers and fruit and attentive devotees, and brandished the two candles in his hand as he began to speak. Instead of some *dharmic* discourse, some inspiring presentation of spiritual principles, he began to comment on how most men wished they had a particular appendage of such impressive proportions as these candles; certainly he wished he did! From this ribald beginning he leapt into bawdy jokes and a consideration of human foibles, desires, and dynamics in the arena of sexual energy and relationship. The whole scene was so far from the serious, principled discussion of universal realities that I had previously held as the ideal in a spiritual community that I could not even call what he was doing the antithesis. It existed in an entirely different realm; and yet, instead of being shocked or repelled, I found myself feeling wholly at home. In an apparently crude yet essentially artful manner, he was breaking open crystallized conventions using the instrument of laughter.

As over the years I have watched other people pass through this kind of initiation into Lee's signature brand of spiritual life, I have recalled that first *darshan* where I could have responded with rigid judgment or rejection, yet found myself softened and surprised into laughter and an unexpected relaxation. By the time I reached that *darshan*, the proprieties of conventional American life had long ago broken open to expose the suffering and self-deceit commonly hidden beneath. I had seen enough of the truths that lay behind the false mirrors of convention that essentially that life did not interest me anymore. This man with his outrageous flirting and vulgar jokes was communicating to me something entirely different from the surface appearance of things. He was transmitting an example of true elegance; not the outer elegance of appearance or even behavior, but the inner elegance of integrity to the real.

After several days of public events in Boulder, there was no further meeting planned with Lee for us newcomers until a community Celebration to be held at a camp in the nearby mountains. After handling the public events and hosting Lee and his traveling company, the members of the Boulder *sangha* were also responsible for the food and logistical arrangements for the three days of the Celebration. To prepare for this gathering of close to a hundred people was an immense task. So my next order of business, after these first meetings with Lee which were already altering structures within me, was simply to work. Having touched something extraordinary, we returned to the ordinary.

A couple of days before the Celebration, a number of people began to get sick. On one level this may have been just a flu bug going around, but on another it seemed to be a manifestation of our resistance and a way of processing whatever in us was in need of inner cleansing. People had symptoms such as vomiting, exhaustion, and upset stomachs.

The day before the Celebration I began to feel a telltale uneasiness growing in my stomach. I was determined that I would not be sick and unable to attend my first Celebration. Uncharacteristically, I simply stopped eating. My normal attachment to food as a symbol of love meant that I would rarely forego eating, even when my digestive system was struggling to handle it. Only short periods of total poverty and a couple of experiments with fasting for a day had ever interrupted my entanglement with food. Yet now I found myself spontaneously choosing not to eat, to let my body focus on handling the digestive bug. It may seem the most obvious thing to do, but it was not something that would previously have been obvious to me, and it was not obvious to most of those around me. Some people who, like me, had only queasiness kept eating regularly. Most of those people seemed to take about three days to move through the illness, with a good deal of discomfort throughout. The few of us that stopped eating moved through it quite rapidly. By the end of twenty-four hours my digestive upset had disappeared.

It seems to me that often, in the newness of our first approach to a school and a teacher, we are given extra energy that helps us act in contradiction to lifelong habits and helps us discover unexpected possibilities. Later, as the flood of energy carrying us through the transition subsides, we become responsible to anchor the new habits through our own efforts. We have been given the pattern of what is possible; then we have to choose to give our own energy to bring this possibility into grounded and permanent action in our lives. A couple of years later I would face this challenge specifically in relation to my attachments around food. But for this first Celebration, I was given help to act differently, and as a result I approached the Celebration with fresh and healthy physical energy. The opportunity to fast on the physical level had helped to create an emptiness, a sense of waiting for the feast, which deepened receptivity to the food at all levels, physical and energetic, which would be given during my first gathering with the community as a whole.

The last event before the Celebration was a *zikr* hosted by a Sufi couple who were friends of Lee's. It was a formal, ritual space of celebration, filled with feasting, chanting, and prayer. Invitations for the evening were extended only to Lee and a chosen

group of intimate devotees. Most of my new friends and co-workers, who were established practitioners, were invited to this
gathering. I wished intensely that I might be invited to participate,
yet at some almost inarticulate level I also understood the importance of a closed circle in which the participants shared a matrix of
developed practice and relationship with each other and with Lee.
To open this kind of sacred space to newcomers would be like
opening the windows in a chamber in which a unique and potent
scent has been created through focused intention and specific
shared rituals utilizing selected flowers and herbs. The wind that
could blow through the window might bring new and enlivening
currents and scents, but they would be unpredictable and would
diffuse and possibly destroy the particular scent that had so carefully been created for particular purposes. I find it ironic, now that
I myself am a long-term student, that having had such a clear
understanding of this principle of exclusion, even if not so clearly
articulated, I have been mired for years in a rescue dynamic around
trying to pressure Lee into including others in his private parties.
It is only after a dozen years with him that I am beginning to
respect the need for other students to live from the principles I
spontaneously understood when I was excluded from a particular
chamber. What the universe offered me that evening was not participation in the coveted gathering, but the chance to support
participation by others who were invited. By caring for the children
of my friends, I made it possible for parents to attend who otherwise could not go.

The day before the Celebration, we spent the morning cooking, cutting cucumbers and carrots, preparing plates of crudité,
and stirring pots of stew. In the midst of this activity a wind seemed
to whirl through the space, as if setting the sliced cucumbers dancing and the carefully arranged olives leaping into the air. The
spiritual master had entered the space, opening the door to the

house and simultaneously resetting the mundane movement of our chopping into the rhythm of a passionate and invocative dance. He passed by me, surveying the trays of brightly colored vegetables and the simmering stew. I felt his passage as heat, like that of coals radiating fire from some other planet. We offered him a spoonful of soup to test, but he would not take even a taste, preferring to wait until the full completion of the ritual, the final presentation of the celebratory meal. Then he was gone, leaving our workspace reverberating with a new rhythm for the rest of the afternoon.

What is it to have one's heart stirred? To have awakened in one's heart both sorrow and bliss that echo the notes pouring into the universe from the Heart of God? This is what lay latent in these moments of meeting: the moment in which I first saw my teacher's eyes; the moment in which he passed casually by me in the kitchen, like the Pied Piper dancing past the unsuspecting children who were compelled by the mystery he embodied to follow him. I came from a Quaker background that taught me to listen to my own inner voice—the voice of God within me—but that specifically rejected the authority of a minister or single leader "guiding the flock." I came from a political background that espoused democratic, consensus decision-making; that focused on institutional changes in the political system and its structures. I came from a radical feminist participation in consciousness-raising that eschewed the patriarch as practically synonymous with the devil.

Yet my heart was being stirred by something that overturned and broke into pieces all these constructs by which I understood the world. At one time I would have said that devotion to a guru was a sentimental attachment that opened the imagined devotee to abuse of authority. I would have said that to focus on life in a largely renunciate spiritual community was to abdicate political responsibility for the real, practical changes in which we, the privileged class, are responsible to participate in order to share a basically decent human existence with the rest of humanity. I would have said that to bow to another human being, no matter how great a teacher, was to misunderstand the actual relationship of human to divine. All these clear ideas which I could convincingly have debated were about to change. They were about to change not because of an intellectual argument but because of an experience of the heart that altered the point of view from which I saw them.

CHAPTER 3

COMMUNITY

⸺

With great anticipation we drove up into the mountains for the spring Celebration, traditionally called the All Fools' Celebration. For three days we would share in talks given both by students and by Lee, and participate in theater, feasting, music and chanting, and formal *darshan*. We would take turns helping with cooking, cleaning, being with the children, and other aspects of practical labor required for the Celebration to occur.

In the first *darshan* at that April Celebration in the Colorado mountains, Lee discussed a consideration that would underlie many of the confrontations and conundrums of my life in this school as my involvement deepened over the next years. The consideration actually stemmed from a discussion that I had had with a friend, which apparently someone then passed on to Lee.

I had been saying to my friend that Lee was strongly criticizing the tendency toward maudlin sentimentality which many of us brought to spiritual work; yet he had been extolling the *ras lila*, the story of Krishna's dance with the *gopis* under the autumn full moon, as a paradigm for the relationship of human to divine. It seemed to me that this story was full of sentiment and romance, and that it indicated there was a place for sentimental feeling in spiritual work and relationship. From my current perspective, I would say that I was confusing sentiment, in the sense of shallow feeling, with deep and objective emotion, but at the time I understood Lee to be saying that there was no place for any feeling or emotion in the Work. This misunderstanding could not have been further from the truth of a school with deep mystical and devotional currents. I also understood his statements to mean that there was no place for romance in this school. Yet I was confusing romance in the sense of fantasy based in vanity and selfishness with the true romance that flows unceasingly from the Heart of God. This kind of romance is characterized by true poetry, beauty, elegance, and innocence.

Lee cut straight to the core of my confusion, without ever having talked with me directly about any of these issues.

An interesting question that I heard today concerned my considerations about bringing maudlin sentimentality to your work. [The person was asking] how does that fit with our discussion of the *ras lila*, which seemed to this person to involve a lot of sentimentality . . . *Rasa* is a word that is associated in Indian culture with a lot of the forms of art, particularly music and poetry, [which] is said to have a certain quality of *rasa*. This has to do with a communication of a particular type of emotion, which has a quality of essential elegance . . . And *lila* means "play,"—play in a kind of light and delightful sense. So the *ras lila* would be the play of Krishna that conveyed objective emotion or objective elegance . . .

Krishna's relationship to the *gopis* was typified by an essentially elegant quality. The *ras lila* is not just a dance. The *ras lila* includes all the forms of the love play that led up to the dance. It includes the dance itself and all the forms of longing and yearning and realization that arose and transpired *after* the dance . . .

The quality of the *ras lila* has to do with the objective emotion or mood of love.

The distinction between sentimentality and emotional elegance is a central discrimination that would underlie many of the lessons that waited to confront me in years to come in my work in this school. I had to begin to deal with both the possibilities and the dangers inherent in a path that strongly involves devotion.

True devotion, based in the quality of objective elegance, grows toward the possibilities of longing and adoration. The distortions of devotion devolve into pathetic flattery, adulation, and sycophancy. We cling to sentimental responses to the teacher that are in actuality efforts to avoid responsibility. We languish in a childish dependence cloaked in a paradoxically patronizing admiration. My own tendency to try to absolve others of their rightful responsibilities and to avoid moments of confrontation for myself or others would require repeated correction over the years. That tendency, which we call a "rescue dynamic," is based in a sentimental view of relationship, of human beings, and of the Work. In contrast, a view based in respect for others, myself, and our work together frees me to both expect and enact responsible action. It requires a willingness to deeply feel the suffering and sorrow that are part of this path without trying to rescue or pretend as a means of escape or avoidance. I have come to see sentimentality as a wallowing in pretense in the desperate effort to avoid and deflect real feeling, with its piercing objective quality. Sentimentality involves a codependent preservation of entrapping dynamics, whereas ruthless compassion has the capacity to set us free.

Toward the end of this *darshan*, Lee spoke of a letter he had written to the community, which he said he might read during *darshan* the following Sunday. "It was a recognition of my own process that generated this essay," he explained carefully, "rather than frustration with any of you. It's important to hold that. If the essay is read I want it to be held properly. I don't want it just to be wasted on you. This essay was generated based on my own process of momentum in this Work as a teacher."

The next *darshan* was on the last day of the Celebration, April 26, 1987. With acute anticipation, we gathered in a large room that I remember as being suffused with light. We sat on our pillows in rows: women on the left and men on the right. An open aisle in the middle led directly to Lee, seated in front and facing us. His presence permeated the room. But even as he sat as a physical focal point at the front, it was the energy of the entire room that stunned me. Lines of light seemed to emanate from each participant, contributing to the intense brightness of the room—a coherent web of light vivified by the individual sparks that were the supposedly distinct and separate human persons. The Buddha taught that the three jewels on the spiritual path are the Buddha, or teacher; the *dharma*, or teaching; and the *sangha*, the community of practitioners. I had met the teacher. Now I was seeing the *sangha* with new eyes, as a newborn sees light and patterns in a new world for the first time. The gathered power of this community encompassed me—rolled over and through me like the waves of an incoming tide.

After a period of chanting while people gave *prasad*, Lee began to speak. He answered some questions, and then reiterated that he had written a letter to the *sangha* which he planned to read at this *darshan*. Immediately the *shakti* energy jumped into a range of such intensity that it was as if some Wizard of Oz behind a screen had turned up the electrical voltage in the field. The energetic lines of light crisscrossing the room flared into fiery strands, and there was an impression of dancing fireballs bouncing and shooting back and forth across the room.

Lee suddenly turned to Regina, a student responsible for much of the writing, editing, and communication in the school. "Actually, maybe Regina can read this. That would be better." Then, as he so often does, he counterbalanced the seriousness of the moment by cracking a last joke as he left the room.

Lee: "Wait a minute! I have to leave before you read it. You know all those stories about 'star people' that Bandhu told? Well, they're waiting for me out in the parking lot! [Laughter] We've called in the flying saucers!" He gathered *prasad* and sang, "De . . . de . . .de . . .de," as in "The Twilight Zone" theme song. Then, looking around the room, he added, as he walked out the door, "If some of your mothers could see you now!"

Somewhat stunned by this sudden departure, the physical absence of the master in the midst of the *darshan* that is focused on his presence (the literal meaning of the word *darshan* is "the sighting of the master"), people quieted still further.

Regina began to read. "April 17, 1987 . . ."

Then the tape was turned off, and the letter was later lost or destroyed. Shocking and penetrating as it was, it lives on only in the memory of those who heard it. So I must try to communicate its power from the depths of its effects on me in this initial approach to a school and a teacher so radically different from almost anything to be found in the Western world.

I found the letter heartbreaking, and I was not yet even a student. In it was such tenderness, such desire to meet us and guide us toward what was possible. It had the intimate invitation and promise of Jesus' words, "I am the good shepherd . . . and I lay down my life for the sheep." (John 10:14-15) Yet in this letter the master was saying that we, his students, had not been able to meet him at the place where he stood. We had not been able or willing to cross the river to find him in the paradise of shared work and communion that was waiting for us, that was the human birthright. He said that he had begun his work with us, reaching to us from a position of enlightened unity. We had not met him there; we had called to him for help from the swamps in which we chose to live. So he had left the gardens of paradise and had come down into the work of the Bodhisattva. Still we had not reached the place where he stood; so he had come down still further into the form of the *Heruka*. This was a more fierce manifestation of the original teaching, which he was to bring us. There was greater confrontation, even greater danger, in taking this form that brought him so much deeper into the manifest universe. He could not rest in the pure, subtle spirit of the teaching and bring us to that meeting place because we would not do the work of reaching him there. Since we still would not come to him, he had come yet further down to meet us. He had now crossed the river and was with us among the forms in which we had chosen to work. If we did not choose to work at this level, then he would have to drop into an even deeper and fiercer incarnate form. It would not be pleasant, for him or for us. And there could come a time when he could come no farther to meet us. This was the moment of possibility, and he begged us to make the effort to meet him here.

A student who had been with Lee almost from the beginning of the community—from the beginning of his teaching work—said later that he left this *darshan* feeling a kind of brokenness. It was so evident that we were not able or willing to meet Lee where he stood waiting for us; that we were not receiving what he had to give.

It may perhaps seem odd that while at one level I did not consider myself a student, I took Lee's communication in this letter with passionate seriousness. Apart from any rational excuses or defense I could have made, pleading that I was not among those who had refused to meet him, I felt this communication reach deep into my heart. It is only now, twelve years later, that I realize that in fact I was quite literally one of those who had refused to meet him where he stood waiting. If I had obeyed my first sense to move to Boulder directly from Atlanta, I would very likely have met Lee over a year earlier, at Christmas of 1985. I could have been receiving his direct teaching and the force of his physical presence for an entire year. This never dawned on me during that *darshan*, yet I had no impulse to protect or except myself from his communication. Whether or not he was my teacher, he offered something that I needed and wanted, and I understood from a place far deeper than reason or explanation that I had not yet met him in the place that was possible.

In considering my own failure to meet Lee the first time I was called, I realize that what blocked me was not just general distrust of myself, but a specific fear that I would be seduced into doing less than what was in total integrity to the work. I was afraid that I heard "Boulder" as my first destination because I wanted comfort, a place that was easy on people. Yet, in fact, once again it was fear itself that was the seduction. I was seduced by my fear of seduction. Although I made dramatic gestures of sacrifice and obedience in the ensuing year after leaving Atlanta, gestures which finally brought me permanently into Lee's company, all of these gestures would have been unnecessary if I had simply obeyed the first and simplest instruction: "Go to Boulder."

Our decisions have consequences. Each choice has a payoff and a cost. My disobedience, even though it was based in the intense desire to enact the highest obedience, cost me a year of my work with Lee. At the same time, the strength of my intention to follow the direction of the Work enabled that year to be held within the stream of energy of that Work, so that I learned profound and permanently useful lessons. If we learn from our mistakes, then we build energy through the process of correction that brings us forward into new possibility. The divine suffers for us these losses in time, and at the same time waits for us to return into the path of its energy, like the prodigal son returning to his father. The paradox of loss and learning that exists in our imperfect movement forward on this path can nourish in us both a sense of urgency and a sense of compassion.

The Celebration in the mountains lasted three days. The theme of the first day was Hindu spiritual life and practice; of the second, Jewish culture and practice; and of the third, the Renaissance. Quite a range to cover in three days! Lee's letter fit perfectly with this final theme. He was asking for a rebirth in his students' work with him—for a renewal that could enable an unimagined epoch to open in the life of the community.

On a practical level, we were invited to dress in costume for a Renaissance feast complete with dinner theater, an excerpt from Shakespeare's *Taming of the Shrew*. The two students who played Kate and Petrucchio gave a dynamic portrayal of the simultaneous repulsion and attraction between the polarities of man and woman. Once again I saw Lee through another facet of the prism that was slowly revealing this teacher of many faces and one purpose. Watching Kate and Petrucchio battle their way through surrender to love, I knew they were portraying not just an encounter scripted hundreds of years ago, but a possibility for relationship that lay at least latent in this school—a possibility that had begun to make itself visible in the developing bonds of community that I observed in the people I was meeting.

In the community publications given to me in August there had been a copy of the community journal, *Divine Slave Gita*, which I had hardly opened. But a quote of Lee's on the back cover had commanded my attention: "The work I have come to do is the same work you have come to do. I have assumed it; you have not." I knew this was true. If there was one thing that drew me increasingly toward Lee and his community, it was the clear knowledge that he was doing the same work I felt called to do. I had seen this in his eyes, and I had seen that he could guide me in this central intention.

The Celebration over, we descended from the mountain in a caravan of cars and trucks. For the first time, I was making not a solitary descent but a descent shared with others. Through this journey, I began to bond into a matrix—a being—larger than myself. Lee and his ashram residents returned to Arizona. Life in Colorado continued with weekly study group meetings, consideration of a new community household in Denver and, for me, gradual engagement of the foundational conditions of practice in this school.

To the extent that we can see things from a wider perspective, it can free us from either pride or shame, self-aggrandizement or despair, around our strengths and our shortcomings. We are simply elements in a field, and we are asked to maximize what we can contribute to that field. Methods of maximizing this contribution include obedience, effective action, commitment, intention, attention, and alignment to a guide—a teacher—who can help integrate us into that field and steer its movement so as to best serve the purposes of the work, the purposes of the divine.

How odd it seems to me now that two students of Lee could so instantaneously recognize that I was moving toward this school, that this was my place, while I myself was still focused on another path that I believed to be my ultimate direction. If I needed confirmation that those around us can reveal to us our blind spots, can often see us far more accurately than we can see ourselves, it was given to me at the very beginning. These new friends read my inner movement at a level I could not yet read myself.

The community household did not work out, and I moved into a house shared by members of the Institute for the Development of the Harmonious Human Being, a spiritual school founded and led by a teacher named E. J. Gold. While I continued to consider the Hohm community my guiding matrix, I began as an adjunct to attend weekly meetings of E. J.'s students as well. Coming from a position of total ignorance of any school other than the one in which I had originally participated for seven years, I was being given a gradual introduction to what I still consider to be some of the best spiritual schools in existence. If I were going to choose the Hohm community as my spiritual path, it would not be a blind choice, ignorant of other possibilities. It would be a choice based in recognition of the excellent work being done in a variety of schools, a foundation from which I could clearly choose the specific path and teacher that was calling me.

Even after my powerful experience of the Celebration, I was still trying to earn money to return east to my first school. Slowly, however, the determination to return east dissolved and died without my even noticing that my direction had shifted, like a sailboat spontaneously coming about in response to the prevailing winds. I was no longer eating at the table of this teacher as a guest with the intent to be on my way as soon as I had completed the meal. I was beginning to send down deep roots into the field of work of the community, and I was beginning to be nourished at that deeper level that becomes possible with a deepening level of commitment.

As an expression of this deepening, the consideration began to arise that part of right relationship to this field of work was to offer financial support, to tithe. After a year of dramatic change and irregular income, I was just beginning to achieve a minimal level of financial stability, and I still had nothing extra. Realistically, I didn't see how I could possibly add tithing to my financial commitments. Yet I had taken actions on faith that seemed totally unreasonable when I was acting solely on my own. Surely I could act from the same faith now that I had all the support of a growing matrix of community in my spiritual work.

The week after this consideration arose, when I received my paycheck I used a major part of it to make a payment to Hohm of ten percent of that month's income. This meant I didn't have enough money for the rent that would be due in two weeks, but I had decided that tithing came first, and that everything else would find its rightful place if I gave it priority.

It could be argued that this approach was irresponsible—that paying the rent and other worldly responsibilities should get top priority. I would say that it depends on context. If the context is essentially one of excuse, using tithing to avoid paying the rent and putting oneself in a position of dependency where someone else has to pay it, it is clearly irresponsible. If, however, the context is one of faith, and a clear decision is made that includes handling worldly responsibilities, the decision can open a door to energy flow. I knew that I would pay the rent, that I would fulfill this responsibility, even if it meant finding an extra job for a month or so.

The next week I got a call from a company that wanted help with a special project. They hired me at almost twice the salary I had been receiving. Having paid the tithe, I was able to pay the rent as well, with money left over.

The next time I saw Lee was the week before the July Celebration—Guru Purnima—in Arizona. Each year at the local Fourth of July fair, the ashram sold fry bread (a Native American invention, flat bread fried in oil with various toppings). This year the plan was to operate a game booth as well. The community sent out a call for help, asking if people could come to work at the fair the week before the Celebration. They needed hawkers for the game booth and workers day and night for the fry bread booth. A friend and I decided to respond and to drive together from Colorado.

PRESCOTT

It was as we planned our trip that I took the map out of the glove compartment in my car and discovered it was folded, from that day of choice almost a year earlier, so as to direct me to Prescott. What struck me as I looked at that folded map was the tangible evidence that there is a plan that guides our lives, a plan we can trust. For me, all roads led eventually to a small ashram hidden among the pines and junipers in the hills just outside Prescott, Arizona. Whatever the detours, through inescapable inner demand, through stubborn perseverance, and through the pervasive influence of an unseen plan, I had finally found my way to my destination.

We drove west through the Rockies and then south through the huge rock formations scattered through Monument Valley in Utah—formations that suggest the bodies of deities, great gods and goddesses, frozen at the instant of transmutation from body to pure spirit. When we reached Prescott Valley, thirty minutes from Prescott, we had to call for specific directions. At that time the exact whereabouts of the ashram was carefully and vigorously protected. Even approaching as visitors and invited helpers we were not given final directions until we were in physical proximity, making the ashram feel a little bit like Brigadoon, the magical community of the Scottish highlands that becomes visible to ordinary humans only once in a hundred years. If the inattentive or indecisive visitor does not seize the moment at which Brigadoon appears and follow directions exactly, the community will disappear from view, continuing on in another realm that is absolutely unreachable to those who could not choose and act in the required moment.

We were entrusted with the directional code for reaching the ashram gates and drove through them just fifteen minutes before dinnertime on a Tuesday evening. We had been told that Lee himself prepared the meal on Tuesday and Thursday nights, and that he followed the meal by a talk about the *dharma* and practice. To me this seemed like unbelievable generosity—that he would make the meal with his own hands, serving us rather than expecting us to serve him; and that he would create a space in which our individual questions could be intimately considered in a small group several times a week. Once on the ashram, I would discover that this generosity, his abundant availability to his students, extended far beyond these two or three evenings. He was present at his desk in the office during much of each day; he gave private meetings with students at their request; he played bridge many evenings, with an invitation to students to bring questions and considerations to the space. And periodically he took the entire community of ashram residents on trips to movies or talks by spiritual teachers or to festive dinners in Phoenix! In addition, he worked in the fry bread booth, a tiny enclosed kitchen, for long hours during the Fourth of July fair each year. To work with him there was both a coveted and feared position, as his demand for attention in the booth was exacting, even extreme. His irascible response when students failed to meet this demand had been felt by many.

The next day I was assigned to the game booth. At one point, on his way out of the booth, Lee paused at the game booth where I was calling out, in what I thought was a loud voice, "Games and prizes! Five throws for a dollar!" Apparently what a rather shy Quaker-bred woman thought was a loud voice didn't cut it for this job.

"You have to *yell!*" the spiritual master instructed me. "You have to shout so they can hear you!"

It was my first direct instruction from him. I had my first opportunity to choose obedience or disobedience in response to his practical and immediate direction. It may seem a simple thing to yell out to a crowd of people I didn't know and would never see again but, given my childhood training, it was not simple. To raise my voice in public above a certain limited decibel was to break a lock that surrounded my entire field of energy, my physical and subtle bodies. This was hardly what I would have expected as my first direct instruction from a tantric teacher on an esoteric spiritual path—to shout as loudly as I could, hawking basketball throws at a Fourth of July fair. But there it was. Spiritual life grounded in ordinary life—as ordinary as it could get. I began to yell with a breath that seemed to come from my toes: "Games and prizes! Five throws for a dollar! Try your skill!"

If only my compatriots in political activism in the '70s could see me now! I thought. Instead of speaking idealistic truths about peace and politics, which was the last time I had raised my voice in public, I was hawking basketball throws. Was this a change in form that I could possibly explain if challenged? My new compatriots in spiritual work would not challenge me; they all shared the view that this activity, inexplicable as it might seem, had profound value. To them, the booths were a way to make money to support the community's life and work. The booths were also, in and of themselves, forms of tantric work, of engaging the divine as found in the most mundane elements of incarnation. For myself, I was starkly aware of the difference between the choice of a life in which each spiritual practitioner potentially becomes a catalyst for consonance with divine direction in the world as a whole, and a life of external, political organizing that seeks to change social structures directly. It seemed clear to me that only by taking the risk of obedience while maintaining an attitude of discriminating evaluation was I going to find out whether this activity at the fair (and by extension, the life of spiritual apprenticeship which it represented) had value, or whether it was an unconscionable diversion from what was truly important and needed.

All day I shouted out my wares until, by the end of the afternoon, I was fairly hoarse. As we returned to the ashram, I realized that my entire being felt lighter, looser. All day I had been "blowing my own horn," not in the sense of vanity, but in the sense of purposefully allowing my voice to flow out of my body in a way that was totally opposite to my tendency. It was as if I had been Joshua, blowing the horn to break down the walls of the city of Jericho. The "city" that was being broken down was the crystallized structure of my own personality, a structure that was too small for the work that was coming. Lee had put me in the position of using the sound of my own voice to break down the entrenched walls of myself. It was my first experience of Lee as the sly man, the teacher who not by forethought but simply by the stream of his movement and choices creates situations in which we dismantle our own inner obstacles in the process of building something of value to a larger spiritual work.

Each day we rode in a crowded van to downtown Prescott, where booths filled the courthouse square. The fry bread booth was the favored assignment because that meant the chance to work with Lee. One morning my friend Margaret, a newcomer like myself, was invited to work on a shift with Lee, rolling the dough into balls that were then flattened and dropped into the hot oil. I was left on our usual shift hawking the games; but now I was without Margaret's company. Immediately, what had been a sunny morning filled with a routine that had become familiar and reliable shifted to an inwardly darkened sky. While externally I yelled out the invitation to throw baskets, inwardly I was struggling with feeling that I was not a worthwhile aspirant, whereas Margaret must show great promise, to be invited so quickly into the inner chamber of the fry bread booth where senior students commonly worked with Lee. Here I was spending my days in a way I could hardly justify to my political conscience, and apparently I wasn't even good at what I was doing, at spiritual work; at least not as good as Margaret.

I sensed that I had an opportunity in that moment to choose right relationship to the teacher. Whatever his choice about where he physically placed me, I had the choice as to how I let this placement affect me inwardly, and whether I let it distance me from him by throwing me into attention on my own sense of failure. Somewhere deep inside, I made a choice to place my attention on his presence, which pervaded the entire space in which we worked at the fair, rather than on his absence in my particular personal assignment at the game booths.

This is a choice I have faced in innumerable moments during my years in Lee's company. Sometimes I have been able or willing to make the wise choice that I made out of the innocence of beginner's mind that morning at the fair. That choice is the choice of real independence—of refusal to depend on the master's physical form but to trust in his energetic and pervading presence in our lives. That summer morning, at the game booths was where I could find him. For me, that was where he was. He had told me this by the simple action of placing me there, without ever saying a word to me.

I could not erase or deny the disappointment, sense of failure, or lack of self-worth that arose in the face of the discrepancy between Lee's choice for my friend and his choice for me. But I could choose to know those feelings, and I could choose to embrace his choice at the same time. In all the years I have now been with him, whenever I have made this same inner choice in relation to his actions and his choices for me, I have found—even in the midst of reactive emotions—a mysterious sweetness. Whenever I have chosen instead to energize my attachment to my own way as opposed to his guidance, I have entered into a series of hells. Not just one hell, but a series of emotional reactions that lead from one to the other like a descending stairway into the depths of the illusion of separation from all things: from myself, from my friends, from my teacher, from God.

That moment when I dealt with what seemed an unfavorable comparison between Margaret and me, where she was invited into the inner sanctum and I was not, was only one of many instances in which my closest friends were selected to accompany Lee in limited or private spaces to which I was not invited. In those early days I had no way of knowing that within only two years I would be living on the Arizona ashram and receiving the daily teaching lessons, difficult as they might be, that emerge in daily life with a teacher. If I had allowed those moments of comparison to define me and my capacity for work rather than using them at some level to deepen connection, I might never have found my way to the door that led into deeper relationship with my teacher and my work.

After the weekend of work at the fair, we entered a week of consideration of *dharma* and specific practice within the Hohm community, coupled with celebratory meals and events. A seminar entitled, "The Power to Create from Nothing: A Seminar on the Mastery of Distraction, Fantasy, and Seduction," focusing on how to manage and purposefully use our emotional and mental energies, comprised the first three days. It was a kind of training that is largely absent in our American culture; even the contemporary interest in psychotherapy is only beginning to bring some awareness of these possibilities.

The seminar was followed by the Hohm Community's version of a Baul *mela*. In India and Bengal, the Bauls, beggars and singers who wander the countryside through most of the year, traditionally gather once or twice a year for shared celebration and worship of the divine presence. Feasting, singing of mystical poetry, and wild, ecstatic dancing to the beat of the *ektara* and the rhythms of their sacred poetry fill the *mela*. In this Western spiritual community's version, we gathered on the concrete floor of an old tennis court on the ashram (a court left from earlier days in which the property was a Christian camp). Feasting, poetry, talks, and theatrical performances filled the weekend, completed by *darshan* on the final night of the Celebration.

Prior to that night, however, we were invited to a vastly different form of *darshan*—a dramatically different sighting of the master. After dinner Saturday night we piled into vehicles and drove to a local bar with a wide dance floor. We danced to a few taped disco tunes while preparations were completed. Then we were ushered into an inner, smaller room, with a stage at the front and a more limited but still ample dance floor. Two years earlier, at the enthusiastic celebration of a triple marriage of three couples in the community, Lee had inaugurated an impromptu rock 'n' roll band. That Saturday night of the Celebration, the band was resurrected, this time with new players for at least half of the positions. The band was called Living God Blues. They had auditioned with the club owner the week before. Having passed that initiation, they were ready to roll. The first notes reeled off the guitar strings and the drum beats began to pound, paving the way for entrance into an altered space, a space totally different, yet intimately related, to the respectful, serious sacred spaces in which we had met the master in the days preceding.

The notes were like a magnet dragging us deeper into an unexpected possibility and dragging the lead singers out of the darkness at the side of the stage into the central spotlight. They swaggered on stage, grabbed the mikes, and began to belt out songs like "Piece of My Heart" and "Under My Thumb." The singers were a woman with a husky, sweet voice and a man in tight leather pants and sunglasses—the spiritual master in an unprecedented guise.

Part of me was asking, Where is this man taking us? First, his version of spiritual life had turned this middle-class Quaker girl into a carnival hustler—a "carny," as they say in the trade. Now he was leading us into an inner room that instead of the communion of the Last Supper offered us the chance to sink down into the thinly veiled passion and primal rhythms of contemporary rock 'n' roll. This was spiritual life? It looked more like a slightly cleaned-up version of "Dirty Dancing"! Not that I looked any different from anyone else. My questions were in my head, but my heart and body were singing and dancing to the rhythms reverberating through the marrow of my bones as the amps were turned up and the energy rose along with them.

Then Lee broke into a song that brought all my questions and unease to a point of intense confrontation. He was singing, "Sympathy for the Devil." He was singing it for me, precisely articulating my conflict. Was I being seduced and tricked into sympathy for the devil? Or was this man skillfully and even humorously cracking open and dissolving my most favored and treasured identifications and assumptions so that I could discover a life so much broader and deeper than I had imagined that it appeared that until then I had tasted only its reflection?

For the Bauls of Bengal what was happening would not be the least surprising. It was the ecstatic evocation of mystical response to divine reality, which Bauls have practiced for hundreds of years. Four years later, when several Bauls from India visited our ashram and performed their sacred dances for us, they told us that rock 'n' roll is Lee's version of Baul music, with its encoding of sacred knowledge and its potential for awakening that sleeping knowledge, that Remembering, within those who hear.

Karuna, who shared the role of lead vocalist with Lee, wrote about that night:

> Lee was growling and coaxing, teasing and belligerent, his teeth bared, eyes flashing. He looked like a Tibetan terror deity, like a lean grey wolf, but I was so close I wasn't afraid. And we danced, steppin' to the walkin' blues . . .
>
> In the bigger picture, the LGB Band is not an instrument of catharsis or just a 'show.' We are *worked* by the powerful 'underworld' energies, the force of unconsciousness that is aroused at each performance. These energies and our interaction with them are Lee's tool for instruction and transformation with the particular experiment that is the Band.
>
> . . . We were *dismembered*—with laser optics . . . More than one dark shadow flickered over nearly every face, the anatomy of our own psyches exposed to us in X-ray. Grounded in practice and with a well-developed sense of the absurd (humor), we move through the X-ray machine, out the other side and keep going. We celebrate, we soar, and why not dance? (*Divine Slave Gita*, Prescott, Ariz.: Hohm Press, July-Sept. 1987, Vol. 7, No. 3, p. 37)

This was certainly a very different form of spiritual work from anything I had encountered previously!

Perhaps always a little slower than the body, by the next day my mind had come to an unexpected and even awed respect for the unconventional methods of this renegade spiritual master. Rather than experiencing the shamed and somewhat unclean "morning after" feeling of having engaged in some indulgence (whether of sex or a physical substance), I felt radiantly bright, as if deeply cleansed. In the field of the primal beat of the drums and the guitar notes alternately ripping through the space, old internal structures had been tumbled and broken, revealing energies long trapped in those forms and making them available for use. Of course we do not, typically, change deeply and permanently in one moment or from one event—although this can happen, especially in the company of the teacher. Yet my experience of a "free moment" provided a reference point to which I could return and to which I could build access through practice.

At the time I had hardly heard of tantra, which had not yet become a trendy staple of the New Age scene. I did not know that ancient tantric texts describe working with the ordinary elements of the common world as potential doorways into deeper reality. Baul practices in particular work through the physicality of the body and its physical substances and emanations. Although I had never read of practices which meet and work with spirit in its most dense physical manifestations, I was being given the chance to experience something of this approach to an inner chamber through the medium of rock 'n' roll.

The experience of the previous evening was for me a glimpse of the process of the alchemy of transformation, something of the central work of this school. In that process, our lowest elements, the "lead" of our human passions—our desires for sex, for food, for drama, for love—are not just allowed or accepted but are pur-

posefully evoked and even energized, under certain correct circumstances, so that the energy locked in them can be released,
refined, and finally transmuted into the "gold" of the higher passions. These higher passions include the bearing of others'
sufferings which we call compassion, and the passionate seeing and
even adoration of the other which is objective love, both of which
are finally transformed into that ultimate human passion which is
the longing for the divine.

The next night Lee held a traditional *darshan*. He sat dressed
in white, serene and regal on a large silk-covered chair on a dais in
front of the hall. Burning incense filled the room with a sweet and
exotic scent redolent of the mysteries of India and of the yet further mysteries of the realms beyond physical place into which Lee
was guiding us. Dressed with respectful elegance, carrying our
prasad, we entered the room and bowed, heads to the floor, before
taking our seats, cross-legged, on round cushions. I, of course, did
not consider myself a devotee. This was not even my teacher, and
even if I had been looking for a teacher, I would not be looking for
the role of devotee. I was looking for the Work. Devotion had little if anything to do with work, as far as I knew. Yet I felt welcomed,
whatever my exact relationship to this teacher and his community
might be. And I was aware that the devotion these students brought
to their teacher created an energy that I found deeply nourishing
for my work. How inexplicable it all seemed.

Chanting in ancient Sanskrit filled the room. Though the
language was totally unknown to me, I sensed the power encoded
into the very sound of each word. I sensed a transmission of spiritual power similar to what I had experienced when I had heard the
Catholic mass sung in its original Latin. There is value to making
scripture accessible to the masses, comprehensible to contemporary participants; yet there is great danger in some of the methods
by which we open this accessibility. In losing touch with the origi-

nal languages in which scripture and ritual were informed and encoded, we lose unknown and perhaps infinite dimensions of ancient knowledge that were esoterically seeded into the frequencies and vibrations of those oral transmissions. In the small *darshan* hall in the mountains of Arizona, in the beleaguered enclaves of Tibetan Buddhism in its own land, and in other half-hidden islands of remembrance, these sounds still nourish dimensions and deities which this planet forgets at its own peril.

As the chanting rose and fell, each of us in turn approached Lee's chair and offered *prasad*. The offering of *prasad* had not become easy for me. Each time I approached Lee in this ritual I found myself filled with both joy and strong reticence. Sometimes we can will ourselves to carry out forms of action even when the experience or quality that rightly fills those forms is lacking. If this action is carried out without inner acknowledgment that the spirit is missing, the action can constitute pretense. But if the effort is honestly carried out as a commitment to give what we can, even when in the moment that gift is only the outer form, then the action can sometimes open the way to the missing spirit.

Giving *prasad* to Lee and bowing in *darshan* has sometimes been such a time for me. Each time I have carried out this action—committing myself at least to the form of giving if I could give no more of myself—there has been a shift at the moment of bowing and then meeting Lee's eyes. The reticence is transformed to tenderness. Not tenderness toward me or from me, simply the existence of tenderness, as a fact of God.

As I sat in my first formal *darshan* on the ashram, I was washed by the paradoxical currents of this school and its guide. This man who had sung guttural rhythms the night before—the man who had swaggered on stage and created visual sexual innuendoes with the mike—this man was sitting with such formal elegance in front of us now, and unmistakable qualities of compassion and deep kindness radiated from him, along with a sense of fierce and uncompromising attention to what is true.

Then the chanting was over. Lee asked for questions and gave penetrating and compassionate answers that spoke directly to the student's deeper question, often verbally unasked. Then in the midst of this formality and perceptive wisdom, he broke into some lengthy and vulgar or bawdy joke. Sometimes he made himself laugh so hard he cried, at the joke or at some ironic facet of the human condition or at some humorous, unshared vision. Then, hardly pausing for breath, he moved into a sublime consideration of pristine *dharma*. Following him in this unpredictable movement was like following some leaping dancer full of the passionate, untamed rhythms of the south whose feet stamp in obedience to an essential order with such flare that the eye can hardly discern the underlying pattern.

During this Celebration Lee asked for people who were willing to move to Aptos, California, to participate in one of the strongest study groups and a lively community household there. Again I felt that clear sense of inner direction. I asked Lee if I could join the Aptos household.

APTOS

Two months later I traveled to the ashram in Arizona for a visit before driving on to California with a friend who was also moving to Aptos. The night before we left for California we shared in a late-night feast with Lee and all the members of the ashram. We were invited to sit in Lee's circle, seated cross-legged on the floor as servers filled the center of the circle with the components of the feast. The menu was planned as a surprise, so we watched with eager anticipation and curiosity as it gradually manifested in front of us.

These feasts late in the evening were a weekly tradition at that time, a space in which ashram residents, living a simple renunciate lifestyle during the rest of the week, shifted into abundant and even opulent celebration, feasting on not only physical food but on the mood of communion which could arise in that space. Underneath all the outer flamboyance of food and storytelling and laughter, it was a space of waiting—waiting for the presence or the merest touch or breath of the divine Beloved. Sometimes the space fell suddenly from raucous laughter into reverent silence. Sometimes from silence we would break into inexplicable laughter.

Often the feasts focused on Middle Eastern or Greek or gourmet creations, from spicy lamb stew to desserts over which the cooks labored for an entire day. But that night the meal could not have been more different. It was the menu of a classic American diner: eggs scrambled or over-easy, bacon, sausage, coffeecake, and strong coffee. After the meal, my friend Dennis and I planned to drive all night across the desert. This meal, planned with no knowledge or linear connection to our small personal plans, was the serendipitously perfect send-off, filling us with the food of an American diner before we took to the road with all the other night-time truck drivers crossing the great distances of the United States and stopping for coffee at the diners that line the trucking routes that connect deserts, plains, and mountains. Like the travelers in the Eagles' song, "Hotel California," we had stopped at a "diner" that might serve coffee just like all the others, but to walk through its doorway was to enter a magical space in which unknown dimensions could open. Like all magical spaces, it held both danger and possibility as two sides of one reality. It was our relationship to this reality that determined what we would find.

We sat in Lee's company, drinking his presence as we drank the coffee, and after he left the space, we sat late into the night with friends in the *sangha*. When we finally left, I was so sharply awake with the piercing sweetness of the evening that I drove all night while Dennis slept. As dawn dissolved the night and we drove out of the mountains into the lush valleys of California, we stopped and drank the last of the coffee from the large thermos we had been presented with before we left. It was definitely a mysterious and magical brew, a black nectar reminiscent of the black skin of Krishna in Indian paintings.

Again there was that sense that the nectar of the gods is not just sweet, but dangerous to our commonly held conventions and the comfortable illusions in which we perhaps survive but do not fully live. Coffee is not part of the usual diet of the Hohm community; it is a forbidden substance, to be drunk only under certain prescribed conditions within which it can offer a totally different possibility than simply making the heart race with caffeine-induced adrenaline. In drinking the coffee served that evening we were drinking a substance that could either toxify or purify.

This is the reason that ancient traditions guarded and pro-scribed the conditions under which ritual substances could be ingested. Their power can either harm or heal, destroy or create, close or open the doors to sacred spaces. I have found that even one cup of coffee drunk in disrespect of Lee's instruction can create a dissonance that destroys a moment of possibility. Repeated choice of such small actions of disrespect and disobedience can finally close doors with a frightening finality. On the other hand, use of such substances in obedience and in consonance with the guide's instructions can reveal and open doors that are otherwise hidden and inaccessible.

The principle that physical food can be irradiated by the sub-tler energies of the divine so that when we partake of it we partake also of the subtle energies that have infused it is an underlying principle in both the Christian ritual of communion and that of the giving and receiving of *prasad* in Eastern traditions. This process culminates in the principle of transubstantiation, in which physical food literally becomes the divine body that has entered and changed its very substance. It is perhaps for this reason that feasting plays a great part in many religious rituals—and certainly in those of the Hohm community.

On a deeper level, every substance we ingest—from a cup of coffee or a fresh garden carrot to emotional impressions—has a potential effect on our work body, physical and subtle. When we "consume" what is convenient and comfortable, on either the physical or energetic level, we shut out the substances created through awareness, work, and alignment to the divine that can make all human life a sacrament of communion: the transubstantiation of the divine into the incarnate world through which it can express.

A few weeks after I arrived in Aptos, Lee and a group of students from the Arizona ashram visited the household for a kind of mini-celebration. Lee gave public talks in Aptos, San Francisco, and Berkeley. There was a celebratory meal prepared by a Japanese sushi chef. *Golub jaman*, an Indian dessert, was specially ordered from an Indian restaurant in Berkeley. The mood was sweet and rich with festivity and the intimate company of the teacher. Except he was still not *my* teacher.

Why would we run away from the gift of the teacher? This is potentially the most profound relationship we can engage in human incarnation, a relationship which colors and transforms all other relationships: the relationship to the transcendent divine manifested in a human guide who stands as a doorway into deeper realms. Yet the entry into these realms is not without price. It is not a superficial exploration from the safety of a tour bus. It is an entry in which we ourselves become the food that is eaten by the deities whom we meet. It is only in becoming that food—in being dismembered, fused into a larger body, and finally remade—that we discover the possibility that lies hidden, yet inherent, in the human creation. I had entered the outer chambers of the community, yet I was still shielding myself, as best I could, from the annihilating force of direct relationship to the teacher, the apocalyptic consequences of commitment. Lee had clearly communicated to me in that first interchange in Colorado that the issue of commitment to relationship would have to be faced if I wanted to penetrate into the inner chambers of work that I sensed and sought, the chambers where the unknown mystery of objective love could open. Now I was walking through the deepening fields of relationship, the process of bonding, which led toward that choice.

I was aware of the bonding that was taking root with other *sangha* members, although I still hid from myself the depth of bonding that was taking place with the teacher. I asked Lee whether it was lawful or irresponsible to continue to participate and bond more and more deeply with the community when I expected at some point to return to another spiritual group. Was I building a matrix of relationship that would turn to an experience of betrayal at my departure?

Lee's answer was that there is only one Work. I could participate in this community as long as it was useful and resonant; if I moved on to another spiritual community at some point, it would not constitute betrayal but simply a shift to another matrix within the one field of the Work. His response was dramatically different from that of teachers who try to frighten or seduce students into participation in their particular school. Implicit in his answer was profound respect for other spiritual communities and confidence in the sustenance of relationships based in a shared commitment to spiritual work. His answer set me free from my fear of commitment to relationship to this teacher, my tenacious commitment to running away.

Among all of the public events and celebratory feasts, one quiet evening remains most memorable for me. The Aptos house was a gigantic structure, a former live-in therapeutic community. It included something like thirteen bedrooms and a spacious living room opening onto an upper porch looking out from the mountainside toward the ocean. A labyrinth of outdoor stairs and balconies led to a small protected rooftop porch, much like the flat roofs on which Jesus taught or the Sufi mystic Rabia prayed. Although Lee usually chose enclosed indoor spaces for teaching circumstances—spaces that were both physically and energetically contained—this particular evening he uncharacteristically announced that he would be on the rooftop porch if anyone wanted to bring questions or considerations. Like iron filings moving into a pattern around the magnetic core, one by one we found our way to the rooftop in the warm dusk of a September evening in California. Some people were still busy with washing dishes or preparations for the next feast and some chose this unscheduled moment for a little personal space—for a time of recovery from the inundation of people and energy in a densely-packed week of teaching and festivity. As a result the group that gathered around Lee was small and full of intention.

In this smaller and more intimate setting, people began to ask Lee questions about their personal practice, about the meaning of the *dharma* in relation to their own individual circumstances, about their relationships with mates, children, and *sangha*. Lee answered each question with care, based in specific perceptions of and relationship with the individual student. Mediated through the verbal dialogue, Lee was communicating a mood, a transmission once again about relationship, this time through example. There was a sense of vulnerability, of intimate consideration of the personal implications of impersonal principles. As the evening deepened into darkness, we could see only the shadowy silhouettes of our companions and the light from a few candles reflected in each other's eyes. Through the words and the currents of energy emanating from Lee, we were being woven into one tapestry, one unified creation. We were being given a momentary experience of the possibility engendered by bonding.

Lee gave particular focus to a question about relationship to children. He spoke about how our relationship to children could give us a reminder of innocence, a doorway through which to return to our own organic innocence. Even if this doorway opened only for an instant, that experience of the deepest reality could reorder the entire set of relationships, the matrix, which lay above it. If the foundation that underlay real relationship became accessible even for a moment, it could permeate and shift and even dissolve the false foundations we had laid over it. It could shift the context of our relationships and our world view because we would recognize that instantaneous experience as most real, most trustworthy, most consonant with the life of the divine which informs us and is the true foundation of our lives. He spoke of having receptivity to each other so this innocence could emerge.

As he spoke he was modeling for us this mood of receptivity, evoking in us something buried and forgotten, hidden by wounds, yet itself unwounded and accessible to someone who knew how to evoke it, someone who knew the way through the labyrinth. He was guiding us through that labyrinth and he was paying the guardians of those secret spaces with his own vulnerability. In the darkened evening, as we talked quietly and laughed sometimes without even being able to see each other, he was providing an experience of the vulnerability and intimacy integral to that innocence. Then the moment was over; that space was complete, and we dispersed into the evening, taking with us the gift that had been given.

During Lee's visit he made trips with small groups of his students to meet various teachers in the area. I was invited to participate in his visit to Green Gulch Farm, a Zen center headed by Sensei Reb Anderson, whose teacher was Suzuki Roshi, the

Japanese Zen master perhaps singly most responsible for bringing this tradition to the United States in a form Americans could embrace. It was my first visit to a traditional Zen center of this kind, and I found it impressive. There was a compelling sense of elegance expressed through simple order. This principle was evident both in the physical structures—the buildings and gardens and the huge single gong at the center of the inner courtyard—and in the relationships among practitioners. There was obviously work going on here.

We were given a tour that included a traditional Zen teahouse that was spectacular in its spare simplicity and its adherence to classical forms. We were told that Japanese builders specifically trained in the art of building teahouses had been brought over from Japan to build it, and it was used only for tea ceremonies carried out in precise adherence to the classic protocols of the ceremony. We did not have tea because the teahouse had not yet been ceremonially dedicated. Yet even prior to actual use, the teahouse radiated emanations encoded into its walls, which became the matrix in which human and divine could meet, through the serving of tea, in right relationship of all elements. It was an outstanding example of the way in which physical spaces and structures can create the possibility for energies beyond the physical to enter our human spaces and become a doorway to the presence of the divine.

After Lee left for Arizona, we returned to daily life and practice and participation in a community study group. Lee had blessed the Aptos house, and this blessing permeated the life of the household even while we struggled with the usual difficulties in our relationships with each other, our jobs and finances, and our efforts at outreach in the California culture so focused on New Age ideas of effortless harmony without the interference of a physical teacher.

One of the members of our household was a man who, like myself, was not a formal student but who was a close personal friend of Lee's and who had been associated with the community for a number of years. His name was Marco Vassi, and in the '60s and '70s he had authored *Stoned Apocalypse* and other radical, sexually explicit literature. Now he was facing AIDS and the prospect of death. After his wild and experimental past, he lived with quiet dignity in a small single room in the household. I was busy with a new job, helping with the children, and participating in outreach efforts, and it was only on a few rare occasions that I found myself engaged in conversation with him. Yet in these conversations, and perhaps even more in his silence, I felt in him a penetrating sensitivity and subtle awareness that are not common. It struck me that Lee attracts those with such an awareness of subtleties—those who can see beneath the exterior play and rough facade that he often presents as a disguise for a teaching of great elegance which is offered only to those who can discover and use it.

At the same time, Lee, both through his energetic presence and through the welcome of the Aptos household, offered to this man a sanctuary that he perhaps had never known. The law of hospitality is one of the most central laws in Lee's teaching, one that he emphasizes and elucidates repeatedly. In offering hospitality to this man who was not a formal or fully practicing student, we received in return an example of the dignity and integrity with which the human can face both life and death.

Marco was a man whose behavior and writings were often shocking in a way that might indicate a harsh lack of any relationship beyond such external forms as indiscriminate sexual encounter. Yet, at his death hundreds of people from all walks of life attended his funeral to express their gratitude and appreciation; to acknowledge the ways in which Marco had touched them, as he had touched me, through an undeniable force of being. It seems to me that it is frequently those who are most sensitive and most subtly aware who have the most difficulty adjusting to the conditions of a society that is so largely insensitive to the basic needs of the conscious human. These individuals may appear wild or crazy or ineffectual, yet have deeply nourishing effects upon us. Such persons not uncommonly recognize Lee and he recognizes them because they share an awareness too sharp to imprison in the common forms of life. The difference in Lee is that he has the wisdom and comprehension to be able to traverse these realms consciously and purposefully, to guide us through them. Awareness without comprehension and foundation in a larger reality can be overwhelming to the point of insanity. The structures that allow us to handle such an awareness are built through practice under the guidance of a teacher.

Each morning we meditated and sang *arati* in our small meditation hall. This hall had been the master bedroom, offering the maximum in luxurious comfort to its privileged residents. It had been converted into a *darshan* hall of simple elegance, filled with the power of intention and consistent practice.

On Sundays, in the absence of the master's physical presence in *darshan*, we gathered for *kirtan*, a time of chanting and listening to a tape of one of Lee's talks. Much as I loved hearing Lee's voice and his considerations, the chanting held an unexpected power of its own. As the *dumbeck* drums beat out the rhythm, and our voices joined in sounding ancient Sanskrit syllables, I sometimes felt we were creating a space that lifted off the ground and lived in a wholly different dimension from ordinary human consciousness. Each element in the ritual—the use of incense, the intention with which fresh flowers were prepared and placed in proper relationship in a vase, the attention brought to the syllables we chanted in a language we did not know—seemed to have a particular function in this creation.

The power of this possibility permeated the following week as we dealt with the practical details of our jobs, our care of the children, our house meetings and even our trips to the movies, reminding us that our lives could be lived from that context of possibility. To contact those realms and dimensions did not mean to abandon ordinary life, but to engage it more fully.

SPIRITUAL WARRIORSHIP

In October we drove to Boulder once again. Lee was scheduled to present a joint talk with a teacher from California whom he had met briefly once before. The talk had been organized by followers of the other teacher and by one student from our school who had been strongly impressed by the teacher at the previous meeting. From what I had heard of that meeting, the man sounded like a manipulative charlatan. I wondered to what degree Lee might have agreed to the talk simply as a teaching lesson for this one individual, who happened to be a senior student and one of the most central participants in the school.

Beyond this service to his own student, it seemed to me that Lee was offering what he calls an "object lesson,"—a lesson in action—for anyone who might choose to hear it. He was giving people the chance to see through manipulation and misuse of a position of authority by offering a contrast in the same space. He would not verbally explain and make the discrimination which people needed to learn to make for themselves; but he would, through his own behavior and communication, expose what was real and what was not for those who chose to make use of his offering.

When the night for the joint talk arrived, the room was full not only of people but of anticipation of an unusual and unpredictable event. The title for the talk, chosen by the other teacher or his students, was "Naked in the Garden," a seductive and sexually titillating title calculated to draw people in with the promise of revelation of mystery. It was quite different from the kind of confrontational challenge that Lee often offers in his talk titles—a strategy that requires people to face and surmount a barrier of reaction just to choose to attend.

After everyone was seated, the two teachers entered the room from the back, walking up a center aisle to the chairs in front. The other man, dressed in dirty sneakers and a sweater and jeans, seemed to be trying to effect an air of casual ease. To me, however, his dress and manner conveyed an internal sloppiness, a disregard and disrespect for those around him.

In contrast, when Lee entered the room, the dignity and clarity of the warrior entered with him. He was dressed in a simple black Japanese kimono, similar to the robes of a priest or a martial artist, and his carriage was simultaneously unassuming and fiercely erect and present. He was ready to fight for the teaching. If the other man was there for the teaching as well, then there would be no fight but a shared teaching. If the other man intended to distort the teaching and try to use its power for personal gain, Lee would unveil him in the aikido manner, which uses the opponent's own energy to disarm him and render him harmless.

In the next two hours, Lee proceeded to do just that. The other teacher proclaimed that he was not there to teach or to manipulate people; he was there to make friends. He said that with him people could find love. He said that everyone is starved for love, for friendship; and he was there to offer to be the best friend they had ever had. He tried to ride on Lee's energetic power one moment, saying that he and Lee were the same in one way or another. Then, when Lee skewered this power play with a dexterous joke, he would switch and make cutting remarks about how Lee was trying to manipulate us but that he would show us how not to be fooled.

Lee never stooped to such tactics. He did not defend himself or attack the other; he simply used a relaxed sense of humor and simple statements of truth to communicate the teaching for those who wished to hear. He said that he did not love the people in the room—that he was not there to offer us love but to expose to us the self-deceit in which we lived and to offer the possibility that, by a life of practice and effort, we might discover a level of living that was more real, a life through which we could serve.

By the end of the evening the other man was visibly frustrated that he had not been able to work his usual magic on his audience. Lee allowed the event its scheduled three hours, and then he crisply closed the space, saying, "Well, we have plans for dessert after the talk, so this is the end of the talk for me." Lee and his students left while the other teacher and a number of people stayed, the teacher desperately trying to snatch "victory from the jaws of defeat."

A student of Lee's wrote a report of that evening for our community journal, at the time called *Divine Slave Gita*. She described how the manipulations attempted by the other teacher were gradually revealed not by any direct confrontation by Lee, but by the simplicity of Lee's direct and real relationship with those in the room.

> Whenever Lee spoke, I perceived a remarkable shift in the room. The space was immediately redefined. Lee was pulling no punches, he was simply real and present. Actually strictly speaking, he *had* pulled a number of punches—on the surface. His inflammatory remarks really riled up the crowd, but I saw that he was perfectly available to any sincere questioner. When Lee spoke the room changed color, it got lighter,

almost translucent to the eye. He looked quite masterful and noble to me. The contrast to T.'s itchy coarse energy and juvenile posturing was becoming dramatic. Next to Lee, T. looked more and more like a sulky punk. T. played dirty with his audience *and* with Lee. Amazingly these manipulations of T.'s were having no effect on Lee. His regal presence opposite T. and his unruffled good-humored response to the goings-on was truly powerful. Lee had nothing to prove. The serenity of his body spoke louder than words. (*Divine Slave Gita*, Prescott, Ariz.: Hohm Press, Oct.-Nov.-Dec. 1987, Vol. 7, No. 4, p. 47)

A year later this same man asked to visit the Arizona ashram. I expected Lee to respond with an emphatic rejection based on the man's display of the ultimate poor taste of trying to use the teaching for his own aggrandizement and personal power. Yet Lee welcomed him and the woman with him and treated them with his usual pristine hospitality. The only sense I could make of this contradiction was that if someone has the capacity to teach, and has the slightest chance of being able to use help to become more able to teach, Lee is both willing and obligated to respond. He was given such help when he himself was beginning to teach, and he gives this in turn. The fact that this man had a lot to learn, first of all about himself, did not exclude the possibility that he could make real use of help, and Lee was willing to give him the chance.

Lee offered a similar quality of unstinted hospitality to a teacher who came from Germany in the winter of 1988. This was the man who had first invited Lee to come to Europe, to participate in the conference, "Atem aus Kosmos." That visit was the

beginning of Lee's teaching work in Europe, which has grown rapidly over the years.

On first meeting, I found this man to have both a brilliance
that could clearly contribute to valuable teaching work and a
demanding arrogance that would make it difficult for him to
accept the help, or even shared effort with other teachers, that
could allow this brilliance to become refined and usable in relationship. Since my teacher has consistently proclaimed his own
arrogance, from the first days of his teaching through his most
recent poems to his Master, Yogi Ramsuratkumar, it may seem odd
that I would find arrogance a stumbling block. Yet meeting this
teacher brought into sharp clarification the different contexts in
which arrogance can operate.

In Lee arrogance is an admitted characteristic which is conscious and clear to him through his own self-observation, and he
intentionally allows this quality, like all other qualities in his character, to become simply an object of use by and for Yogi
Ramsuratkumar and the Work. In the visiting teacher, arrogance
was an unconscious attribute, which he did not admit and could
not therefore use or allow to be used in service to the Work. Even
what we may consider our negative qualities can be useful to our
spiritual work if we are clearly aware of them, without defense, and
if we dedicate these attributes to the use of the Work. If, however,
our unconscious intention is that these characteristics be used for
our own aggrandizement and the domination of others, they are
unusable and indeed indigestible in the field of work. We are
forced into a position of denial, of lying to ourselves, by our own
attachment to these characteristics and their potential selfish uses.

In contrast, when we dedicate ourselves, as we are and as we
may become, to the service of the Work, then the Work both uses
and changes these forms as needed. E. J. Gold has said that our
chief feature, our chief negative characteristic, in fact becomes our

major asset, the doorway through which we enter into deeper work. The apparently negative or dark side of the characteristic, our weakness, is only the shadow side, the unredeemed appearance, of our deepest strength. As we own and come into relationship with that weakness or darkness in ourselves, the very remorse and suffering of our own interior wound makes us vulnerable to truly feeling the suffering of others—perhaps even the suffering of God. Through that suffering we are able to come to a true responsiveness, a willingness to accept full responsibility in the Work.

I remember seeing Lee sitting on the front steps of the main building on the ashram, talking with the German visitor. Lee's entire aura was transmitting his intention to serve this man as a developing teacher, if the man could be served. In the man's aura, two intentions struggled for dominance. One was a real desire for this help that a senior teacher could give. The other was pride which could not admit the simple fact that he was not the equal or superior of the man so freely offering him sustenance, offering respectful support for his own development. In the end the arrogant pride won. This man had to denounce and reject Lee in order to hide from himself his own refusal of gift and the implicit consideration that he had something still to learn—something he could learn from Lee.

While Lee is quite willing to expose, when necessary, the manipulations and abuse of the teaching by a teacher who lacks clear commitment to the Work, he has always been more passionately concerned with affirmation of the work of those he considers real and trustworthy teachers. In particular, he has been a fierce advocate for those he considers real teachers who are attacked and rejected, often by their own communities, for particular actions that the community finds reprehensible. These may include questionable sexual conduct, use of money, or other behaviors that the *sangha* finds inexplicable. Some of these forms of behavior have been commonplace in ancient traditions of crazy wisdom in the East. At the same time, similar outer forms have been used by recent charlatans in the West who try to justify their abuses of power with *dharmic* excuses. While Lee teaches his students the need for piercing discrimination, he is highly critical of those who reject a real teacher for actions that merely outrage Western conventional thinking. In an interview by a student of Andrew Cohen's for the journal *What Is Enlightenment?* Lee was asked what he would most like to be remembered for. He replied that he would like to be remembered as an advocate for real teachers who were misunderstood and maligned because their behavior confronted contemporary conventions and orthodoxy. (This was an interview by Hal Blacker for the Summer 1995 issue; this particular exchange was not included in the published article.)

TAKING IT TO THE STREETS

In November of 1987 I visited the Arizona ashram again for the Appearance Day Celebration, or the birth of the guru, a traditional ritual in India among devotees of a spiritual master. The theme of this Celebration was "The Streets." To go more deeply into the meaning of this theme than simply listening to talks, we were encouraged to dress in costumes and take on the character of someone living on the streets. This might be a homeless person, a drug dealer, or a con man savvy in the reading of other people's weaknesses and dynamics. Without deep thought about my character, I chose to dress as a New York street prostitute.

I took the invitation to "become" a street person more as a game than as a serious exercise. It was a chance to be flamboyant, to act out a somewhat different persona from shy Quaker girl with high political ideals. The "game," however, did not last long. Within a few hours of donning the costume I began to experience a deep distrust of Lee as a teacher. Why was he initiating such an exercise? This persona felt degrading, not inspiring. After a few minutes of enjoying the shock of presenting myself as someone entirely different from my usual self, it was not much fun. My own character and those of the "pimps" and "pushers" around me felt far too real.

I could not understand why we would choose to take on roles that degraded the human being. Why not go straight to what is most real in us, and share that with each other, in celebration? Why feed with our energy the forms of degradation of the human being: prostitute, addict, pimp, bag lady, derelict?

At that moment I felt a deep and frightening distrust of Lee and of what he was doing—a distrust of at least his awareness and competence, and, harder to face, perhaps even of his motives and intention. Was he mistaken in the direction he was guiding us? Was he wrong? Finally I made an effort of will to tune inside and let arise the guidance Lee would give if I were able to ask for his help in that moment. The answer was clear and simple. He would say, without any of the fear or pressure or dramatic intensity that I was energizing, "Just try it out and see how it goes. See what you get from it, or don't get."

So—try it out, try out something unfamiliar and repugnant to me. This meant *really* try it out, knowing I would evaluate it afterward, rather than never really doing it and therefore having no real evidence or experience to evaluate. This meant really being the hooker whose clothes I was wearing.

The moment I chose to really try it out, everything began to change. It became clear that what was unbearable was the stark and isolated pain of who I was as a prostitute. I was already feeling her experience without recognizing that simply putting on her clothes had taken me so far into her life. But as I owned her experience as my own, I discovered that I had been holding onto this level of pain to avoid facing a much deeper level. This was the core pain—the grief—that arose in response to selling myself. And as I faced this pain, I realized that I am no different from that prostitute. I sell myself; and like her, I sell only *part of myself*, withholding that which is most real. Day by day, moment by moment, I give less than what is true, less than I know, less than I am capable of giving. I give less than who I am. I give only what will "sell," in an attempt to procure approval, control, affection, or love. The prostitute gives the form of sex without love, for money. I give the form of myself—some "acceptable" part of myself—for no more praiseworthy returns. The men who come to the prostitute do not choose to pay for love, for to pay for love would be to give themselves, wholly, to a relationship involving daily intimacy, compassion, and responsibility. The men ask only that the prostitute give them the form, for which they can pay with no strings attached—no strings such as human relationship, human Being.

What is the pain of being a hooker? It is the pain of relating as thing to thing, rather than as being to being; the pain of relating to *how I am seen* rather than to who I am. It is the pain of living as less than that divinity which we are—the pain of selling our place in the Great Work for the "pottage" of survival, approval, or love. To be a hooker is to provide what people want on a surface level and to receive a surface reward in return. It is very easy, at one level—and in that kind of ease the being is suffocating and dying.

To the extent we hold ourselves as hostages and prostitutes to the things we think we need, Life can only touch us—reach us—by breaking down our structures. So it broke down my concepts about how a Celebration should work, what my role should be in life, and how I should relate to the community. The learning that night came through trusting Lee enough to try out something that seemed questionable to me; living my question; and trusting myself enough to know that I could evaluate and make choices about experience after engaging it.

After traversing my own crisis in trust and relationship to Lee's guidance and his methods, I sat at the following meal next to a couple who had been students of the Indian master Osho (Rajneesh). They had recently begun participating in the Hohm community, and this was their first or second Celebration. We began discussing the Celebration, its theme, and the experience of dressing in costume and taking on a character in relation to the theme.

"Some people seem to think Lee is just playing games with these costumes and characters," the man observed, with obvious respect for Lee's way of working and recognition of the demand it placed on us. "They think we're dressing up just for fun. They really don't get what he is doing. This guy is playing spiritual hardball."

RETURN TO PRESCOTT

Sometime that fall Lee had announced that a major ashram business was for sale and asked if any members of the *sangha* living in outreach wanted to take it on. A number of people responded, among them several from the Aptos household, and plans were made to move the business to Boulder. As a result, we decided the Aptos household would close at the end of the year. At the same time, we received a plea for help from the ashram in Arizona. They needed help with community businesses, cooking, office work, and the community bookstore in town and were inviting people to come for two to six weeks to help support the small ashram crew. I volunteered to work in the office for six weeks, and several of my friends volunteered to assist with other ashram jobs. We left Aptos in a van once again, stopping at the headlands of Monterey to feel the ocean waves splash us one last time before we departed for renunciate dwelling at the edge of the desert.

103

We arrived in Arizona in December of 1987, in time for the community's first Baul Feast, between Christmas and New Year's eve. Friends were gathered from all directions, even from across the ocean. After the trip to India in 1986, Lee had been invited by a teacher he met there to participate in a conference in Europe the following summer. As a result, he was beginning to gather a group of dedicated students in Europe as well as in the United States. Some of these students were making their first visit to the Arizona ashram, adding an international flavor to our gathering, which was so large that a new, makeshift, dining hall had to be built for the feast.

An ashram that began with only twelve founding residents was expanding into an international *sangha*, and the physical space was densely packed both with human bodies and with high currents of energy. The Feast menu was rich with gourmet creations, from spiced nuts and wine to roast goose, with French chocolate *gateau* as a climax. After Lee left, some of us stayed late into the night, drunk not on wine but on our mutual passion for the *dharma*, our gratitude for the discovery of this small hidden sanctuary where the heart could open, and on the mood of communion fed through this lovingly prepared meal and the Host who served it out of his heart, through the hands of his devotees.

It was the end of 1987, the end of my first year in the company of Lee Lozowick and the Hohm community. At the beginning of that year I had been without a home for heart or body, isolated in the midst of winter ice and snow. I had come down out of the cold mountains into the heat of relationship with a teacher and a body of practitioners. Now began the process of deepening, a process as precise and penetrating as a surgical knife and as gentle and embracing as the breath of the heart.

PART II

SETTING ROOTS

CHAPTER 4

ASHRAM LIFE

―❧―

I began to work in the ashram office, answering phones and helping with bookkeeping and other details. The six weeks to which I had committed passed quickly and I had no interest in leaving. I continued to work in the office and began also to help with the children and to work at Mudra, the community bookstore.

One weekend Lee announced that he would be taking the entire group of ashram residents, minus children, to a movie in Phoenix—Eddie Murphy's new concert comedy, "Raw." It was my first experience of Lee's community trips. Every so often he would decide to take the entire ashram to a talk by a spiritual teacher, to a movie in Phoenix, or to a dinner of thick hamburgers and french fries at a local burger joint. One man would stay at the ashram as a guardian for energetic as well as physical sanctuary while the rest of the ashram residents crowded into the back of one of two huge old vans.

On this particular ride I found myself in deep conversation with one of the women. Donna had come to the ashram to visit in November of 1985—the same month I had made the decision to leave my first spiritual group. At the end of her visit she boarded a train for California to continue with her previous plans. As the train headed west she wrestled with a compelling inner sense that she had to return to the ashram rather than continue her journey. Halfway to her destination, she got off the train, traded in her ticket for a ticket back to Arizona, and called the ashram to ask for someone to pick her up at the station.

From that day Donna settled into life at the ashram. A month later she was invited by Lee to participate in the upcoming trip to India as the person primarily responsible for childcare. There were four children between the ages of five and eight on this ten-week journey through India. The group of twenty traveled as the Indians did, in third class rail carriages and buses so packed that people rode on the roof or held onto the outside. It was not an easy job, and Donna told me she had sometimes been in tears over her relationship with the children in this first major responsibility given her in the community. Yet she forged with them a friendship that has deepened as they have grown into adults.

This woman arrived at the ashram the same month that I would have arrived if I had followed my guides' first instruction. And, unbelievably, she had come from the tiny New England village where I had lived before entering my first spiritual group. I felt a resonant commonality with her, anchored far deeper than the external parallels.

I began to talk with Donna about the process of my own transition from my first taste of the Work in my original spiritual group through my solitary journey west, my retreat, my wanderings, and my final stable contact with the Hohm community. I could hear my voice change, deepening energetically, as I spoke with her. I was owning something about the power of my own connection to this Work, which had led me through many twists and turns to the field that was now opening as I settled into ashram life. I was bringing something of my past into the present so that it could be used. It was her listening that helped to make this possible, to reach into my past and retrieve that which was useful, to integrate it into the present. Strong feedback had deeply served me at one point already; now I was being served by a different facet of the *sangha*. Lee has said that sometimes what is most useful to another *sangha* member is not any kind of feedback or observation, but simply to "listen and bless" (a term he borrowed from another friend of his, Rebbe Zalman-Schachter). I experienced this quality of listening and blessing in the way Donna received me.

We arrived in Phoenix after a two-hour ride packed into the back of the vans like pieces of a puzzle. The van spilled us into the parking lot outside the movie theater. We were ready to laugh uproariously at a raw humor not unlike that which peppered our *darshans* and talks at home.

Although these trips with Lee to various venues might look like a respite or a game to balance the intensity of inner and outer work required in our daily life with him, they are not vacations but simply another facet of work with him. They may involve play and humor and getting down into the nitty-gritty of life, like the Celebration of life in the streets. For a serious idealist like myself, this aspect of play can sometimes be the most unexpected, and therefore the most effective, at slipping through the walls of defense to open hidden spaces of spontaneous responsiveness and receptivity. Taking students to a production of "Raw," which begins with Eddie Murphy's hilarious childhood considerations about the process of human excretion, may not seem fitting to a purveyor of the pristine *dharma*. Yet tantric masters have always used shock as one of the methods of opening their students to deeper work. In our contemporary times, the small shocks of crude humor may sometimes serve just this purpose, and at times Lee uses this possibility to the utmost.

After the movie we met the children, who had gone to a different movie, and we filled a local shop reputed to have the richest ice cream in town, of which we consumed major quantities. Some years later Lee assigned me to give a talk on "the *pushti* path" (grace given through abundance). Moments in an ice cream shop with Lee definitely confirm that we are on the *pushti* path—a path which embraces abundance, generosity, and even opulence at times, as a way of expressing and receiving the infinite abundance and generosity of the divine. We are a school of paradoxes. At the same time that we demonstrate the path of *pushti*, we cleave to a path of renunciation and asceticism so severe in some ways that Yogi Ramsuratkumar, Lee's own teacher, after questioning him about life on the Arizona ashram, once said to him, "You must not have very many people on your ashram!" Although his remark was met with laughter, it is also quite accurate.

Rumi communicates the mood of the *pushti* path in a poem in which he says: "...the love of lovers makes their bodies into bowstrings, while the love of beloveds makes them happy and plump." (Chittick, W. *The Sufi Path of Love: Spiritual Teaching of Rumi*, SUNY Press, 1983, p. 209) At the ice cream shop we grew fat with joy as Lee delighted in opening this space of abundance, this use of the simple pleasure of taste to open our hearts to divine gift, always hovering at the edges of our lives.

Every so often Lee would take us as a group to hear a teacher or speaker in Phoenix. Some of these speakers seemed to have something of value to offer. Others appeared to have little, and it seemed to me that Lee took us to hear them for exactly that reason. He wanted us to be able to learn from other teachers, within the context of our own teaching as foundation, and he also wanted us to learn to discriminate, to recognize for ourselves what was useful to us and what was not. In particular, it seemed he wanted us to learn to deal with the charismatic attraction that some so-called teachers could generate—to deal with the force of fascination. Even teachers whom he himself greatly respected could become a distraction and a fascination for us if we had not learned to recognize and handle this powerful vector. If we had faced our own tendency to fascination, then we would be able to draw on these sources without losing our footing, our attention to our own teacher and particular path.

After one of these presentations, about twenty of us went to a restaurant for dessert and discussed the evening. Someone asked how to make use of the talk that had been given, which had not been outstanding.

"The only way you can make use of it," Lee responded, "is if you understand the communication in the essay 'How Not to Act Superior When You Really Are.'" (A reference to a chapter in Lee's book, *Laughter of the Stones*.) It seemed to me that Lee was suggesting that we could only make use of these presentations if we could dispense with arrogance and self-righteousness and use the lectures as an opportunity for objective observation. Part of this objective observation was to be able to recognize when a speaker had little or nothing of use to us. Gurdjieff taught that the human being needs three kinds of "food": physical food, impression food, and subtle food. If we could recognize that the food being offered was not of a quality equal to what we usually ingested, and we could make this evaluation without feeding judgmental superiority, we would learn a process of discrimination that would be of use in many other situations.

Living conditions on the Arizona ashram were so rustic that many Westerners would consider them unlivable. A small geodesic dome, built according to the blueprint outlined by Buckminster Fuller, housed about half of the residents. I lived in a tiny upstairs room, with a skylight through which the moon shone at night. Three people shared this space, so small that our beds took up the entire floor space. Our personal belongings had to fit on a few shelves and in one dresser. The dome was heated by only a wood stove. Having lived with wood heat and primitive conditions on mountains in Maine and Massachusetts and Colorado, I felt right at home.

One of the other residents was nonplussed at my easy acceptance of ashram living conditions. "You don't seem to have any problem with the diet," he observed quizzically. "Most people start out complaining and going into town to get some snacks at the supermarket."

Perhaps living on rice and beans—or sometimes nothing at all for a day or two when I was most poor—made the fresh garden salads and raw oats with almonds and raisins gracious bounty by comparison. Or perhaps I was so filled with the energy I was consuming daily in this new life in Lee's physical company that the food seemed rich to me in a way I couldn't explain.

Not everyone enters spiritual work experiencing such a honeymoon period. One of the most hard-working students in our community left her first *darshan*, her first encounter with Lee, so enraged at his arrogance and disgusted by his crude jokes and rambling talk that she was convinced she never wanted to see him again, let alone consider him as a teacher. Yet gradually, in the succeeding hours, it began to dawn on her that the intensity of her reaction suggested there might be something of value in Lee that was threatening to her comfortably established life.

Indian scriptures recount the story of a man who was furiously angry with Krishna. His anger itself became the mode of total attention, which he turned toward Krishna. Total attention, regardless of the mood, allows the devotee to fully receive and unite with the diety. Through his laser-focused anger, this man achieved unity with Krishna. Similarly, the prospective student who had left *darshan* gradually recognized that Lee had wholly captured her attention through the mood of anger, and she felt compelled to investigate further what it was that had so engaged her. Within a few months she had not only become a student but had moved to the ashram as office manager.

But for me, life on the ashram did begin with a honeymoon phase. Having run in the other direction in the face of repeated invitation into Lee's company, now that I was finally living in it I felt such gratitude that the basic conditions appeared to me not as difficulties or irritants but as the natural response to the master's gift. Sometimes we would dance late into the night at a club where LGB was playing; yet the next morning at dawn I would find my body rising for meditation in spite of my mind suggesting that I might indulge in a few extra hours of sleep instead. There were, of course, innumerable inner and outer struggles and difficulties; yet this underlying mood of gratitude permeated those first months and shifted the context in which I saw many potentially difficult circumstances and events.

At one point soon after moving to the ashram I went to Lee to ask him about my relationship to him. Now the question was not just about bonding into a *sangha* that I might later leave; now I knew that my relationship to Lee was entering a level of deeper bonding. Was it right to allow this to continue when I was not committed to him as my teacher? I was beginning to trust him more and more deeply, and while I was grateful for this process, at the same time I was frightened by it. How did I know that he could be trusted? How could I turn to the very person whose trustworthiness I was trying to evaluate for help with that evaluation?

Lee listened to my entire presentation without interruption. His answer was not in words, but in the way that he listened. It was the deepest listening I had ever experienced. In the field of that listening my questions revealed their roots, and the tangles among the roots dissolved. I knew that he could be trusted.

Lee's final words as he ended the interview were, "It will be all right." He looked at me intently, as if to read in my eyes and body and whole aura whether I had received his transmission. "It will be all right." That simple statement was so replete with his own trust of the universe, his own resting in a reality whose nature is, as Chögyam Trungpa Rinpoche called it, "basic goodness," that he gave me a transmission about trust far deeper than the words he spoke.

Remembering that moment I am reminded again of the words of Julian of Norwich, "All shall be well. And all shall be well. And all manner of things shall be well." That knowledge flows from a direct and personal relationship with an impersonal reality; from a life founded in the divine in such trust that all circumstances, no matter how difficult at one level, become part of that divine harmony because we are resting in the level of underlying causes and the reality of one Source, rather than in a separative interpretation of particular events. Lee taught me something about trust that morning not by what he said but by who he was. It was his own relationship to the divine that taught me something about the possibility inherent in my relationship to him.

A couple of months before the April Celebration Lee announced that people could try out for parts in a production of "Jesus Christ Superstar," which would be performed at a classic downtown theater in Boulder during the Celebration. It was an incredibly short time in which to prepare for a full-scale production. People threw themselves into practice of their parts, preparation of costumes and sets, publicity, and all the tasks a theater production requires. When the night of the performance arrived, those of us in the audience who had watched the patchwork development of this play sat in the darkened theater amazed. Some of the main characters who lived in different states and even different countries had not been present for rehearsals until a few days before the actual event. Yet, the performance was riveting. The entire company of players somehow coalesced into one living organism. Of the play's powerful libretto, the song that most stayed with me was Mary Magdalene's poignant cry, "I don't know how to love him." It is the cry of the stumbling human heart turned toward something it recognizes as greater than itself. In that cry is the longing of the devotee to live in expression of the love which the teacher and the divine evoke in our hearts.

The day after the performance, back at the camp in the mountains where the Celebration was held, Lee lit a bonfire in a great open field. Onto that bonfire the members of the theater company threw their costumes, pieces of the set, sheaves of pages of the script, and whatever other materials had been part of the play. In the production they had opened a sacred space in which we had all shared. That space had been completed, and Lee dramatically closed it by burning the material forms that had been part of it. Repeatedly, I have seen him destroy the forms when a certain energy has done its work. He demonstrates a vastly different relation to the death of forms from that of conventional sentimentality, which clings to forms and remnants of the past as mementos. Lee constantly clears the way for the birth of new forms of work.

In June Lee traveled with a small group of students to Germany. Those of us who remained on the ashram juggled extra responsibilities to cover for those who had gone with him. The experience of his absence revealed to me how much his presence had permeated the field of being which I took for granted as daily life. At the same time, this sharp absence had a sweetness to it—a sweetness made up of both his energetic presence, which could not be denied even while he was physically thousands of miles away, and of looking toward his return. In that sweetness was a stirring of something akin to love, of some preliminary taste of that great possibility which Lee has named Longing. While my days were filled with the mundane details of bookkeeping, answering phones, and selling books at Mudra, my relationship to the *sangha*, the children, and the spiritual master was deepening and setting roots.

After five weeks of traveling and teaching, Lee returned from Europe, and the steady rhythm of ashram life continued. Each day was filled with almost more than we could do. While we nourished ordinary life with family and children, we also participated in a packed daily schedule that included morning meditation, daily labor in the office, workshop, or bookstore, writing for the community journal, evening talks, and intermittent band gigs. Always there was the unexpected spice of Lee's creative ideas, from a community trip to Phoenix to enthusiastic enrollment of the entire community in a multilevel marketing company.

Twice a week we gathered for a meal prepared by Lee and served in his dining room: huge bowls of fresh green salad, often with extra treats that were not on the usual ashram diet, such as grated cheese or walnuts or even slices of sausage that someone had brought him from Germany as a gift. In addition, he would serve large bowls of fruit filled with luscious pineapple, bananas, and whatever fruit was in season: peaches, plums or perhaps some exotic slices of mango. Community dietary recommendations include eating vegetables and fruits separately, rather than mixing them at one meal, so we had to choose between two bounteous gifts, embracing one and relinquishing the other. After the meal, Lee would give a talk, answering questions about practice and *dharma*, speaking about particular considerations he wanted to raise, and reading from a wide variety of literature he considered useful to us, from books by other spiritual teachers to poems by Charles Bukowski or Rilke.

Often I would look around at this intimate gathering of *sangha* with a sense of grateful amazement. It seemed to me astounding that Lee would so frequently invite us into his home and serve us food prepared with his own hands, and that he would make himself so available to personal involvement with our practice and questions. I had expected that we would give our effort to supporting his work, rather than that he would give such copious time and attention to supporting ours. I felt the reality of his statement that he had come down from higher realms to meet us where we stood.

At one of these talks I asked Lee how to develop compassion. I felt the pain of my own self-righteous judgment, directed toward both others and myself, and I saw the essential need for compassion in order to deepen relationship in community so as to establish a field from which we could work together rather than criticizing and competing with each other. The hardness of my own heart, in the light shed by Lee's daily company, caused me sorrow.

As when I asked Lee about trust, what I remember is not so much what he said as how he was. His response to me was itself an example of compassion. In the face of my idealistic demand that I manifest compassion absolutely and immediately, he said that compassion is something which grows in us over time. We can nourish it by small daily choices; we can feed it through study of those who offer us great examples of compassion; and at the same time we can have compassion for ourselves in the process of growth, rather than demeaning ourselves because we have not achieved the perfect ideal. I said that compassion involves the word "passion," and that I wanted to have the passion for kindness and the passion for this work that I had for fulfilling my own petty desires. He answered that this deeper passion is something that grows gradually, and part of our work is to learn to nourish growth rather than to demand instantaneous achievement, in ourselves or in others. The sense of a larger view, a larger acceptance, and the context which he held as he spoke of this process of growth gave me a living model of what it is to approach oneself or another with acceptance rather than with critical rejection for our humanness.

While Lee could exemplify acceptance and relaxation in one moment, he could manifest fierce anger and intense demand in the next. Sometimes, as I sat quietly handling accounts, he would be yelling with passionate fervor at a devotee who had, through lapse of attention, caused a snag in the operation of a community business or other project. Since his anger was not (at least for my first two years in the community) directed at me, I had the chance to observe without reaction or judgment. It seemed clear to me that this forceful correction came only after the devotee had had many chances to pay attention and had instead enacted a consistent and even predictable pattern of sloppiness and unconscious but effective sabotage of work possibilities. This side of Lee did not frighten me or create doubt any more than the wild fields of energy or the ascetic diet. It seemed clear to me that he was working with his students with integrity and essential respect, even when he was yelling at them.

I continued with my work in the office, and as the needs of the ashram pressed on anyone available to fill the work force, my responsibilities progressively expanded. Once a week we took the ashram children to a local indoor swimming pool. It was always a rowdy and joyous event. One day we loaded the children into the van for the trip home and reached the ashram before we realized that one of the children was missing. In shock at our lack of attention, two of us drove back to find the missing child. She was a confident and gregarious girl of about eight. We found her just coming out of the gymnasium. She had gotten absorbed in conversation in the locker room with a new friend.

When I told Lee about our gross failure in attention and responsibility for the children, I expected a passionate reprimand from him. Instead he responded with incisive yet quiet instruction: "Just make sure it never happens again." I had made a mistake, and a serious one, leaving a child at a pool without a supervising adult. But it was the first time I had made the mistake, and I was clearly deeply conscious of its seriousness. His quiet, concentrated response, with its expectation that I would infallibly obey what he said, actually penetrated far deeper into my psyche than any forceful, shouted correction would have.

In working with children, I have seen how often adults rob them of the opportunity to experience conscience. When a child has hurt another child, even intentionally, there is often an instant of real regret and feeling for the other child that can be seen on the offending child's face. An adult intent on forcing the child to "be good" while believing that in fact he is essentially bad will begin to lecture and correct him. The adult firmly believes that he is teaching the child to have conscience. But the fact is that the adult is burying the child's conscience. In the child's moment of vulnerability—of his willingness and ability to feel the pain of another which he himself has caused—the adult, instead of nourishing that spontaneous experience of remorse, callously hammers upon the child in a way that forces him to put up a defense that walls him away from his own true feeling and from the adult. The result is that the child learns to obey outer strictures for fear of punishment and rejection, but loses contact with the natural experience of conscience that the adult meant to inculcate.

In this experience with Lee I saw that Lee recognized my natural experience of remorse, of conscience. When that was present, he did not need to shout at me, to add external force, but simply to concentrate his own attention, added to mine, on letting that experience penetrate and be felt so deeply that I would not forget again.

The music of LGB had become one of the major focal points in our community development. Each band gig took us into realms of both underworld and upperworld, facing our demons and angels as we danced with abandon or listened quietly from the shadows of a corner table. Lee wrote the lyrics for many of the original songs in the band's repertoire. He claimed there was no esoteric meaning to these lyrics, that they were simply to be taken at face value as songs about love, sorrow, the revenge and spite of wounded lovers, the innocent vulnerability into which love could open.

The lyrics were powerful enough taken at their surface. Yet many of us heard in them reverberations and reflections of esoteric instruction encoded in the traditional Baul way, and of the haunting longing for the divine. I was not alone in my reading of these intertwined levels. After a band gig in Boulder, someone observed with amazed gratitude that "a year and a half of therapy and hundreds of dollars couldn't do what two lines of a work song and one man wailing into a microphone did in one night."

That fall I moved back to Boulder. Several of us formed a community house—an old, roomy place with a large front porch, shady trees, and a garden. There was a large living room for study group meetings, *kirtan* on Sunday nights, and other community gatherings. Since it was located on 10th Street, we gave it the utilitarian name of "10th Street house."

We worked hard building a matrix among the *sangha* and doing outreach, inviting people to study group meetings, organizing women's meetings, men's meetings, and household meetings, and working with community businesses. But although these activities demonstrated my growing commitment to life in the community, the areas of dissonance in myself and in others also became more evident as we worked together. It seems clear to me now that I was offered feedback both verbally by those close to me and through circumstances that could have saved me much time and suffering if I had listened and used this input rather than resisting it.

For example, after *kirtan* we would hold an evening gathering at which we shared tea and small treats such as strawberries or chocolate that had been given as *prasad*. It was an intimate space that I treasured, and I wanted to nourish it as deeply as possible. One way I saw to do this was to provide extra treats of various kinds—to buy some cheese and crackers, or prepare some fancy hors d'oeuvre such as warmed brie on baguette. These were not items on the diet, nor were they a gift of *prasad*. They were, in fact, my stubborn pushing of luxury on a space that could usefully embrace abundance but only when it came through clear channels of gift and consonance with the spiritual master.

One of the senior students was indignant at my insensitivity to the protocol demanded by this space. He told me that Lee did not encourage such luxuries, and chose to have simple food such as mint tea and nuts as the usual fare in these gatherings. What I was doing, in his view, was actually a manipulation of the space based in my personal attachments, even though I adamantly maintained that I was trying to feed the space.

Years later, living in Lee's closer company, my attachments around food would be one of the areas in which I faced the deepest confrontation. If I had listened to the feedback from the *sangha* years earlier, the energy that got tied up in dealing with my neurotic relationship to food would have been available for more useful work.

CHAPTER 5

CLOSING DOORS

❧

While the door deeper into Lee's company was gradually opening, another one was closing. Even though I was deeply involved in the activities and life of the community, I still had not let go of my attachment to my first group. In 1989, sometime after the beginning of the new year, I wrote to my former teacher, asking if I could return to my work with that group. In early spring, the letter came back to me, unopened, marked "Return to sender. No forwarding address." All possibility of contact with that group had ended. My relationship with my first teacher and my first spiritual group was dead. I had not told anyone, even Lee, about this letter. When I took the letter and my heartbreak to a friend in the *sangha*, he was gentle, yet objective.

"You've never been through the death of your mother or father," he said. "When your parents die, the world changes. You discover things you could never know before. You're facing a death now, and the grief of that death. What you don't know is that because this door has closed, another door can open. There is possibility in the world that you can't imagine until you go through the kind of shift of context that opens through death."

I had asked to participate in Lee's trip to Germany in May, and he had accepted my request. The trip would involve a tour of Germany by LGB, as well as Lee's usual speaking engagements. As a result the traveling group was unusually large, including band members, families, and children.

While I worked to make money for my plane ticket, Lee and two large vans full of students were traveling through the southern United States on another band tour, officially named, "Not A Pretty Sight." Along the way, the group stopped in Atlanta, Georgia, for the community's April Celebration. Those of us not on the tour flew in from all over the United States. We met in a large rented suburban house, where the women squeezed into one large room to sleep on the floor at night and rolled up our bedding to make space for Celebration talks and meetings during the day.

It had been a little over three years since I had left Atlanta, and here I was back, in an entirely new circumstance, with the teacher I felt to be at the source of that memorable energy on a spring afternoon almost exactly four years before.

Unexpectedly, I descended into one of the deepest hells I have experienced in my life with Lee. As I listened to the talks and prepared for the final *darshan* on the last night of the Celebration, a mist seemed to be descending over him, or between him and me. He looked to me progressively darker and more untrustworthy. The distrust I felt was like a storm cloud brewing, gathering energy, spinning all my doubts into one sucking vortex. By the time I entered *darshan* Lee looked to me like a devil complete with black cape and horns. The man I had known—the man of gentle intimacy and fierce demand, of rude but funny jokes, of embracing compassion—had disappeared behind a veil of darkness, like night falling over sunny slopes. I did not trust him, could not trust him, and did not see any means of evaluation I could use to discover whether this distrust or my earlier trust of him was the true ground on which I should stand. I sat in *darshan* caught in a vice that squeezed my ribs against my heart. I had left things and people and work before. Was I to leave this teacher also? Was he just a painted distraction along my path, and now the paint had worn thin and I saw him in his true colors, which were no colors at all, but an enveloping darkness?

For a long time I could not give the *prasad* that I had brought. I sat paralyzed in sorrow, terror, and pain as doubt ravaged my heart. Finally, without resolution, I rose from my seat. I would give him the *prasad* I had brought, even if it was the last *prasad* I ever gave him—even if this was my last *darshan* and the end of my work in his company. Whoever he was, he had given me something real. For that I was grateful. The *prasad* had been bought for him, and it was right to complete the intention of giving it. I walked forward, bowed, and handed it to Lee.

As I gave him the *prasad*, something shifted. The darkness of doubt did not disappear, but there was a point of light. It was as if, in the choice to give to the master, I had opened a channel through which he gave something to me; his clarity repelled the clouds from around that centerpoint in my heart. From there, he left me to do my work myself.

The shift from doubt to trust that began that night was not instantaneous. My reservations about whether I was on the right path and with the right teacher continued as I returned to my job and my life in Boulder. But the direction was in motion and momentum began to gather, not in the brewing of a storm, but in the clearing of the field. Within a few days, that passage of doubt was a memory, and Lee's image burned steadily in my heart again. From that moment in *darshan* a choice had been made. I would trust, and persevere through doubt. That choice has been made and remade innumerable times since; but a pattern was set that has helped to carry me through each subsequent confrontation with the darkness of doubt.

The trip east to Atlanta provided me the chance to finally close the storage lockers which I had rented three years earlier. Before the Celebration, while visiting my family, I traveled to North Carolina to close the locker there. When I opened it, I discovered that the few things of monetary value, such as a stereo and a sewing machine, had been stolen. In my dramatic exit from Durham three years earlier, I had failed to read the fine print and had not realized that the storage company provided no insurance. I had been paying rent for three years on a locker containing nothing but some mementos and household items that might have brought a few dollars at a yard sale. I finally left them at a donations box, as I should have done in the first place. My written journals, the one thing of real value to me, had either been stolen as well or I had unwittingly buried them in the boxes I took to Colorado. In Atlanta I found the storage locker full of equally useless baggage. Between the two lockers I had paid almost a thousand dollars as the price of disobedience to my inner sense. What I thought would be a cost of perhaps one hundred dollars at most, based on my certainty of a quick return east, turned out to be a hugely expensive infraction.

I returned to Boulder and continued working to make the money I needed for my plane ticket to Germany, but every paycheck seemed to dissolve into payment of various necessary bills. Finally I realized that the money would not come first. What had to come first was total commitment. In the wake of that commitment, the money would follow. I had faced this circumstance repeatedly before, and the laws had not changed. I had to pay with risk, to make myself vulnerable to the universe, and then the universe would lawfully be able to help me.

I was inputting an engineering manual at an aerodynamics company one morning when this realization dawned on me. I had learned that realization demands action or it fades into the useless terrain of mental insight devoid of life. I knew that if I did not take a risk—that unless I acted in faith in the moment—I would never get the money for the ticket. I called the travel agent, booked the cheapest seat available on a flight from New York to Germany, and sent in my check. Once I had made the choice, everything else did in fact fall into place, and a few weeks later I was driving east with another member of the community who had taken a similar financial risk and booked the same flight. We were on our way to meet Lee and his entourage in Munich.

We arrived at the airport in New York to find that the airline had overbooked the flight. When we were finally admitted onto the airplane, we were seated in their only free seats—each about as big as a bed, in first class, instead of the coach seats for which we had paid. Looking backwards down the aisle before the stewardesses closed the curtains to guard our first class sanctuary, we could see the coach section packed as densely as a cattle car. Meanwhile, stewardesses were bringing us hot towels and toothbrush kits before serving dinner with linen napkins. Commitment, plus "the Influence" (Divine Influence) working through Lee, had manifested in a luxurious flight for these Baul beggars flying across the sea.

It seems that to follow this path we must give everything—and the divine will only take from us if we are truly willing to give. Yet the same reality that demands everything paradoxically returns more than we gave. Having sacrificed all luxuries and many comforts in order to purchase these tickets, we found ourselves met with abundance beyond anything we had even asked.

The point is not to act on faith with the expectation that we will be given more than we sacrificed. Such action is not faith but manipulative bargaining. Yet the fact is that real faith opens the way for a flow of energy in the universe that is full of abundance and blessing beyond our imagining.

When we got to New York, my companion and I discovered that neither of us had the arrival time of Lee's flight into Munich. I called the Arizona ashram and got a response of relaxed unconcern. No one knew when Lee was arriving in Germany, or even what day, and those who might have been able to find out seemed to feel that it was an unnecessary and unreasonable request on our part that they exert any effort to do so. All we had to do, we were told, was wait at the Munich airport and sooner or later someone would pick us up or Lee would arrive. So we got on the plane in New York with no idea whether Lee had already arrived in Germany and taken off for some distant city, or whether we would be waiting at the airport for endless hours. When we got off the plane in Munich, the German *sangha* leader was waiting for us, and Lee was due to arrive in ten minutes. Our plans could not have been more synchronized. In a few minutes, huge dollies full of band equipment were rolling across the airport floor, ready for LGB's first tour of Germany.

Based on former trip stories, I was prepared to drive all day to our first seminar in Switzerland and resume eating, sleeping and general human functions somewhere between twelve and twenty-four hours later. What a surprise when Lee said we were going to a park for the day. We would eat, sleep and swim until it was time to go to our German hosts' homes that evening. We would drive to Switzerland the next day.

At the park, Lee and one of the male students prepared a huge salad for lunch and magically produced a spread of German cheeses and bread. Chocolate materialized from somewhere. The children rowed in red rowboats among the ducks on the pond. We talked and napped in the sun. German friends appeared and disappeared throughout the afternoon, gathering around Lee and engaging him with questions. He talked with simplicity and depth about basic aspects of the school, which I had never heard so coherently explained.

Someone questioned Lee about the band and how it fit with spiritual work. It seemed to the questioner a strange combination. Lee talked about shamanism, about the band providing a doorway into the underworld and an avenue through which he can serve as a shaman so we make the journey of transformation rather than getting stuck in the dead-end corridors and seductions of that world. Surely I had heard these words before, but the coherent power of Lee's communication was such that in that moment I *saw* the door, I recognized where he was leading us, and something in me was engaged to follow him into that world in a new way. My many resistances to the work of the band just fell away.

We met back at the picnic table and divided up to go to our respective hosts' homes. I noticed the blips of reaction in myself and in others as Lee chose who would stay at the same house with him or who would ride with him or shop with him. But these blips were nothing like the level of friction I had feared from others' reports and forewarnings. I found that inasmuch as I could take each situation he chose for us as a door to an opportunity that he was offering, the situation—whatever it was—became a gift. That night the gift was a surprisingly spacious apartment to share with five women and four girls. (I was prepared from reports of previous trips for one room with wall-to-wall bodies.) We had salad and bread for supper, went out for an evening walk, and watched the sunset.

I realized that day that the teacher is always present, always knocking at the door of our hearts. At each instant we have the choice of whether to receive him—to let him in and know communion—or to shut him out and agonize in separation because he has not come in the form we would choose at that moment. Maybe he comes through other people and a meal together, when we were attached to time alone. Maybe he comes through time alone when we feel desperate for his physical presence or for that of the *sangha*. He is always standing in our hearts, waiting for us to recognize and welcome him. We have the choice whether to receive or reject the Guest.

After this day of gentle introduction, the next morning we crowded into vans that were no longer in their prime of life and began the trip south to Switzerland for Lee's first seminar. Toward evening we began to drive high into the Swiss Alps, winding through hairpin turns on a tiny road that gave us a stunning view of the valley, looking directly over the cliffs at each turn. Some people found it too frightening to look down; others, myself included, were overjoyed to be ascending into the high mountains. This was the kind of terrain that had been the locus for my solitary passages through deep transitions; now I was entering the mountains as part of a committed and working group, as part of a community. The polarities of my life were being knit together as we drove up into the heights still brushed by snow even as spring flowered around us.

Finally we reached Schweiben Alp, the retreat center, an immense chalet perched on the side of the mountains, with still loftier snowy heights rising beyond it. The air was clear and brisk. Gardens lined the side of the mountains: rows of vegetables, flowers, and herbs carefully kept by the spiritual group that ran the center.

The first time I heard Lee offer specific instruction about the use of breath and sex—two central areas of practice in Baul *sadhana*—was at this first seminar on this tour of Germany. The mornings began with an *arati*, a waving of lights followed by a joyous ringing of bells. After that Lee began the seminar sessions. He spoke with unusual directness and depth about various considerations. I was surprised that almost without preliminary he was giving profound answers to people's questions without setting the usual traps and snares of coarse comments or bawdy humor that often appear to deflect the questioner's attempt to get serious.

Suddenly, one morning he began to describe with deliberate exactness a type of breath that we might find useful in spiritual practice. The description was precise, yet limited; it was clear there was much more to be discovered than he was voicing. He said that in practicing certain technical or yogic breathing we are aligning ourselves with a much larger process of breath, the breath of the universe. He added that if we breathe in this way with an attention to sexual energy, we can discover something about the relationship of sexual energy—the energy of polarities—to universal energies and fields of work. Rather than being simply a pleasure engaged for satisfaction of our own desires, sexual energy then becomes a process through which we can feed the field of a universal work. This possibility for relationship to a universal process is not dependent on physical sexual activity. It can also be accessed, using this breath, through conscious intention to allow our sexual energy to be useful to a larger field. Through that shift in the context and orientation of sex, we also open, as a side effect, the possibility for sex to become a process that alchemically catalyzes our own transformation.

I could feel the entire field of energy in the room vibrating with the power of the hints Lee had just dropped among us. At the same time I sensed that some people in the room had barely heard him; they had not registered the power of the offering he had just made because they were not ready or willing to engage it. It was another example of the way in which work tools and work energy are cloaked and made invisible even when they are set right in the middle of the room. Jesus said, "He who has ears to hear, let him hear." (Matthew 11:15) We hear what we are willing and ready to use.

No sooner had Lee dropped these cosmic hints than his mood totally shifted. "All right, lunchtime!" he exclaimed with great practical enthusiasm, banishing all traces of the subtle communications he had been offering. The chamber was complete and he closed the doors at the height of the energy, leaving the space sealed and simmering while he went on to eat his lunch.

It was clear from this strong beginning that Lee intended to use the tour through Germany as an opportunity for a powerful transmission both of specific teachings and of energetic possibility. A later seminar took place in northern Germany in a huge old seminar house run by a devoted Sufi named Atar. We spent days in *dharmic* considerations and evenings, gathering in the great central room lined with dark mahogany and furnishings that somehow made the space feel like a great ship, tilting as we lifted out of the normal earthbound parameters into the waves of a reality founded in higher dimensions. Then, shifting gears in a way that incapacitated our rigid defenses and tumbled us into spaces of confrontation, innocence, or joy, Lee ended the seminar with an outdoor performance by LGB (which somewhere along the way had metamorphosed from Living God Blues to liars, gods and beggars). Among the rhododendrons bodies leapt and whirled, ecstatically moving to the rhythms of the dance. Germans may be rigid and stiff when the music is off, but turn on that beat and they relax into an almost boneless undulation that we named "magic dancing."

The trip continued with seminars, public talks, afternoons spent at sidewalk cafes where Lee offered informal teachings, and band gigs at clubs and fairs throughout Germany.

One day Lee suggested that I might handle some basic logistics, such as activities for the children and food while traveling. I realized that I would never have offered to do this job without being asked—not because I was unwilling or incapable, but simply because I assumed my contractions were so much larger than my capabilities. As a result I didn't realize I was able to serve, and didn't initiate taking responsibility. It reminded me that self-reference is not just gross selfishness but simply seeing the world through the veil of self, so that one misses seeing the real needs and possibilities of work. Lee didn't seem to care about my many neuroses; he just wanted someone to see that there was food for each van on traveling days, and caring attention to activities for the children. This I could do.

I realized that the requirements of that particular job, and its opportunities, were also those of much of our daily life in Lee's company. It was not my responsibility to open chambers or do any fancy higher dimensional work, but to see how minor practical details can either block or feed the higher possibilities and to handle those details. If this is done well, the *sangha* as a body and Lee as the guide are free and in position to be able to work when possible. To the extent these details are not handled, energy is drained and fragmented that could otherwise be more profitably used.

We traveled on to Berlin, where students had organized talks and band gigs. Our living conditions there were crowded. What amazed me was the way in which Lee shared living in these cramped accommodations. There were nine sleeping spaces in the small room he had been given. Watching Lee in this circumstance was an instruction in innocence and "being that which nothing can take root in," one of the community's practices. He just didn't get hooked by anything. The result was that the energy space around him was simple, clear, and spacious, regardless of how many people were clustered into the room or queued up waiting for the bathroom.

He also had no fear or reaction to the energy of the "cat" (with claws out) that I find so despicable in myself and in other women at times—even those I respect and love most. Women seem to me to have the constant potential to flip from angel to devil in an instant when our sense of territory, possession, security in love, or even vanity is threatened. When we are truly women, we feed, sustain and engender. But somewhere in me I have been almost constantly on guard against the potential to flip. Lee was not on guard. He simply recognized and handled that potential in us.

Often I would cry just at the sense of his presence. It wasn't a feeling of joy or sorrow, but a depth of awareness of the gift that he gave us simply in being there with us, in accepting us into his company. That gift was being constantly given, and the simplicity with which he lay down and went to sleep and woke and walked with us, in the middle of all our never-ending "stuff," pierced my heart.

Back in Munich Lee invited his students and another teacher from the U.S. to a dessert cafe. Watching quietly from one end of the long table, I was struck by what Lee was giving to this teacher, and at how in some way this giving seemed to feed Lee as well. The thought I had was of obligation, in a spiritual sense. Lee has said that he was given help when he began by teachers ahead of him, and it is his obligation to give, in turn, such help to teachers who are beginning after him. My impression is that most people who consider themselves teachers are in fact too arrogant or threatened to accept the kind of real help Lee can give. The teacher we met in Munich seemed able to receive, and it opened a channel where Lee could discharge something of his obligation and feed a flow of energy in the Work that is larger than any one teacher or master.

Driving in the van down the autobahn one day, Lee talked about how he worked under his own teachers; for example, his judo teacher. He said that when his teacher started tossing him around at each class, Lee didn't say to himself, "I'll show him I can take it," or "I'm not going back," or "Why is he doing this to me?" He simply said, "I'm going to study my teacher." That was the attitude he held, no matter what was happening: to learn what the teacher had to give. Simply, "to study my teacher."

On the last day of the tour we were invited to a lovely outdoor dinner in the country at the home of a German friend. After food and wine, we gathered around Lee and there was a spontaneous consideration of the trip and what we could learn from it. It was not so much any specific issue we talked about as it was seeing Lee's eyes look alive that said to me that a trip with him and the community is a "domain of possibility" (a phrase coined by Werner Erhard). It is a circumstance through which invention and creation can take place, through which we can enliven our own work and that of others and, at least in moments, possibly touch what is Real. The question I took with me was not one to answer but to hold in my heart, perhaps as a koan: How can we bring the life and intensity of work that emerges on trips more fully into our daily lives so that we totally engage the real Journey on which we have embarked together?

After Lee left for the U.S., I remained in Munich for another week. In spite of his physical absence, his presence was everywhere. Whatever transition I had been making from that night in December of 1985, when my sense originally told me to go to Boulder, the transition had finally been completed. The door behind me had closed, like the closing of the locks on a canal that allows a boat to be lifted from one level to the next. The entire energy field in which I moved was filling up with Lee's presence now that the doors had been sealed. Over and over in our work with a teacher we face transition points where certain doors to the past or to our past attachments must be closed so that the field can fill up with new possibility. Until we close the back doors through which energy can be leaked or wasted, we may not be able to glimpse the possibilities that are awaiting our demonstration of reliability.

CHAPTER 6

IN THE TEACHER'S COMPANY

～

A ppropriately, I returned to the U.S. on July 4, Independence Day. I was in the process of building independence from the rule of the mechanical self—from the emotional habits and attachments that comprise who I think I am, rather than the expression of that One who is essentially present in each of us and beyond us all. It was an independence—an inner liberation—that could give me the freedom to recognize, honor, and obey rightful authority. It was not a goal of independence that most Americans would even understand, let alone desire or seek. The original American concept of political and religious freedom has been distorted into an excuse for license—for indulgent excess—whether of money or guns or greedy consumption. It is a warning that every spiritual school can use to remind us of the power of distortion that can warp great intentions and original ideals, turning them into caricatures and parodies in spiritual life as well as in the political arena.

The seminar preceding the Celebration in the summer of 1989 was titled "Cults." The parents of one of the community's members were active participants in a group that worked to pinpoint cults and deprogram cult members. They were guest speakers at the seminar and talked about the characteristic that distinguishes cults from legitimate spiritual groups. They said that while cults focus on manipulative control of their members, healthy spiritual groups nourish an unbiased exploration of truth. Again Lee was exposing the community to a wide range of viewpoints and emphasizing the need for discrimination and clarity, even about our own community and its leader.

The night before the Celebration began, the community presented an ambitious, almost four-hour production of Nicholas Kazantzakis' profound play, "The Buddha," at a local Prescott playhouse. Because of the length of the original play (about eight hours), it had never actually been produced on stage. This was its world debut, in a somewhat shortened form. Lee appeared as one of the three gods—the god Vishnu, sustainer of creation, who also incarnates at another time as Krishna. He was accompanied by Brahma and Shiva. As is usual with projects Lee initiates, the play had been produced in an incredibly short time. Some of the cast had had only a few weeks of practice. Yet it held the audience of almost 600 people, mostly local citizens, enthralled with its considerations of the purpose and meaning of life and death. This was the inauguration of a permanent theater group, the Baul Theater Company, which has since given riveting performances of Lee's rock opera, "John T.," and earned a three-year contract at the Arizona Renaissance Festival for its humorous *la Comedie Dell Arte*, Italian Renaissance comedy.

After the Celebration I traveled to Colorado to collect my belongings and move to Arizona. I wanted intensely to live on the ashram; however, I had been told there was no room available. Instead I was assigned to a household half a mile away. On my return to Arizona, I moved my few belongings into the house, but

I never slept there. The ashram was like a magnet pulling on my heart so intensely that I could not leave. I would stay till the last evening gathering was complete, then wrap myself in a blanket and sleep on the living room floor of what was then the women's house. I felt as if I was caught in a current streaming toward a waterfall I could not see. I couldn't get out of the current; I didn't even want to get out of the current, yet it was taking me into the total unknown. There was no familiar frame of reference to make sense of the territory through which I was passing. Everything was changing at such a rate that my ordinary eyes could not process what they were seeing; the dimensions were beyond those they could interpret. All I could do was write Lee copious letters about the details of my process and observations without understanding the meaning of this deepening intensity and this irresistible pull toward the ashram that had told me it did not have room for me.

Within a few weeks a room unexpectedly became available. I moved onto the ashram, into the daily company of my teacher and the community of residents.

In October we traveled to Colorado for a week, for Lee's annual teaching visit. During that visit I had a chance to see aspects of my psyche arise in response to being given a favored position that were not pleasant to observe. I was fortunate enough to participate in every special dinner and fabulous feast that the Boulder *sangha* could offer in honor of the master. I had always thoroughly enjoyed our community feasts and had eaten heartily. But now I found myself manifesting a compulsive, even devouring energy that grasped at every delicacy and consumed it in huge quantities. It was so visible that we laughed about my new post as the devourer, the food vacuum. I had been moved into a position where temptation to indulgence was available to me at a level I had not experienced before, and I was providing evidence that I had not mastered this temptation, that I was susceptible.

I can't say even now that I am free of susceptibility to these temptations and indulgences; but I feel that I have painstakingly gained a degree of maturity that I did not have then. Shocked as I was at my own immaturity, I saw that the indulgences available to those in power offer a temptation that has entangled many secular leaders and even many spiritual teachers. I was not alone in my susceptibility and in the need to wrestle with the character weaknesses that showed up in a different light once I was in a position of relationship to those forces, even if that position was only in a small renunciate spiritual school with a body of perhaps one hundred students, and the trappings of privilege were no greater than a breakfast with the master or the chance for a steak dinner at Boulder's most exclusive restaurant.

There was another factor at play in my ravenous and devouring energy; this one harder to define, yet even more central. It had to do with the great ache of emptiness at the core of the experience of separation and loss of love. This core emptiness, normally buffered and repressed in the hopelessness of the infant's experience of abandonment—an experience of almost epidemic proportions for Western infants—began to percolate toward the surface in the face of the possibility that here was a love, a divine love, large enough and real enough to begin to heal it. The ravenous devouring was in a way a healthy step toward contact with that emptiness, the first tentative outreach from that place toward my conscious world. The more I listened to the driving force underlying that ravenous energy, the more I could find my way to the innocence buried beneath the emptiness.

Sometime later Lee had a number of quotations written in large calligraphy for posting on the ashram. One of these, attributed to Gurdjieff's father, read, "*A man is satisfied not by the quantity of food but by the absence of greed.*" It seemed to speak directly to the devouring energy I found arising in myself during this trip.

Because I did not seize the opportunity to penetrate to the roots of my dynamics around food, the same issues arose repeatedly over the ensuing years.

At the same time that I was experiencing tremendous vulnerability to this circumstance of traveling closely with Lee, and was profoundly grateful for the opportunity, I found myself feeling an anger toward him that I did not understand. He had not done anything that I could see to make me angry. He was respectful, demanding as always in his teaching, yet also supremely gentle and receptive in his guidance.

One day, as we returned from some public event, he commented humorously about me, "She looks perfectly calm until I look into her eyes, and see the fiery anger blazing at me!" I had been working inwardly to understand and digest the anger so that it would not be felt by my teacher; but since it was obvious that I was not succeeding, I turned instead to asking for his help. I asked if he knew why I was angry, and how I could work with it more effectively.

"I think you're angry," he replied, "because you experience that you have no choice [about this movement by the divine]. You experience me as being responsible—responsible for this happening to you. Yet the fact is, I have no choice either. I have no more choice than you do. The choices are made by the Work."

Lee's answer made perfect sense to me. Although we are responsible for our choices, a major part of that responsibility is to use our free will to choose alignment to a larger movement with which we can act in consonance; ultimately to surrender to an all-encompassing Will, the Will of God. I could have refused the current of movement that had brought me into this circumstance, but I could do so, as in earlier choice points, only at the peril of my own inner integrity, my inner life. The anger was actually at this larger movement to which I wanted to align but which I experienced as moving me in directions that took no account of my personal desires and preferences. It was the person of small desires and fascinations that was angry, even while the deeper inner being found wholeness and the breath of life in movement in this direction.

One day as we drove through the Colorado mountains toward some meeting, I questioned Lee about how to handle the stormy currents of my own process as I moved more deeply into my work. I said that in the past I had gone alone up into the mountains to process many things; that I found a clarity and spaciousness in the high mountains that helped me to face my inner storms and move through them. Lee said that this was no longer the optimum way of handling my personal process, that I was now part of a body, the body of the *sangha*, which could process the currents of individual emotions through its group field in a way that would be much more effective. I had a dim sense of what he meant. It was as if I was now part of a larger circulatory system. The group body is a more complex body, just as the individual human body is more complex than earlier life forms. With greater complexity comes greater capacity for consciousness. I could make my way through my individual emotional labyrinth with greater clarity and consciousness and therefore greater capacity for usefulness if I used the group body. As a corollary, the group body would be strengthened by my use and trust of it.

A student of Lee's had met students of another teacher in Boulder and found their work impressive. Lee's student arranged for Lee to meet with this other teacher, whose name was Andrew Cohen. Their meeting was respectful, as they seemed to recognize in each other a common commitment to meeting the demands of the Work regardless of the radical or unconventional actions this might entail. At the same time, Andrew seemed to be questioning Lee in a way that gave Lee the chance to offer help.

Andrew was one of only a few teachers other than Lee who I had seen show receptivity to help in their teaching work. I felt that in Andrew Lee was meeting a teacher who had enough experience to bring a strong contribution to the space and at the same time was able to recognize the value of a kind of reciprocity that Lee could offer him. He questioned Lee in a vulnerable and challenging way that I had never seen another teacher do. He demonstrated a willingness to ask direct and confrontive questions and to thoroughly consider Lee's answers. I had the feeling that this might be someone with whom we would remain friends, which has, in fact, become the case. Lee and Andrew meet regularly when their schedules intersect and even occasionally teach together.

We returned to Arizona, and while an intensifying level of inner work continued for me, on the external level I took a job teaching counseling methods at a local college. I had debts to repay from the bank loans that had enabled me to make my leap into the unknown and which had brought me to this place where I was now putting down such deep roots. The distances spanned by my inner and outer life sometimes seemed like the two sides of a great chasm. Although teaching and interacting with the students in my classes held value and enjoyment for me, the entire structure of conventional life, even the concerns of an environmentally-oriented college, seemed to me like a thin rind of outer skin, largely ignorant of the many-dimensional body of which we are a part. Meanwhile my inner experience was beginning to penetrate into deeper layers of these dimensions, especially into glimpses of the focal relationship of this school: the relationship of longing.

Seeing Lee every day on the ashram, I was beginning to have to come to terms with a driving impulse that I see in myself and in most Westerners to personally capture the teacher's attention. When I asked Lee how to work with this tendency, he told me that I could turn this personal grasping in the direction of longing for the divine. Essentially he was suggesting that I take the grasping that results from our primal experience of separation and use that to reconnect myself to the essential impulse of the being, which is to rediscover a unity with the divine that has in fact never been lost, but only forgotten and misperceived. Every instance of grasping, used correctly, can take us not toward useless clawing at the teacher's attention but toward experience of the deepest level of being which underlies the impulse to participate in the Work and in all relationships.

Lee's recommendation is profoundly simple, but to carry it out in practice is, as he says, "simple but not easy." It requires a constant reorienting of our habitual mechanical response until we begin to build a new habit in alignment with the deeper being. At that point, energy from that deeper level can flow through the new habit pattern, enlivening it so that it begins to have a magnetic force of its own. We create the possibility for this deeper level of help through our perseverance at the mundane level of simply redirecting our attention when our entire body of habits is screaming that in order to survive we must grasp the master's personal attention—that without this attention at this immediate moment we will die. Other goals can demand our compulsive attention equally strongly, but the master, because of the high level of energy that is flowing through him, can become the most attractive and consuming level of candy for which we grasp like hurt and wounded children.

The November Celebration in 1989 included one of Lee's intermittent surprise guest speakers. This speaker, Father James Redington, might have seemed an unusual guest for a school based in Baul traditions that were radical and renegade even in the East; a school focused around a guru and drawing also on Fourth Way teachings. Yet he turned out to be one of the most memorable speakers we have had, and has remained a friend of the community, exemplifying the kind of friendship in which differences of approach become aspects of the bridge we build between us. Father Redington, a Jesuit priest and theologian and a professor at Georgetown University, shared with us a surprising common interest: the penetrating considerations by Vallabhacarya, a devotee of Krishna, which Father Redington had translated into English under the title *Vallabhacarya on the Love Games of Krsna.* Through his translation he had made possible the in-depth consideration of the *Bhagavata Purana* and their commentaries, which had been a focus of study in our school for years.

Father Redington spoke to us about the illumination of the relationship between human and divine that is provided through the story of Krishna's love games with the gopis. His sensitive and perceptive reading of these passages deepened and expanded our own study. We invited him to speak to us again on later occasions and were privileged to read also his further research in an unpublished manuscript. His presentation was a striking example of the interweaving of the same principles in outwardly vastly different traditions. He spoke of the fact that it was not the *gopis'* scriptural knowledge or even their virtuous actions but simply their complete attention on Krishna in "total love" that released them from earthly attachments and delivered them into the pure joy of his play with them, the dance of love under the autumn moon. In the Christian tradition, he noted, Jesus tells Mary and Martha that although Martha has devoted herself to service and virtuous action, caring for the needs of Jesus and his company, Mary, who simply sits at Christ's feet in utter devotion, "has chosen the better part, and it shall not be taken from her."

Father Redington's elucidation of Indian scriptures communicated a sensitivity and intimate understanding of the principles involved that provided a memorable example of respect for and blending of both Eastern and Western traditions. I found myself thinking of him as a "Christian Baul," a priest able to draw on Eastern wisdom and devotion in a way that strengthened and deepened his living of his own tradition, the classically Western path of the institutional Catholic Church. Throughout my years in Lee's company, I have seen him bring to the community these rich contacts with the most devoted and knowledgeable practitioners of traditions other than our own, whose teaching provides inspiration and a kind of cross-fertilization between paths.

During a visit to California in late fall, Lee took our traveling party to dinner at a sushi restaurant called Matsuhisa's, frequented by the rich and famous, in the Hollywood section of Los Angeles. We were ushered to a table for four in the center of the dining area. At the nearby sushi bar, diners could watch Nobu, the chef known for his superlative creations, at work on his masterpieces. The most expensive option on the menu was a selection called "chef's choice," which consisted of whatever items the chef chose to serve, including any special creation he was making for that night. Lee chose this selection for our entire party, and after a wait honoring the great care that went into each dish, the waiter began to bring us one creation at a time, enough to be shared among the four of us. Each dish was perfection unto itself. As the meal proceeded, the mood deepened into a level of communion that might be expected at an intimate dinner for two but was totally extraordinary for a group of four sitting among the poshly dressed celebrities of Hollywood. The food, already perfect at its own level, was transformed into the stuff of communion, the physical substance which becomes divine body and blood so that we may eat of the divine and become that which we eat.

The sparks from the fire in which we met must have been visible even through the glitter of famous faces. Someone walked up to Lee and said, "I think I know you . . .?" Obviously the questioner took Lee to be some movie star or celebrity whose name would be recognizable. He did not understand that what he was recognizing was something he had lost within himself and wanted to remember.

By the time we left the restaurant we had spent almost five hundred dollars on a dinner for four people. I had never experienced such opulence; yet it was clear that this expenditure was the furthest thing from a personal indulgence. I had been grasping for more and more and more; yet at the core my grasping was distorted longing. When I found myself in the field of the divine heart that was what I most deeply sought, distortions melted away and there was only communion and gratitude. Back in the ordinary world, the next day and in the next years, I would have to struggle with my food cramp again. But for that night I experienced food as it has the capacity to be, an alchemical element to which, through my teacher, I found for one evening perfect right relationship.

Lee's willingness to spend abundant amounts of money on celebratory meals and gatherings is in sharp contrast to his miserly grasp on every cent in other circumstances. After years of trying to clean the ashram of desert dust with a couple of ancient vacuum cleaners, we were offered a donation to buy a brand new vacuum.

"We don't need a vacuum," Lee responded, settling the matter. "I'd rather spend the money on something else; on things we need, like producing albums for the band."

In his journal *The Eccentricities, Idiosyncrasies, and Sacred Utterances of a Contemporary Western Baul*, Lee says, "If I am going to spend money, I'd much rather spend it on entertainment, meaning travel, food, theatre, concerts, movies, than on 'things.' Entertainment feeds the soul, 'things' (accumulations, furniture, clothes, doo-dads, technology) feed the Ego." (Lozowick, L., [Prescott, Ariz.: Hohm Press, 1991], May 1, 1990, p. 9)

In the same journal, Lee wrote about the delicacy of the
energetic fabric that can be created when a space opens into the
sacred, into a space of communion.

> The ideal of course is to be sensitive
> enough, or intuitive enough, to recognize the
> existence of such an energetic dynamic, whether
> it is between two people, a group, or a person
> and a "thing" (book, piece of music or art, task,
> etc. . . . .) and simply "wait one's turn." Most
> people, through naiveté, or downright mean-
> ness, wade into such dynamics causing a
> rupturing of the membrane, therefore a
> wound. Such dynamics can rarely be repaired
> but fortunately can be recreated at another
> time, free of the damaging element(s). Such
> dynamics could be called a Chamber. If many
> people are involved, it is more difficult to rup-
> ture (the skin is tough and not easily pierced)
> but when the dynamic is between two individu-
> als (two children—extremely fragile; an adult
> and a child—fragile but less so; or two adults—
> tougher unless the chamber is a sexual one,
> then as fragile as the dynamic between two chil-
> dren—tender—tentative—gentle) it is easily
> torn, like a tissue. Life is very simple if you are
> awake, and intricate, confusing, bizarre, unbe-
> lievable to the sleeping. (p. 12)

What we had shared that night at Matsuhisa's was a chamber,
a delicate membrane interwoven from the substance of the being of
each person present. In that chamber, work could take place that

would feed eternal verities. To pay five hundred dollars for the food that became an alchemical element in that process of fusion was a small price.

This moment of epiphany at Matsuhisa's notwithstanding, when we returned to Arizona, I was back to dealing with my daily habits. Essentially, I was not yet willing to let go of the comfort that I felt food was bringing me. As a result I was not open to the deeper comfort of right relationship that can emerge when we release our defensive protections, which, in fact, serve as barriers. Several years later, Lee came up with a phrase that described the separative environment that was created by my relation to food. He said that I went into a "food trance," and the result was that I was not attentive to or even aware of much that was occurring around me, including the needs of children.

About a year after this, in the fall of 1990, Lee gave me an "exercise"—a specific and usually temporary practice intended to bring a particular dynamic into more acute consciousness and help the student to develop a new and more useful habit pattern in some area. He recommended that I eat no sweets of any kind for a period of two months. What was curious to me was that, once I engaged this exercise, my desire for sweets, typically a driving interest for me, largely dissolved. There was no question for me that I would not disobey the recommendation in the slightest way. When preparing food for others, I would not even lick my fingers if they had honey on them.

I was absolute in my engagement of the exercise. What I saw was that as soon as the grasping dynamic knew for certain that it could not engage my energy in attaining sweets, it simply shifted to other possible goals. Craving for sweets virtually disappeared. What I wanted was not the sweet; it was something that I experienced as being carried by the sweet—essentially love—and if I could not have the sweet, I simply started grasping for love in other forms.

Although the sweets lost their hold—their attraction—the basic dynamic remained in place. Nevertheless, the exercise revealed to me that the addictive, grasping energy I experienced around sweets and special food was, in fact, a lie. And seeing that the linking of the sweet to love had been a lie, I knew that all the other forms for which I grasped were not in fact necessary in order to experience love. Love could use these forms, but did not need them in order to flow.

Just after the two months for which the exercise had been given ended, we had a celebratory meal that included a dessert of a rich chocolate cake. I looked at Lee, wondering if I was to eat this cake or forego it, as he had not yet released me from the conditions of the exercise, even though he had originally said that it would end at this time.

"You can eat the cake if you first tear up all your credit cards," he told me.

My credit cards, originally a gift that had helped me to reach this school, I had later used to build up a heavy debt. I was still working to repay that debt. I no longer used the cards, but I still had them, holding onto them as I had held onto many other things, such as my storage lockers full of useless objects. I cut up the credit cards and threw the pieces in the trash can, and we all ate cake.

Lee's teaching includes an emphasis on handling ordinary responsibilities in the world as part of building a reliable matrix in which we can receive and use higher and subtler energies responsibly as well. He teaches that we must learn to handle money, food, and sex (a phrase coined by another teacher, which we have found apt and useful) as part of learning to use our human machine as an alchemical instrument. Alchemical practice begins with the simplest of disciplines: with absolutely clean equipment, careful mixing of precise amounts of various elements, and attention to the practical realities of time and space. An alchemist who casually mixes an extraneous element at the wrong moment could produce an explosion. Lee's teaching leads toward transformative work in subtle domains, but this possibility is based in responsible action on the simplest and most basic of levels as a foundation. He released me from the exercise around food by using my desire for sweets as a motivator to move me through my resistance to making a shift in my relationship to money. He was working as a "sly man," a man of skillful means, who sees us so clearly that he can use one of our dynamics to help us penetrate another, thereby releasing us from habitual patterns in two domains at once.

ON THE ROAD AGAIN

The next trip I made with Lee was to the New Age mecca of California. Six of us drove to a conference titled, "The Energies of Transformation: The Dynamics of Spiritual Emergence in the Body," sponsored by the Spiritual Emergence Network and the Institute of Transpersonal Psychology. Living close to the master may appear as a ticket to paradise, but I was finding some of the ramifications of this gift sobering. The difference between my state of being when I was traveling with Lee in Germany and my state of being on this trip to California was such that in the face of it I went numb and silent. In Germany I expected nothing, was often given nothing in the sense of formal acknowledgment or inclusion, and was grateful for everything. I was in a state of profound appreciation for Lee, the *sangha*, and our work together. Now I was given many things, such as inclusion in this trip, and I was finding that I often expected or wanted more. Living on the ashram, I was up against trying to live as a mature human being in Lee's daily company. In many ways it was easier to worship him from a distance. One of the speakers at the California conference said, "It is easy to love the beggar children on the streets of India. It's a much harder spiritual practice to be a human being with your husband or wife or child, with the people you live with—to really live in relationship day-by-day."

The trip to California began with Lee's typical departure some minutes before the scheduled time. His relationship to time and sleep on a physical level are imbued with hints about relationship to the sleeping and waking states in terms of consciousness and about the way to build patterns in physical space and time that create an alignment in subtler domains through which higher energies can enter and work. In his company I was beginning to find myself acutely aware of my own choices in these areas and of their effects.

We were to leave at 6 a.m. I knew from experience that this probably meant 5:50. I was so intent on being on time that I unconsciously set my alarm twice as early as I intended, and woke to its ringing in the middle of the night. In the darkness, staring groggily at the lighted numbers, I realized what I had done and went back to sleep. At 5:45 a.m., ready to go and waiting in the kitchen, I saw that Lee had not yet appeared. At 5:47 he emerged from his room, and at 5:54 we were driving through the ashram gate. Still tired from a restless night, I went to sleep in a back seat.

A conversation in the front of the van woke me intermittently. One of the men was evoking an extended consideration from Lee about their visit with Yogi Ramsuratkumar the previous December. Lee was pointing out particular teaching lessons that the men who traveled with him failed to report in their journals, lessons that he said were some of the most useful moments of the trip. Up to now, in response to repeated questioning, Lee had refused to discuss what those missed moments were. So I was aware that this was a unique, vital conversation. I wanted to be awake for every moment of it. At the same time, after only three hours of rest the previous night, sleep was blissful. I made no movement to wake myself; I just drifted in and out between a deep sleep and lines of the conversation. Only afterward, when I was finally fully awake, did I realize the opportunity I had lost (slept through, to be exact), and remembered that what I wanted was to be awake, to hear Lee's teaching. But it was too late.

By the time I was fully awake and involved in the conversation again, we were driving along winding roads past green hills and fields. To ask a question that is important to me always requires a kind of gathering of forces, of attention and intention and an effort toward courage or willingness to truly hear the answer. As Lee sped around the curves, up and down the hills, I gathered energy to ask a question I had been holding for weeks. He had said at a recent talk that people in the *sangha* in general have more of a chance to really work than people living in close proximity to him do. He said that when people don't have his continuous physical presence, the inner demand for his energetic presence generates work as a way to be in touch with him. When his physical presence is more constant, the likelihood is that people will just live as parasites, with him as Host. He didn't suggest that people living close to him should move away so as to contact that inner demand and motivation. He simply said that there is this tendency. So in the van I asked him, if we live in his close company, what can we do about this tendency?

All I remember about what came next is a simultaneous imprinting of the curves of the road and the words and energy of Lee's answer. My outer attention seemed to rivet on the visible road almost as a side effect of a riveted attention on the inner road he was describing, the journey of this common work. And yet, with all my intent attention, at one point he said that he had laid out for me my blind spot, what I have to work on—laid it out on a golden platter with neon arrows flashing—and I missed it. I tried to repeat back to him what I thought he had told me. First he said that was not it; later he told me that I may have repeated his words, but without the real tone or meaning, without understanding. Later still (as I still tried to retrieve the moment and unlock it), he told me simply that I had missed it, that there would be other chances, and to let go and go on. I realized that time and space do not wait, suspended, for us to retrieve missed opportunity. The movement of time in which we work creates a circumstance in which we must face remorse and use that to deepen our response to the next opportunity.

What I do remember is his discussion of the tendency to be parasites living on a Host. He said that those of us living with him day to day receive a continuous level of refined food through our contact with him, which means that the inner demand to *generate* that food ourselves is less strong. I extrapolated from this that we need to find or access within ourselves another level of motivation that will impel us to create our own work *while* receiving the daily food of his physical presence.

I said to Lee that I experience at times an inertia that I have to move through to do the work that is in front of me and especially to move out of a parasitic dependence on his presence and his work. He said the solution to inertia is simple: "You just do it. If your work is to write, you just sit down and write. You just go ahead and do your work."

At one point, someone said that it seemed we all already know the answers to the questions we ask him. I commented that while that's probably true, I'm not in touch with the place in me that knows. I thought part of the purpose of having a teacher was to help us access those answers. I thought if we reached the point where we were in touch with all the answers for ourselves, we would be able to work fully on our own. "Then," I asked, "why would we need a teacher?"

"That," said Lee, "is a very good question." And he said no more.

I remembered that Lee often quotes J. Krisnamurti, who said, "On the path of love there are no questions." And clearly, on the path of love one follows a teacher out of the call of one's heart. So questions and answers do not seem to hold, necessarily, the place of value in a student-teacher relationship that I had assumed. (Another illusion down the drain!) So the question remained: What is the real purpose in having a teacher? And what would a working relationship with a teacher that did not have this endemic tendency toward dependence be like?

As our road trip west continued, Lee spoke about the attitude we can bring to learning from a teacher. He said that, for himself, he finds that another teacher is generally either ahead of him or behind him. If Lee has something to offer to a teacher who is coming after him, that teacher has to choose to use him, to receive help. He commented on how many of us say we want his advice and recommendations but then choose not to follow suggestions he does make; and how often we are offended if we aren't given the attention we want from the teacher. He told us how another teacher once told him to go sift sand, and Lee just did what the teacher told him. "If I go to another teacher to learn something," Lee said, "then I just do what he says. If he says, 'go sit,' I would never get arrogant and say, or even think, 'What do you mean, telling me to go sit? I'm a *teacher*!' I would just go sit."

I have heard Lee bring an attitude of arrogance to interactions with others in some circumstances; yet he seems to bring none of this to his approach to teachers from whom he wants to learn. It seems to me that most of us are controlled by habitual attitudes, and that these attitudes become filters through which we consistently and inescapably approach the world. In contrast, Lee seems to have choice about using arrogance or not, depending on his purpose. When I questioned him about this, he said that arrogance is something he *has*, not something he *is*. This relationship of choice in regard to personality attributes means that "the machine becomes a tool of essence rather than a handicap to essence."

We arrived in California and reported to the conference site. In marked contrast with the crisp and reliable way in which Lee had left the ashram even before his scheduled departure time that morning, the conference began with energetic and physical chaos.

The six of us were attending on volunteer scholarships, since that was the only way the community could afford for us to go. This meant that we did work for the conference interspersed with attending talks. Our first job was to help with the registration of more than four hundred participants. Lee took up a place at the registration desk signing in people with last names starting with "S" through "T". I was given a position at the troubleshooting desk— and there was plenty of trouble. The computers had broken down two hours before, so the entire registration process had to be carried out manually. In addition, the conference itself was beginning late, which was only a precursor of things to come. At 3 p.m., when registration was due to begin, the volunteers had not even been instructed in what to do. I thought of Lee's consistency, an example being the way in which he departs and arrives on time or early. During the ensuing chaos of registration—with continually changing orders from the organizers, when we got any orders at all—Lee commented that the entire affair was an example of the failure of Western culture, and in particular the New Age culture, to understand the meaning of spiritual *practice*.

During the first talk, Claudio Naranjo, a teacher who is a good friend of Lee's, saw our group sitting in the balcony, and he came up to greet Lee. As I remember, they hardly touched. If they did, the physical touch—whether hug or handshake—was not the point. There was a meeting of being that was so tangible it did not have to be expressed in any form, or dramatized or used to garner attention. They simply recognized each other, and in that recognition I could see that each was fed. And we who sat nearby were also fed, without any direct acknowledgment or inclusion, simply by the fact that something real was taking place and we were lucky enough to be there, and to be able to see.

There was a quality in the meeting between Claudio and Lee at that moment and each time they were together during the conference that seemed to me instructive for all our human relationships. It was a quality of respect, receptivity and honoring. After his own talk, later in the week, Claudio told Lee that he appreciated having a "real" person present so that he had "someone to talk to." Not just in words, but in energy, they seemed able to speak to each other because the other was listening.

I wondered what we would receive from Lee in our daily lives together if we gave that quality of receiving, honoring, and respect for what he has to give us. I wondered what we would find evoked in each other if we gave that quality of attention. I also sensed that to give that attention we have to be willing to receive it—to allow ourselves to be recognized and honored in our essential being and to cease the self-indulgent dramatization of our self-hatred and insecurity.

Before Claudio's talk there was an incident that Lee hinted was worth reporting. While Lee stood at the doorway of the conference hall, four of us from the ashram were seated in the back row, talking about events of the trip. When we had gotten into the van at eight o'clock that morning to drive from our motel to the conference site, most of us had been exhibiting fairly strong waves of energy while Lee drove steadily along Route 1. At one point he turned around to look at us, comfortably distributed throughout the van, and said, "You're an alive bunch this morning!" Someone was now repeating this comment to someone else, and we added that Lee had said this "with his usual complimentary tone." I saw Lee looking over at that point with his ears pricked and an interested yet enigmatic expression on his face. I told him that we were just discussing his "complimentary tone to us," to which he replied, "Well, take it while you've got it, it won't be there once we're back home."

I looked at him almost in shock. The implication, if I understood it correctly, was that there might actually be things he could truthfully compliment us about, but he wasn't going to dilute or ruin our work at home, on a daily basis, by risking compliments. (He said once that one compliment could destroy a year's worth of work, and that to learn to handle compliments so they don't disturb our momentum can be an important aspect of our work.) The implication was that on the road, in the particular chamber and momentum created by that movement together, he could risk a broader freedom of movement, including even the occasional compliment. It had never occurred to me that his statement that morning might actually have been complimentary or appreciative.

I had the definite impression at that moment that the spiritual master cares for us, individually and as a *sangha* body, with a softness, almost a tenderness, that he keeps generally invisible so that it doesn't distract us or give us something we may not be able to handle correctly at that point. I suspected that there are times when he could express compliments or appreciation and that he doesn't, for the sake of our work.

Because of his unique function, a teacher must handle his relationships with students with great circumspection. The teacher may engage relaxed conversation, humor, and intimate daily life with his students. Yet at the same time, he is constantly confronting a tendency in the students to fixate on the teacher rather than to use the teacher's guidance to become responsible and able to work. An analogy from the Zen tradition is that the teacher is a finger pointing at the moon, and the tendency of the student is to become so fascinated looking at the finger that he or she fails to even notice the moon.

At the same time, on a devotional path the teacher or guru is by nature a central focus of attention for the student. On this path, the guru serves as a tuning fork. By gradually coming into resonant vibration with the tuning fork, the student comes into resonance with the larger field of Work, which the teacher serves as well. Our particular school combines devotion to the guru with a commitment to what in Fourth Way schools is called "the Work." The result is a demand that both students and teacher enter into a relationship that is simultaneously intensely personal and sometimes shockingly impersonal and objective. While this paradoxical yet constantly deepening relationship may seem at times impossible to embrace, to whatever degree we do embrace it, it leads inexorably toward its prototype, which is the shattering relationship between human and divine, a relationship both intimately personal and infinitely impersonal, a relationship that can open into what Lee has called the ultimate human possibility, to live in longing for the divine Beloved.

It is because in our school we work and learn in large part through our relationship with the guru that refining and purifying that relationship becomes so important. If we are dependent on the guru in a way that obviates our own contributions to the Work, we build ourselves a cul-de-sac that is difficult to escape. Even his help can feed our dependence; and we can use his availability to support our unwillingness to act with initiative and responsibility for ourselves. On the other hand, if we try to maintain independence in a way that is actually stubborn refusal of his help, we end up working largely alone, much more slowly and ineffectively than we could with receptivity to his guidance. As students in this school we are constantly faced with the challenge of finding our way to responsible participation neither as blind followers nor as stubborn loners, but as practitioners resonant to the master and the Work he serves.

One of the volunteer tasks that Lee often chose was the job of monitor, standing at the door before a presentation and checking people's badges showing they were legitimate conference participants (had paid their money). Toward the end of the conference, there was a large gathering of most of the participants for a panel discussion. Lee was at the door, quietly and almost invisibly serving as monitor. From my point of view he was on subtle planes fulfilling a totally different function as he stood there with the blessings of Yogi Ramsuratkumar flowing through him out into the entire field of transpersonal psychology and the field of contemporary spiritual work, some of whose major weaknesses had been demonstrated in this conference. Although many participants had a sincere desire to do spiritual work, few gave evidence of having developed even a rudimentary will to work. Without that will and without a teacher, trapped in the stubborn defense and trust of their own subjective viewpoint as their only guide, most of these people were suffering fragmentation and dissonance in their lives at a level of suffering that was starkly visible to the uninvolved observer, yet would baffle them if they even allowed the tip of that iceberg to emerge into consciousness. From the point of view of the conventional New Age perspective, they were doing everything right: they were free of materialistic greed, committed to personal exploration, and open to spiritual domains. Yet they were largely encased in the limitations inherent in egoic control of idealistic presumptions.

As the ragged stream of latecomers straggled through the door and those already seated waited for a presentation that was predictably and interminably late, Lee exploded into sudden, totally unexpected animation. He began to spin through the empty space behind the seated participants, his arms spread wide like an angel circling over these suffering humans—or like a great bird of prey aiming its piercing gaze at the hidden roots of egoic dynamics, roots which he could pluck out with one fierce grasp of his beak and talons if we would only give him real permission. He spun faster and wider, a smile more mysterious than that of the Mona Lisa illuminating his face, dancing as the child of God dances, without thought or purpose beyond the spontaneous response to the ever-present music of the divine. We stared at him, some of us entranced, some of us embarrassed, some of us sneaking glances at the audience rustling in their seats as they waited for the presentation to begin.

Most people in the audience, with their backs to Lee, eyes focused on the empty stage, did not even notice his spinning parody of their own dancing during the "experiential" sections of the conference. He took a form that had been made vacuous and laughable by its sentimental enactment in the vain pursuit of real experience, and in one spontaneous moment he made the form real and vivid, as he wholly filled it with his play. Almost no one felt the power of the energy emanating from the spinning vortex that Lee had created at the back of the room. Here were people desperate for real experience, yet they felt nothing and sat restlessly waiting for "real life" to appear before them on the stage.

A few people did sense some unusual energy in the back of the room and turned around to watch. Of these, most cast a disdainful and critical glance at the lone, twirling dancer. Their cramped hold on the idea of spontaneity extended only to the field of conformity where four hundred people did the chicken dance together the first day of the conference. For someone to dance spontaneously, by himself, visibly free and uncontrolled by the opinions of onlookers, created a threat that they could handle only by criticizing and rejecting him.

No matter what anyone thought about it, Lee danced on. He was a whirling dervish spinning rainbow strands of light through a field of slumbering consciousness, throwing sparks that among all those hundreds of conference participants might fall on a few dormant coals ready to ignite.

In the van driving home, we asked Lee why he would go to a conference where what he has to offer is not recognized, where he simply attends the talks and actually works on a scholarship. His reply was that it is essential to confront self-importance.

"I have an ego, too," he said. "It doesn't matter who you are, it's essential to confront self-importance, in circumstances where *you're* not pulling the strings. I could be the greatest Avatar on Earth, we could be doing the most real Work there is, and we still have to confront self-importance—to just be a monitor, to just be a volunteer, and nobody thinks of you as anything. This is 'the streets' for us. LGB and playing in bars isn't the streets for me. LGB goes into the underworld; that's a different thing; that's being a shaman. This is 'the streets' for me, just going into a conference where there are all these 'spiritually evolved' people around and to them I'm just an asshole. So much of our work is in a rarefied domain. We don't want to get so we live on an ashram and freak out just getting on an airplane."

We ate apples and popcorn, Lee pumped gas for the van, and we discussed considerations as we drove or watched the changing earth in silence. And all the while, in this most ordinary living of the day, something else was going on. Sometimes the mystery is so tangible that I feel us being pressed and poured into wine for some unknown feast of the divine.

MONEY, FOOD AND SEX

Food was not the only area in which Lee was working with me directly and sometimes publicly during this period, using my personal dynamics as examples for the rest of the *sangha*. Another area was money. The use of credit from the bank had originally come as a gift that fueled my leap into the unknown and allowed me to leave North Carolina for Colorado. But as I've said, I had continued to use it past the point of right timing. It had become a seduction and I used it to make choices that I could not pay for in the moment. Perhaps many of these were good choices; perhaps not.

Credit enabled me to leave Boulder for the household in Aptos and to participate in leading the study group there before I had found a new job. Credit allowed me to leave Aptos for the Arizona ashram and to work there for five months before I had to take a paying job again. These times of transition were times of powerful growth and bonding into the *sangha* and Lee's company. Perhaps if I had used credit only for these opportunities, and had ruthlessly eschewed all other comforts that the credit card might give, such as an occasional restaurant dinner, I might have created a lawful matrix through which I would have been able to generate the money for repayment. The fact was, however, that I used the credit card for many small leaks of energy, for buying and paying for various small comforts and conveniences that I could not afford.

The result was that when I made the transition into life as an ashram resident, I brought with me an albatross of debt. It was clear that I could not work at any full-time paying job and meet my responsibilities to ashram life. Teaching part time at a local college enabled me to make my monthly payments but left me facing the prospect of taking years to pay off the bulk of my bank loan, which was thousands of dollars.

As it turned out, personal friends, learning of my financial situation, offered to pay the entire loan for me. I felt that, all things considered, it was best to accept their gift. Yet to accept it left me with a profound sense of obligation, not so much to my friends, since I knew the gift was offered without expectation of return, but of obligation to the universe which had paid for me through them. To accept such a gift created a shock in me; the shock of realization of the level of my obligation, not just for this large payment of money, but for all the payments that are made for me, by my family and friends, by my *sangha* mates, by the community as a whole, and finally by my teacher. Specifically in relation to money, I made a decision that I would never again use it in this profligate way. I would not buy anything for which I could not pay. I would not accept a loan or credit to stretch time, to allow myself to grasp something now and pay later—not even something for my work. I had been given immense help to get where I was. Others had paid for part of my transportation into this community, and the repayment I could make was from now on to pay for my work in the moment.

On the level of money I have been able to keep my commitment. If I cannot pay for something, I do without it. On a practical level this has sometimes led to great creativity, such as in giving homemade gifts to friends when I have no money to buy something. Yet in the process I have made a much greater discovery. When I stop trying to stretch money beyond what I have, when I accept the absolute limitation of the ashram allowance to each resident for personal "disposable income"—a level of income so radically small compared to that of the typical middle-class American as to be laughable—a paradoxical circumstance occurs. This small amount of money begins to appear infinite, to be constantly multiplied, like the loaves and the fishes. I seem always to have more than I need. When I stop fighting and grasping to have more, I discover that I do not need even what I have. A small stipend has come to seem generously abundant, whereas an income of thousands of dollars used to be insufficient to meet my needs and responsibilities. Many things that once seemed to me absolutely essential now seem not only unnecessary, but totally uninteresting. They have lost their seductive power. But this shift occurred only as a result of sacrificing the desire while it still raged and demanded satisfaction. In accepting limitation I have discovered abundance beyond limitation. In taking only what I need, I find that I am given continually more than I need, or even asked for.

In the same way that a debt was paid for me on the level of money, a payment is constantly being made for me by my teacher— a payment toward the possibility that I will someday be able to work at a level that repays not him but the universe for what has been given. To become both willing and able to make our own payment, fully and responsibly, in the moment, is the purpose of the entire apprenticeship of disciple to master.

I began to see that my attachments around food were costing not only myself but my teacher; he was paying energetically for my indulgences. When I first came to live on the ashram, many of the residents ate our healthy but somewhat spartan diet at regular meals but made not infrequent trips to town for "treats" at local cafes and pastry shops. We justified these as small celebratory spaces in which we could share "communion" with each other in a relaxed, intimate, and festive environment. I, however, began to realize that these spaces felt less and less celebratory to me, and they created more and more a sense of dissonance and distance from Lee, even while I was thoroughly enjoying the company of my *sangha* mates. Lee was making increasingly critical comments about our trips to town and our treats at local cafes.

On one level, Lee's concern about the small treats we bought in town seems inexplicable. How could eating a piece of cake or a few cookies have any noticeable effect on the central issues of spiritual work such as development of compassion, wisdom, and service? Even practitioners in ancient traditions such as the austere and rigorous approach of Zen often have meals that include sweets and other "comfort" foods. Yet when ordinary life is being used as a matrix in which extraordinary energy is collected, conserved, refined, and used, precise distinctions among what may seem mundane elements become crucial for protection and strengthening of the matrix. Persephone ate only six seeds in the underworld, and the result was that she was condemned to live six months of the year with the lord of the underworld forever after. It became clear to me that, for Lee, our small treats in town were an excursion into the underworld—the underworld of our own indulgence and its roots in hidden motivations—that could have serious results for our work, beyond anything we imagined. It was not the substance itself but our relationship to it that was the issue. Sugar given and received as *prasad* was a substance which could have untold benefits to our work. Sugar grasped and devoured as an escape from our work, as a small symbol of independence or comfort, could contribute to the maintenance of addictive relationships not only to sugar but to other substances, energies, and even other people that substantially compromised our ability to work.

The next summer, while Lee was traveling, I made a decision not to make occasional use of the leftover jam that sat in the refrigerator in the long interim between celebratory meals. Previously I had taken advantage of access to the kitchen to give myself these small treats of jam while I knew he was feasting with his hosts and traveling company. I was amazed at how this simple choice to forego such treats dissolved my experience of separation from Lee while he traveled across the ocean. In this small choice of consonance with his wishes I opened a door to his energetic presence, which was always available but to which I had to open my own access. Through my small, even tiny, sacrifice, I had opened myself to his energy, which poured like a river of unexpected blessing. I had given up the jam and in so doing I discovered that the very thing I sought to reach through the jam, the elusive experience of love, was already present, only waiting for me to give it my attention. I had only been distracted by the jam, which was in fact a barrier, while I saw it as a door. This principle frequently applies in relation to our indulgences and addictions: the substance that we believe offers us comfort or surcease or love, in fact serves to distract and even bar us from the very thing we seek. In letting go of the substance of comfort, we discover that a deeper comfort is waiting only for us to be free to receive it with our full attention.

Another lesson involving food occurred late one night when we were tramping through Geneva, Switzerland, looking for an ice cream parlor after an inspiring public talk which Lee had given. Lee had sent one woman ahead to scope out the choices, and she returned with information about a couple of sidewalk stalls. We walked to within twenty meters of a place that was all lit up but had no place for us to sit. Lee stopped short in the middle of the sidewalk and explained to her with great emphasis, "These places won't work. I am looking for ambience. I am not just looking for ice cream. I never want ice cream. I never want just a hamburger. I never want sausage. I want an ambience in which work can take place." He was delineating a totally different relationship to food from that of greed or even of common nourishment.

Some spiritual schools recommend celibacy and work with the purification and sublimation of sexual energies. Although these processes can situationally be part of our school, in general we engage relationship whenever possible as part of our spiritual practice. For many people these relationships include marriage, sex, family, and children. Purification and work with higher sexual energies takes place through committed sexual relationship rather than through the absence of sex.

Many schools that encourage abstinence in regard to sex have no such guidelines in relation to food, and practitioners may feel free to eat whatever diet they choose. In contrast, relationship to food is a major area of work in our school. Food, like sex, is used as a sacred element which is intentionally prepared and selected so that the outer form serves the inner possibility. There are examples of this kind of attention to food as a sacred and sacrificial element in many traditions, ranging from Christ's use of bread and wine as the elements of the ritual of Communion to Gurdjieff's gourmet feasts.

When we first begin work with a teacher and our work is not yet highly refined, precise discriminations about food, or use of money, or protocol in a space, or even about sexual relationships (one of the most fiery fields in which we can work) may not yet be required. But as our work matures, we become responsible for discriminating choices that provide a foundation for work with higher energies. The maturity of our practice gives us leverage to use small elements to create large possibilities. Yet the reverse is also true: that small dissonances can have large and destructive effects.

HOUSECLEANING

In July of 1990 Lee traveled to Germany for five weeks of teaching in Europe. For those of us remaining on the ashram it was an opportunity to forge a deeper connection to his essential Presence during this time of his physical absence.

When he returned, I moved into a different room on the ashram. It was a chance to confront the chaotic state I created in my physical environment and the inner chaos and confusion that it represented as well. I had an entrenched habit of procrastination combined with a packrat attachment to a myriad of odds and ends that produced, as an end result, a stack of boxes in the storage room full of old magazines, half-finished sewing projects, unanswered letters, and other material items that I knew generated a substantial drag on my work. I also had a number of huge boxes containing the remains of my old life before entering the community. These were the boxes I had left in storage when I moved west and for which I had ended up paying hundreds of dollars. I had brought them to Arizona intending to go through them and retrieve what was useful.

One afternoon, just prior to the move into the new room, Lee came to me and said, "Let's get rid of those boxes tomorrow morning." In the morning we carted the boxes out into the fresh air under a juniper tree.

"Are you willing to let me do this?" he asked.

I was not at all sure I was willing. I didn't know what things of value might be in those boxes, from journals and other writing I considered precious, to gifts with "sentimental value" (just what he wanted to release me from!), to small caches of money I might have stuck away to be saved for a time of need. My (correct) perception was that Lee did not have the same sense of value that I did. If I let him handle it, he might dispense with things I considered irreplaceable treasures. Once I gave him permission, I was not going to argue with him; I would have to trust his decisions. At the same time the weight of these boxes was a tangible burden and I knew that simply holding onto them was costing me energetically far more than any material or even emotional value they might hold.

"All right," I said. "You can handle it."

He proceeded to rummage through several boxes with deft and incisive intention, pulling out an item here and there and relegating the rest to trash. "That's done," he said enthusiastically after a brief ten minutes. "Next!" He continued through my hoard of boxes until the entire collection had met its final judgment. Most of it went into the huge garbage cans at the edge of the ashram.

Just after we finished, a trash truck drove up, and its ravenous mouth devoured the contents of my past life. It was as if, in slicing through those boxes with his keen and unsentimental sword, Lee had unknotted and erased the trail, with all its burnt bridges, its delays, and its epiphanies, that had brought me to the community. Now I could enter into a new life, free of the old body.

In clearing out those boxes, Lee's energy had washed through my life like a great cleansing wave, but to eradicate the pattern that had collected the boxes was up to me. Something inside me desperately desired to surround myself with clutter, to bury my writing, especially any poems or anything I considered creative, under impenetrable mounds of dirty laundry, old appeals for money for social and political causes, and any other handy form of camouflage. My awareness of the pattern was not a sufficient force to interrupt the dynamic. I began to collect clutter and chaos once again. Repeatedly, Lee and my *sangha* mates would address me about this dynamic, which was brazenly apparent to anyone walking into my room. I knew with a passionate comprehension that the deities I sensed and wished to serve could be repelled simply by a dusty *puja*, let alone by a room that even a determined human could find it difficult to enter and traverse. Yet I persevered in maintaining my armor of chaos.

Years later Lee would recommend to me with finality, "If you want to get your room clean, if you want to be different, let your friends do it for you! Let them tell you what is useful to keep and what is not!" I refused his recommendation. The idea felt to me like an invasion that I could not find it in myself to embrace or even tolerate. The result of refusing his direct help in this way is that I am still struggling with the tattered remnants of a dynamic that I am intensely aware presents a significant obstruction in my work.

It may seem totally indefensible that a committed and serious student could allow such a blatant disregard of the simplest requirements for creating an elegant and dignified space. Many of our struggles in spiritual practice involve confronting our habits at the simplest and most basic level. To change these habits at a root level is often a challenge that takes years to accomplish. Sometimes change comes through confronting the habit or dynamic directly; sometimes it comes through the gradual development of a matrix of maturity, which allows a new habit to imperceptibly replace the old. Some habits and dynamics are not in our way for long periods, if at all. Yet those detrimental habits to which we cling with persistent self-reference are often essentially forms of addiction—not the chemical addiction of drug dependence but an emotional addiction based in primal imprinting of patterns we experienced as necessary to survive. Addiction and the accompanying denial—whether to substances such as caffeine or nicotine, or to activities such as gambling or shopping, or to dynamics such as violent expression of anger followed by sentimental and exaggerated tenderness—interrupt and distort the flow of life energy.

Lee had offered me a chance to deal with this addiction cold turkey, and I refused. A year later, realizing that my confidence in my own methods had been unfounded, and finding myself still struggling with the multiplying collection of a packrat's treasures, I asked Lee if it would still be useful to follow his recommendation. Without any judgment or gleeful declarations of "I told you so," he replied simply, "No." The usefulness of the exercise depended not only on a willingness to obey but on doing so with immediacy. The same action without correct timing lost its power.

As we grow in spiritual work, there is a constant refinement of the demands upon us consonant with our ability to meet them.

A level of physical chaos in our personal space or a level of unpredictable anger in our emotional space may be digestible to the powers we serve at the beginning, just as roughly chopped vegetables may be quite acceptable at an ordinary lunch. As we develop, we become aligned and useful to increasingly subtle energies and beings. To become fully digestible requires a refinement similar to the precise and delicate preparation of a gourmet meal. Sometimes the sacrifices we make in our commitment to this process of refinement may seem almost beyond our power to endure. At other times we may find ourselves filled with profound gratitude for the newfound freedom from the heavy shells of our old habits. In either case, our movement into these higher possibilities brings us into relationship with universal energies that feed and enliven us even as we become food for these great processes, increasingly conscious participants in the Great Process of Divine Evolution.

"FRED" AND FRIENDS

The November Celebration arrived, and as part of the theme men dressed as women and women dressed as men. People chose a wide range of characters. Some men dressed as their mothers, and looked so much like them that we were stunned. We knew that women had to stalk conditioning that would cause them mechanically to imitate their mothers, and men similarly to stalk the family patterns of the masculine. This similarity of the men to their mothers, however, offered a graphic demonstration that we take on the family lineage carried through both parents, not just the parent of our own sex.

Lee gave some of us specific characters or types to enact. He told me to dress as a construction worker and gave me the name of "Fred." Released from my normal constraints by this character so far removed from the guise of the leftist idealist and feminist through whom I normally met the world, I found myself "hanging out" in a way that was vibrantly freeing. I was whistling at the women, relaxing with a can of beer, and speaking in a deep and assertive voice. In contrast to the deeply painful experience as a prostitute at one of my first Celebrations, in this case I was actually having fun. The crystallizations in my character were being dissolved rather than cracked open.

For weeks after that Celebration a process continued in which I would find myself speaking as various strongly assertive male voices.

"Pass the carrots, would ya?" I would suddenly demand in a rather rude male persona that we named "Harry." Another voice was "Steve," an aggressively rebellious persona with a rather coarse sense of humor. (I didn't let him out quite far enough to tell the dirty jokes he had going on in his mind!)

To a conventional psychologist, it might seem that Lee had inadvertently tumbled me into a process of psychological disintegration, evidenced by the discrete personalities through which I might unpredictably express at any moment. To an alternative therapist versed in the methods of R. D. Laing, it might have seemed that Lee was running one of those live-in therapeutic communities where participants could descend into the depths of disintegration in order to reintegrate at a higher, more coherent level. Seen from the perspective of spiritual work, however, Lee had simply made available a space in which higher energies could dissolve some of the buffers and release some of the repressions that had made aspects of myself inaccessible to me. The process in this case was not even difficult; like Lee himself in many circumstances, it was humorous and funny. The skilled master does not always need to hammer on his material, but sometimes only to apply the lightest pressure or influence at the precise moment and angle that can release old forms and engage new ones.

FEEDBACK

The confrontation with my food cramp continued. Just before the November Celebration, Lee had given me the exercise of eating no sweets. As if planned and synchronized to intensify the teaching lesson, the schedule included an unprecedented space each afternoon for gathering around "*amrit*," or the nectar of the divine. A small booth, run in part by the children, offered sweets of various kinds, from chai to cakes and cookies, at these afternoon gatherings. During Celebrations Lee has occasionally, although rarely, included an entire day of sweets as the only food (which can become quite challenging to digest and enjoy, as anyone knows who has tried eating only sweets without other foods to balance them over a period of time!). More typically, a dessert is part of one or two of the Celebration meals. This offering of daily *amrit* occurred at only one Celebration in the entire history of the community, as far as I know. That Celebration was the one at which I could not eat sweets.

Some people think that Lee consciously plans arrangements like this that heavily confront us with our desires and attachments. My experience is that he does not plan them and does not need to plan them. He simply works in consonance with universal currents, and these currents provide the necessary synchronicities, confrontations, and opportunities.

A friend suggested that it would be useful to me to have weekly meetings with a few members of the *sangha* to confront and work on some of the issues that were showing up in my life at this time. Lee agreed that this was a good idea. Up to that time, except for some meetings about my food cramp and other small issues, we had never had such regular meetings. Now we began to meet once a week, and I was the focus of the meetings. Looking around at the many imperfections in others in the group, some of whom had been in Lee's company many years more than I had, I thought it totally unfair that the meetings were focused almost solely on me. But when I went to Lee with this complaint, he was absolutely unsympathetic. He was equally unsympathetic when I complained that the motivations underlying people's feedback to me were often a confusion of real intent to help mixed with unconscious power plays.

"You need the help," he told me. "It's up to you to take what is given and use it for your work. Just listen, and don't argue. Later you can make your own discriminations about what is useful. It doesn't matter what people's motivations are, if they are saying things that are true. You can use hearing the truth for your work."

These meetings went on for almost two years. A friend of mine, not a member of the group, commented to me at one point, "You must be ready for the fast track, because that's what you're getting." I did not feel in the least ready for the fast track. I felt resentful at being the object of meeting after meeting, correction after correction, from people who were not asking for or receiving corrections regarding their own issues and behavior. I felt angry and deeply disappointed that my sincere efforts were met with such an experience of rejection and criticism. I did not understand how Lee could be so kind and accepting and even playful with me one minute, in the larger public environment of an After Dinner Talk, and the next minute level such piercing observations at me about my personal dynamics and about my failure to hear and respond to the work at hand. Yet I had one thing that I discovered I could rely on. I could persevere.

Vijay Fedorshak, a psychotherapist in our community and author of *Shadow on the Path*, speaks about the "yes" and the "no" which he has seen dramatically present in every person who comes to him for counseling. When Lee was kind and playful with me, he was speaking to the "yes" in me; and that "yes" must have been to some degree available for me to be able to feel and respond to his kindness. When he harshly criticized my tendency to fall into a "food trance" and ignore the genuine needs of others, he was speaking to the "no" in me. It was up to me to use the "yes" in myself in order to face the "no" and move through it. It was not that *Lee* had a split personality, as I used to think at times, but that *I* did. I still have this split within me, but through years of self-observation and feedback from others, I have a deeper awareness of it. I am no longer stunned by feedback that shows me a moment where I was stuck in the "no"; and I am no longer so trapped by an unconscious assumption that if I am not perfect I must be rejected and left without love.

Ten years later, looking back at those days, I see things quite differently. It has become easier, if not yet easy, to accept feedback, and I see myself, others, and Lee differently in this process of observation and feedback than I did then. Those two years broke down a wall of protection, a wall that caused me more pain than any of the observations that people could make to me. Beyond that wall I have found that other people's observations of me, including Lee's most piercing commentary, are some of the best help I can find for moving in the direction that I most want to go, the direction of more effective work on this path. So while I may not welcome feedback even now in the way that I consider ideal, I do seek it out, in contrast to those early years when I wanted mainly to escape from it.

A LIVING CULTURE

In early 1991, we had a chance for a meeting of worlds as a Baul from India named Sanatan Das and his two sons arrived at our ashram for a stay of several weeks as part of an arranged tour of the western United States. This man and his sons brought with them a living culture, a way of life still intact, from their patchwork jackets made of scraps of cloth, to their *ektaras and dotaras* (musical instruments), to the poetry they composed and sang as they danced ecstatically, creating a mood of the sweetness of longing for divine presence that transcended language. Our Celebration that April included a "gypsy day," in which we dressed in vivid costumes and gathered around a gypsy fire at the edge of the woods behind the ashram. Our Baul visitors played their haunting melodies and danced with abandon around the fire. A few days later they attended an LGB gig, where Lee leaped and sang on stage while we danced in our own ecstatic mood of invocation. It was after this that Sanatan Das said of Lee, "He is a Western Baul Master, and his rock 'n' roll songs are Western Baul music."

At home in India, Sanatan Das continues to beg each day as part of his spiritual practice, even while he now lives on a small ashram with his family rather than wandering constantly, as did most early Bauls. Lee's spiritual father is also a beggar, and although our lineage is founded in Yogi Ramsuratkumar, who comes from the lineage of Papa Ramdas, our path has spontaneously emerged in many ways in consonance with these beggars of Bengal. The Bauls use sex, music, and breath as part of their tantric practice; rather than rejecting the ordinary forms of life, they embrace them and find God through these forms. The practice of begging and of wandering serves as a reminder that all things come from God, that all is impermanent except divine reality, and that God can be found not through aggrandizement of material things, but through attention to that reality. Lee's choice to use community resources for feasts and the music of the bands rather than for furniture and embellishment of the ashram clearly expresses similar principles.

TIMING IS EVERYTHING

A couple of months before the Bauls' visit, Lee had given me a project. He had written a journal over a period of three months, making an entry each day during that period. He planned to publish the journal, and he said later that while his other books were *about* the teaching, this journal and the two that later followed it *were* the teaching. He wanted the text of the journal typeset for publication, and he wanted it proofread with utmost precision. He did not want a single comma changed in the text without his express permission. When he first gave me the project, he asked for it to be done in five days. When after five days we had completed only a fraction of the text, he extended the deadline to two weeks. He wanted me to handle the project because I was known for punctilious exactitude in proofreading.

The project was not an ordinary proofing job. Lee had written the journal in his own inimitable style, which involved sentences two pages long at times, often devoid of commas in any of the places that would be considered grammatically correct, and sometimes with commas added at unexpected points. The journal was handwritten and the writing was reasonably legible but not always clear as to whether a word began with a small letter or a capital. He used capital letters with obvious specific intention but without consistent alignment to grammatical norms. Throughout the book the fine points of grammar, capitalization, style, and even layout on the page reflected and exemplified the radical and unconventional view of the world that he was communicating from his perspective as a spiritual master. Yet his handwriting made it difficult to be sure I was reading his precise choices correctly. In addition, he wanted to know if I found an entry unclear rather than just confrontive. If conventional use of a comma or a grammatical correction could increase the clarity of communication, he would sometimes change the original text. If I thought a comma would clarify his meaning at any point, I had to ask him specifically about that instance. The result of all these precisions was that I had to review the entire manuscript with him almost word by word.

Gurdjieff taught that there are three forces at work in any endeavor: the affirming force, the denying force, and the reconciling force. My own experience is that on projects of major importance the denying force often exerts itself with a strength proportional to the affirmative value of the project. This was certainly the case in the production of this first journal in Lee's trilogy. After painstaking proofing and copyediting, the changes to the manuscript had been entered into the computer, and only a few final changes remained to be completed. Suddenly the printout of one of these final proofing copies came out with errors that had already been corrected some days ago. Aghast, we looked carefully through other final printouts and discovered that they also contained some of these earlier errors. There was no pattern that we could discern as to which pages were coming out with old errors reinstated. The only solution was to proofread the entire manuscript once again. Later we deduced that under the pressure of those last days someone, probably me, who was inputting changes must have accidentally replaced the main copy, with its final corrections, with a backup copy that had not yet been updated. Then corrections were made to this new version of the original, so that it contained an unpredictable mixture of old errors and current corrections. This kind of error dogged the final days of proofing, to the point that I began to question whether it was possible to get the journal printed at all, let alone have it completely free of proofing errors, as Lee wished.

At last, late one spring night the entire project was complete and we packaged it to send to the printer the next day. We were euphoric that it was finished, and we knew the work on it was as close to flawless as we could make it. Yet we had not met Lee's timing. He said to me near the end of those weeks that, for him, the project was dead. Because it had not been completed within the necessary time frame, it lost an essential quality of life.

The journal was published nevertheless, followed by two others, and Lee was clearly enthusiastic about the communication in these journals. Yet, for me it was an unforgettable lesson in the relation of time to life. Lee had been holding two elements as crucial to the life of the project. One was flawless proofing, so that the communication he originally intended was not distorted through changes in the text during typesetting. The other was completing the project within a certain time frame. We achieved only half of the equation. It was rather like creating space without time. Without movement there is no life. For Lee the project died because it did not move as required.

A MOOD OF MEETING

While Lee was in Europe that summer a confrontation took place regarding one of my relationships within the *sangha*. Demanding as it was, this confrontation would eventually bring me into relationship at a level I had thought I wanted but for which I had not yet been willing to pay the price.

Sarah and I worked closely in the community. Consciously we were making an effort to support each other in the engagement of work and practice. Yet unconsciously we were locked in competition and critical judgment of one another, rejecting each other's strengths and focusing on each other's weaknesses as each of us tried to be the best worker and the best practitioner. It is a common human dilemma that is highlighted and even exacerbated at times in community, where we live so closely together. We must face choosing between either projecting our difficulties on those with whom we work closely, driving a wedge into potential working relationships, or nourishing and supporting each other's work, in which case we reap the benefits of the other's growth as well as our own. Sarah and I were both aware of our tendency to polarize and were working, we thought, as hard as we could to overcome it; yet we were not admitting the depth of mutual rejection that divided us.

Finally, another woman in the *sangha* confronted us. "You're going to be working next to each other in this community perhaps for the next twenty years or more," she observed, pointing us beyond our present difficulties to the pattern we were establishing for the future. "You have to make a choice whether you're going to live in polarization for the next twenty years, or whether you're going to share this work and become friends."

It was one of those times when Lee spoke through the *sangha*. I heard the teaching in the woman's words and I made a decision. As it happened, Sarah made a similar decision, and the result was an exponential deepening of relationship between us. The two inner actions bore outer fruit in shared engagement of the challenge of spiritual practice over the ensuing years. Yet, in addition to the reward of our particular relationship, I learned something for myself about the power of decision. Regardless of what choice Sarah had made, the relationship changed for me from the moment of my own decision. It changed from the moment that, within myself, I chose relationship over polarization, and made the decision that I would pay the cost of that, whatever the price.

Even with both of us working diligently, it took months for those changes to manifest in reliable outer harmony and trust between us. The price of change, for me, was repeated letting go of the impulse to judge, to reject, to react. The other person's choices, in this situation or in any other, were not my business. It was my business to use all circumstances for deeper self-observation and for the practice of basic teachings Lee had given us, such as "Be that which nothing can take root in" and "Draw-no-conclusions mind." From that foundation relationship flowers, because regardless of what the other person gives or is willing to receive from us, we are in a mood of meeting. In every person is an essential being who can be met. The Quakers express it as "that of God in every person." Chögyam Trungpa Rinpoche calls it "basic goodness." To act in faith in relationship to this basic goodness is to open a door to transformed and transformative relationship; to the possibility of discovering, in the meeting between two human beings, the organic innocence that rests at the core of all life.

WHO AM I KIDDING?

One of the basic practices in this community is that of enquiry. Our form of Enquiry is a quintessential example of Lee's use of humor and parody to slip past the sanctimonious shell of what Chögyam Trungpa Rinpoche called "spiritual materialism," the tendency to let spiritual life become a new form of aggrandizement and source of competitive pride. During the early days of the community a student made glowing promises to Lee about how he would contribute great quantities of money to the community as soon as he made his first big sale in real estate. When the student actually did make the big sale, he thought to himself (and later passed those thoughts on to Lee), "Who am I kidding? I'm going to keep that money for myself!" Shortly after that he left the community.

Lee was "struck with revelation" in that encounter and announced to the community that our form of enquiry was to be, not "Who am I?" as taught by Ramana Maharshi, but "Who am I kidding?" Humorous and foolish as it may sound, I have found "Who am I kidding?" to offer a highly effective method of penetrating the various defenses and illusions with which I surround myself.

Once, in the middle of intense reaction to some feedback I had just received from Lee and others, I walked out the gate of the ashram into the magical grove of trees that guards our entryway. I was mumbling, "Who am I kidding?" without any release from the series of emotional waves in which I was foundering. I knew the point of enquiry is not necessarily to escape reactive emotion, but simply to allow the process to work in its own unpredictable way. Nevertheless I wanted release, and it was not happening, and that was added to my list of grievances. All that enquiry seemed to do in that moment was drag me deeper into the sloughs at the bottom of each wave: from anger to pain to fear to distrust to despair.

Suddenly it was as if the bottom of that world of emotions dropped out. They floated above me—an interwoven matrix of illusion. I saw them as one sees patterns on the surface when looking up toward the sun from within deep water. In the place into which I had dropped, those waves did not touch me; they had nothing to do with me; they were insignificant swells of motion increasingly far above me. The place into which I was falling was not in fact a place, but the absence of a place. It was total absence. It was emptiness. It was an emptiness which, freed of all content, could reveal itself as the most full and rich reality, beyond anything I could have imagined. In this emptiness even "Who am I kidding?" fell away. There was nothing; and nothing was the same as everything. In the place that was no place and the space that was no space, the two met, however paradoxically. In emptiness I met Someone. And the door to that emptiness where meeting could take place was this little phrase, "Who am I kidding?"

The Pushti Path

The theme of the July 1992 Celebration was "Who Are We, As American Bauls?" Lee asked me to give a talk titled "The *Pushti*

Path." While other talks considered the sacrifices and ascetic practices demanded of a Baul in the East and in our path in the West,
mine was to consider the aspect of divine abundance. While the
Bauls of Bengal beg for their food and wander without a home
throughout the year, they regularly gather for feasting at Baul *melas*
which are rich with food, song, dancing, and invocation through
celebration of the divine Beloved. Our American path includes
similar feasting, in addition to singing and dancing in the mode of
rock 'n' roll, our original music which Sanatan Das had called
"Western Baul music," and the use of traditional Sanskrit chants in
our *darshans* and Celebrations. Lee frequently showers his students
with gifts ranging from his own cooking to sharing of special foods,
such as European cheeses which he adds to his weekly salads. He
also passes on barely-worn clothing that has been given to him,
from embroidered vests to T-shirts with provocative messages.

I had experienced a great deal of abundance on this path during my five years in the school, and I was happy to have the chance
to express my appreciation and gratitude. In the talk I said that I
grew up with the Western Christian ideal of Christ as a paragon of
absolute sexual purity, conceived through immaculate conception
and celibate throughout his life. In contrast, the Eastern traditions
spend an entire book of their scriptures on the ideal of Krishna,
who makes love to 16,000 women simultaneously in such a way that
each feels that she is the only one with him, the only object of his
total adoration. There is a place for sexual energy, for energies of
polarity, and for gracious abundance—for embracing the divine
found in ordinary life rather than turning to the divine as escape
from the mundane.

At the same time that our path includes abundance and festive celebration, this gracious richness must be used correctly. In
the talk I gave an example of wrong relationship based in my own
desperate grasping to take care of myself rather than freely receiv-

ing the gifts offered by the teacher. Our weekly celebratory meals often resulted in some gourmet leftovers that might be served the next day as additions to our usual spare and healthy diet. (At the present time, our everyday meals, while closely defined by guidelines for healthy nourishment of the work body, have great variety. But at the time of this example, before we learned to work more creatively with the dietary guidelines and during a time when the ashram was extremely poor, our meals were often repetitive as well as ascetic: a continual replay of brown rice and salad.)

The practice of the cooks for the celebratory meals included an effort to plan quantities with precision so there would be plenty for everyone at the meal—usually forty or fifty people—but with no leftovers. This was a difficult challenge to meet, and often there was some error on one side or the other. I looked forward to errors on the side of leftovers, even though I well knew that this was not Lee's preference and that there was an important principle underlying his preference.

One of the ways to conserve and use the power of any space is to close it crisply and completely when it is time. The food that was served in the celebratory gathering was prepared with specific intention to help invoke a sacred space. When that food was later served as leftovers, it not only lost something of its energetic quality but it could actually rob the original space of some portion of its power. The food that had been intended as an invocational element became instead a small leak of energy when it stretched into the next space, which may be one whose purpose was best served by the simplicity of fresh carrots and celery. I understood all this quite well. But I craved the tastes and sensations of the special foods; food was still filling the space of love for me, in spite of Lee's exercises and assignments, in spite of the cracks in the dynamic that had been created by the exercise of eating no sweets for two months.

Lee often served the leftovers with his "After-Dinner-Talk" meals. I began to harbor an unspoken assumption that I could eat these leftovers not just when he served them, but whenever I wanted. One day Lee came into the kitchen while I was sitting alone at the table eating a piece of pound cake that was left from the special meal the night before. I was not trying to hide what I was doing. I had reached a point of taking for granted that these leftovers belonged to me. Ten minutes to myself to have a cup of tea in the morning had become something I sought like the Holy Grail. I was still searching for love, though it was staring me in the face.

Lee spoke to me in a tone I find difficult to describe. It was so unusual in my experience, in our culture. It was not shaming. It was not physically forceful. Its power lay in its neutrality, in the space it left me to discover my own real answer to his question.

"What has happened to you?" he asked with a quiet force that penetrated straight into my heart. "You used to be a really strong practitioner. And now—look at you!"

In that moment I saw myself. I was sprawled out across two chairs at the kitchen table, without the slightest remnant of decorum or respect for a sacred space. This was not a mood of relaxed relationship. This was slovenly disregard for any protocol. This was sloth. I was indulging my enjoyment of the leftover pound cake, in isolation, without the slightest pretense of using food as the alchemical element for which it had been created, without even the pretense of sharing it in communion. I had not even a remote consideration that I might wait until Lee offered it, or until, from my own discrimination, I recognized that it might be used to serve a group space rather than to serve my lascivious greed. My access to the kitchen had become for me a doorway to privilege instead of a doorway to service.

"Do you know what I mean?" Lee said to me.

"Yes," I answered.

He left the room. No more was needed from him. It was not his responsibility to take steps to remedy the situation; it was mine. Further discussion would only have buried the instant of penetrating self-observation that had just been given me. The fact that I was not alone in my indulgence, that others had also developed some assumptions that we had a right to license, was no excuse. I was responsible for my own actions and my own practice. That responsibility involved discrimination about where the group mind was supporting indulgence and where it was supporting practice.

Years later a friend complimented me that I seemed to have come to an inner decision that enabled me to live with an authority I had in the community without being seduced into the majority of indulgences that position made possible.

"I did get seduced at the beginning," I told her. "I got heavily seduced."

Those seductions still exist; they are inherent to a position of privilege in any social system, no matter how small or how spiritually dedicated. There are still many choices that I face on a daily basis, and many times that I take advantage of this position rather than adhering to pristine integrity. Yet I now consciously wrestle with these challenges, and the weight of my relationship to privilege has changed. The decision to handle this position differently began in that moment when, through confrontation with a real question from my teacher, I was able to see myself for one clear moment. A dedicated French teacher, Yvan Amar, said in a talk at Arnaud Desjardin's ashram, Hauteville, "To be seen by the *guru* is to be seen in one's original nature. To be seen in that way reestablishes our dignity." (*La Lettre d'Hauteville*, "In homage to Yvan Amar," July 1999, p. 6) I was able to see myself as I was in that moment through the light of original dignity in which Lee saw me, an original dignity which I myself had forgotten.

I had begun the talk on *pushti* by giving out a chocolate truffle on a stick to each person in the room. The truffle was in the shape of a heart, made for Valentine's Day by a woman in the *sangha* who had a business as a chocolatier. As I finished passing them around, someone said, "You forgot to give one to yourself." It was true, a commentary on the "rescuing" pole of my dynamic—the pole that takes care of others and forgets myself. I took a truffle stick and began the talk. The considerations ranged from gratitude for the *pushti*, the grace and abundance that are part of our path, to our responsibilities to receive these energies correctly so we can use them to feed our work rather than to feed indulgence. Finally, there was the consideration of the play of Krishna, the dance of love, which leads ultimately into longing, the relation of lover to Beloved, the ultimate possibility between human and divine.

GERMANY

In August of 1993, Lee made a trip to Germany, which again combined seminars and teaching presentations with a totally different mode of teaching, through the music of LGB. We stayed at the largest community household in Germany, an old farmhouse so full of rooms it felt to me like a beehive, in a small village called Hohenavenbergen. Although we usually traveled with Lee to seminars that were held at traditional German seminar houses in the vicinity, we stayed at the farmhouse when he traveled with the band to distant clubs and festivals. Occasionally there would be a gig at a nearby weekend festival, and then we would excitedly pack into vans or tiny European cars and go with the band for an afternoon and evening.

While Lee traveled to distant gigs and seminars, those of us left behind explored Hohenavenbergen, a tiny classic German village. We picked blackberries along the back roads, fed the sheep in the pasture, visited the working dairy next door, and followed walking paths that led into forests lush with ferns and moss and little red-dotted toadstools like the ones in the illustrations for Grimm's fairy tales. As idyllic as our days were, it was tempting to compare them with the "high life" that we imagined others were enjoying and to feel that we needed to fill our days with more exciting entertainment.

I began to plan trips to a local river where we could swim, to a picnic area, and to the town market. One morning when Lee was with us I asked him about some of these plans. He commented obliquely, "It's a good thing we have a social director." From his tone and manner, it was clear he did not think it was a good thing at all.

As my enthusiasm smashed up against the wall of his disapproval, I questioned him defensively. "We traveled all the way to Germany to get rich 'impression food.' Is the impression of one German village all we're going to get? Are we supposed to just sit in a farmhouse and take walks in the woods for the entire month? Doesn't it make sense to make some plans and excursions?" My motive was patently selfish, but at the time I was not willing to admit it, though the truth of the situation nagged at the edge of my awareness like flame licking at the edges of wet wood that refuses to burn.

Lee responded with equanimity. "There are plenty of trips and impressions that occur through the natural progression of the month here. You don't have to force things. And just being here in this village is in itself an impression that is worth the trip. To live in a village in the countryside where people still grow their own food and milk the cows, where the matrix of community life has not been destroyed by technology and greed—what better impression could you possibly ask for?"

Still driven by my own deep-seated desires for entertainment and the stimulations of night life at the band gigs and *dharma* discussion at the distant seminars, I muttered some reflexive grumble. Yet I knew he was right. How ironic that he should be the one reminding me of the values of village life! I was the one with the zealous political and social ideals, the environmental advocate, the champion of radical political changes to support a sustainable human lifestyle. And here was my teacher, who had repeatedly confronted the element of fanatical rigidity in my political ideals, reminding me that this was a chance to experience an integrated and sustainable village lifestyle rooted in generations of respectful relationship with the earth and with other human beings. What a reminder of the shallowness of my ideals if I forget them in an instant when the drive of my desires demands a different point of view. This simple interaction with my teacher showed me the difference between hypocritical attachment to ideals and a real, living comprehension of those ideals based in a willingness to live by them without either hypocrisy or zealous fanaticism.

The fault line that Lee had revealed running through the terrain of my ideals offered a microcosm of the inherent weakness which has sabotaged many political revolutions from within. In the gap between our high ideals and our own unexamined desires lies a great hidden trap. Innumerable political idealists have shown themselves to have pure and even puritanical commitment to their principles as long as they did not have the power to gratify contradictory desires, but, once saddled with the responsibility of political power, have used that power for their own aggrandizement. Religious fanaticism as it manifested in the Christian Crusades, for example, is one example of abuse of idealism to serve the acquisition of power. Robespierre, the Russian Bolsheviks, and the peasants murderously operating the guillotine in the French Revolution also present vivid portraits of the capacity of the human to lose sight of ideals such as "liberty, equality, fraternity" in the overwhelming rule of desires for revenge, for self-righteous vindication, and for raw power.

Yet there are those who have taken the opportunity for political power as an opportunity for compassionate service and wise leadership. Leaders like Martin Luther King in the United States and Nelson Mandela in South Africa have offered examples of power used to serve rather than to dominate and of leadership used not to acquire and incite but to teach forgiveness and a spirit of love. To carry out this kind of leadership requires rigorous and continuous self-observation and confrontation with inner temptation, along with a living surrender to the action of the divine in our lives.

The tour that year had been made possible by an independent German record company that had signed a contract with LGB for a tour and production of a CD. One of the final gigs was a performance at the Frankfurt Music Hall. To play at the Music Hall was a rare opportunity; it was a venue usually reserved for well-known and established musicians. The mood that night had the taste of rare wine, the distillation of the many flavors of the band's offering into one quintessential delivery overflowing with pure magic. As Lee's gravelly voice rolled out across the aisles, the bass notes reverberated in our bones, and the guitar melodies tumbled us into a roaring river of delight. People left their seats and flooded into the empty space in front of the stage. The entire audience was dancing, lifted on angel wings, plunged down waterfalls into murky depths, reminded of the hidden chambers of the heart, which it is our deepest desire to unlock. Leaping, kneeling, drawing lines of music out of the ethers into manifest reality through the musicians who had become one seamless expression of this master magician, Lee was the whirling dervish at the center of a holy rite, spinning creation itself out of his dance.

"Angel Still," a song inspired by a woman who showed up at one of LGB's early gigs, was a poignant description of every one of us: hardened, distorted, demeaned by a sordid existence under the rule of selfish desire and all the suffering that brings. Yet we were, at the core and in the Presence he was invoking, angels still, born to live in the reality of the divine.

> Oh what is it about this world
> That turns innocents to whores
> She's a drunk and lonely goddess
> Who no one will adore

DEATH AND DYING

While we were in Germany Lee received a message from a woman at the ashram in Arizona who was ill with terminal cancer. Ursula was a relatively new student, having joined the community only a year or two before. She had gone through a confrontation with bone cancer before meeting Lee, and the cancer had spontaneously gone into remission. Shortly after she moved from Germany to the ashram, she discovered that the cancer had recurred. She tried a number of healing methods, but the cancer continued to progress. She told Lee that she had essentially no relationship with her family in Germany, and that if she were going to die, she would like to die on the ashram. He accepted her request.

As the cancer advanced, she began to need constant care, twenty-four hours a day. A team of devotees became her full-time caregivers. She sent a message to Lee during our trip to Germany saying that she was terrified she would die while he was away and that she wanted to wait until he returned to die. He sent a message back that he would be with her no matter what happened, but that she could wait to die until he returned—that she could simply tell her body that she wanted to wait.

We returned to Arizona in September. As Ursula moved toward death, she entered a state that was increasingly childlike. Sometimes she would seem to disappear into a stark reliving of primal experiences of abuse. She would scream, as if she were a very young child, "Don't hit me! Don't hit me!" At other times she would have an undisguised, unguarded innocence almost like that of an infant. It felt to me as if in this movement toward release from this life she was healing deep wounds whose roots could emerge under Lee's influence and protection as the shells of both body and spirit fell away.

One day in November I had a strong sense that I needed to visit her. I walked through the fall woods and collected a bouquet of sage and wild grasses to bring her. She received them with a gentle appreciation, and we talked for a little while. Then she was tired, and I left her to sleep. That morning when I brought her the grasses and she accepted them with a childlike appreciation was the last time I saw her alive.

A few days later a message was brought to Lee that Ursula had just died. He sent a message around the ashram that we would meet the next morning for a burial service. It is Baul custom to bury the body in the earth, as part of the approach to God through the body, through human existence. As I understand it, the body and whatever substances of spirit have been built in it are returned to the body of the earth to feed the spiritual development of the larger planetary body as well. At the same time, the individual body which has been the matrix of practice is allowed to disintegrate so as to release the spirit fully into its new level of work. Although this was not the first death in the community, it was the first death to take place on the ashram, and the first such transition in which we had participated as a community throughout the process.

It had snowed recently, and the world was shrouded in its white coverlet. In the morning we crunched through the snow in our boots to gather at the house where Ursula's body lay. Those who had cared for her in the last months had washed her body and wrapped it in a sheet. Now they carried the wrapped body out into the crisp early winter air. We looked at Lee uncertainly; he had said he wanted chanting, but we were not sure when to begin. There was an awkward silence for just a moment. We were new in the immediate face of death, and there was a silence born both of uncertainty and of a natural awe.

"Start chanting!" Lee exclaimed with unsentimental directness. "What are you waiting for?"

We began to chant as the bearers descended the porch steps. A path opened through the crowd of devotees, as if the energy of death parted the waters. The bearers passed through like Moses passing through the Red Sea, and the crowd closed in behind them and followed them across the dry creek bed to the woods at the back of the ashram. There a deep hole had been dug by a number of strong men taking turns over a period of many hours. Between the dryness of the arid climate and the effects of freezing temperatures, the ground was rock hard; it had required intense labor to prepare the body of the earth to receive this woman's body.

Gently, somewhat awkwardly, the body was laid in the ground. Someone threw a rose on top of it. Then Lee picked up a shovel and threw the first shovel-full of earth into the grave. Some of us threw dried rose petals and other flowers as each person took a turn throwing a shovel-full of earth. Then the men who had dug the grave began to fill it, again working hard.

When the earth was level again, Lee made a sign to end the chanting. He turned and began to walk briskly back toward the ashram buildings, and we all followed him. Suddenly, as he crossed the creek bed, he stooped and picked up a handful of snow.

Quickly he shaped it into a snowball and threw it in a strong, graceful arc toward one of the men just approaching the creek. In seconds snowballs were flying in every direction. Lee played with great intention and apparent enjoyment for a few minutes; then suddenly he turned and walked on, back to his desk in the office. The process of death had been completed; the process of life went on. With the snowball fight, he had banished all traces of sentimentality or any mood of grief or fear. The moment of burial was filled with absolute respect and attention. The moment after was a new moment, filled with play and embrace of life as it is. Then he went on with his work.

After Ursula's death, the young children in the community were curious and thoughtful about the place of death in human life and in their own lives. They brought questions to the adults off and on over the next weeks. One way they processed this new experience was to create stories in which death played a major part. The children who questioned me did not evidence any fear about death. They seemed quite clear, from their own inner sense, that it was a transition in which life continued free of the body, and quite clear that someone could be ready to die at any age, young or old, and could know when that time was.

It is my observation that especially between ages two and three, when children have enough language to communicate to us something of the subtle realms they recognize and before they begin to lose touch with their innate awareness, they demonstrate a natural communion with wide and subtle realms. In his seminal book, *The Magical Child*, Joseph Chilton Pearce observes that at about age four the majority of children begin to experience nightmares (Pearce, J.C. *The Magical Child* N.Y.: E.P. Dutton, 1977, p. 121). It seems to me that it is between four and five that children begin to lose touch with their natural awareness of realms of spirit and begin to take on a perception of the physical world as the primary reality, a perception that divorces them from the world of spirit. As a result, they begin to experience mortality as a frightening event of separation rather than as an aspect of a natural and continuous movement into higher states of bonding and exploration. The appearance of nightmares is a common response to this dramatic narrowing of perception. To the degree that we honor the awareness of subtle realms inherent in young children we can help them build a bridge so that they do not need to forget what they have known in order to embrace what they have come to learn.

SHIFTING FOCUS

As I focused more and more deeply on Lee in the months and years ahead, I found that my inner experience changed in more ways. I had always experienced God as a direct, both personal and impersonal, living, present Reality. Essentially this experience did not change, yet the focus shifted toward Lee, as if he became the focusing lens and the guiding force, the immediate doorway to the divine. I was being asked to come into a direct, responsive, working relationship with that doorway so that I could become usable in a larger process. All distractions were drawn away. Even my relationship with the All could become a distraction if I used it to undercut or disempower or diminish the focus of attention on my teacher.

The *Guru Gita*, an ancient Sanskrit scripture, says: "There is nothing greater than the Guru" (Verse 96) and "The root of meditation is the Guru's form . . . The root of liberation is the Guru's grace." (Verse 76) "To contemplate the form of one's own Guru is to contemplate infinite Shiva." (Verse 54) I was beginning to learn something of what these instructions meant in my own apprenticeship.

Our culture worships movie stars and famous figures almost without regard to the reasons for fame. Yet as a society we tend to reject the idea that some humans have a spiritual power and wisdom that qualifies them and indeed obligates them to guide and teach others. The idea that we could learn from masters in the spiritual domain as people once learned from masters of physical crafts strikes us as anathema. This culture enslaved to licentious consumption and individual greed masquerading as individual freedom is terrified of the simple possibility of responsibility and commitment. Yet perhaps the deepest drive in the human is to embrace the profound responsibility of living from our divine nature. To trust a teacher strikes us as an abdication of our inner authority. In reality it is a recognition of our responsibility to make use of spiritual guidance, the gift of the divine made more immediately accessible in our lives.

While this principle was theoretically clear to me, I questioned at times whether I had lost something in my relationship to God through focusing attention on my teacher; whether something in my relationship to Lee could be blocking the direct experiences of God's Presence which had been such a strong part of my life. I felt I could not ask Lee for help with these questions because they were questions about my relationship with him; I needed help from a different angle. Soon afterward, an opportunity presented itself.

Just after Lee returned from India in December of 1993, we had a momentous visit, a harbinger of a relationship that was to grow and blossom over succeeding years. Arnaud Desjardins is a widely respected French spiritual master and a disciple of the great Advaitist Indian Master, Swami Prajnanpad. Arnaud had an ashram in France called Font d'Isière. Lee and his traveling party were invited to the ashram during their trip to Europe in the summer of 1993, and a friendship was established that continued to deepen. In return, Lee invited Arnaud and a group of his students to visit our ashram in Arizona.

Since I had not gone on the trips to France, I did not meet Arnaud until he arrived at our ashram that December. Immediately there was the sense of recognition of a real teacher. This was someone steeped in the Work over many years, someone able to transmit the power of that Work simply by his presence, apart from any specific content or conversation that he might offer. Arnaud's presence was broad and deep. It had the power of a river that has gathered many apparently contradictory currents into one steady and pervasive force that moves irresistibly toward its destination.

We had prepared a myriad of teaching spaces and festive events in welcome and appreciation of Arnaud's presence at our ashram. At one of these events we gathered in Lee's living room for an elegant dessert party intended to create an invocational space in which students of both teachers could question the other teacher. It was a way for each teacher to empower and clarify the work of the other teacher's students, since another teacher might be able to offer an angle and input that could not be so easily received from the student's own teacher. This was a chance for me to ask for help in the area of my relationship to Lee and to God.

We entered the living room and sat down on the floor in front of the two teachers, who were seated together on a wide sofa. The food servers, who were dressed in crisp and elegant black and white, brought in the desserts—gourmet creations that had taken perhaps two days to prepare, the kind of desserts one might be served in the finest of restaurants. Yet these desserts had something that even the fanciest gourmet restaurant cannot provide; they were filled with the trained attention and invocational intention which the cooks had brought to their preparation. They were truly "soul food," through which I felt myself being softened and touched by the tenderness of divine love. I looked around, and I could see the same effects in the faces and bodies of others in the room.

As faces softened and bodies relaxed into a mood of vulnerability, people began to ask intimate and revealing questions about their own work. Gradually, my own question began to clarify and I found myself speaking almost without conscious volition. It was as if the core being within all my personality structures and habits recognized a place that was safe and appropriate to reach out for real help in my work.

"For many years I had strong, direct, and frequent experiences of the Presence of God," I said to Arnaud. "These were especially strong when I lived alone, with almost no external human relationship. I felt that I had a personal relationship with this Impersonal Being. I know there are a lot of levels to the experience and expression of the divine. Maybe I was just coming in touch with angels or divine emanations. But I felt it strongly as direct experience of the Being of God. Now I have a teacher who is the focus of my attention; to whom I turn as the immediate guiding force in my life. And I live in community, continually involved in relationships with other people. All that feels completely right to me. Yet since I have been with Lee, I rarely have those direct experiences of God, of that universal Presence. I have ecstatic experiences of unity or bliss or compassion or even the fact of Love, but all these experiences seem somehow to come through Lee; Lee is the doorway that opens into these spaces. Am I doing something wrong? Is there something about my relationship with Lee that is not correct, that is blocking my direct relationship with God? Or is that kind of experience of direct Presence of a universal Being not the point right now, not the focus for my attention?"

Arnaud looked at me with great compassion and gentleness. Before he said a word, I knew through a kind of silent communication that this change in my inner experience was lawful and

197

correct. It was not an indication of a barrier in my relationship with Lee or between me and God. This shift was a part of the same focusing of attention to which my guides had turned me when they said goodbye. I had a living teacher now, and he was the focus and guide in my spiritual apprenticeship.

Arnaud began to speak, "It seems to me that you have something to heal in the world of *samsara*. It has something to do with family, with this family." He looked around at the members of Lee's community, as we sat together in front of him. "Your work when you were alone was real and useful. But for this healing you have to come down into the world of the human; you have to come into relationship. Whatever healing you have to do comes through this life in community, with your teacher."

It was such a simple answer, yet I knew the rightness of what he was saying. I could stop questioning the difficulties and abrasions in this deepening life of relationship. I could stop holding my life on the mountaintop as some more pure existence. I could embrace the work I was given, here with these other humans including this teacher in a human body, this paradoxical encounter of both human and divine in ordinary life. The work on the mountaintop had simply been the introduction to this life and this work. The mundane impurities and mechanicality that I saw in myself and in others were not something to escape by returning to some ecstatic hermitage; they were themselves the raw elements of the work I had to do. It was relationship itself that I had to confront and engage.

As we continued with our questions to Lee and Arnaud that winter evening in Lee's living room, the servers brought out bottles of a dessert wine made in Alsace-Lorraine. Glasses were poured and a toast was made. One sip of this wine revealed it to be of a different quality than any wine I had ever tasted. Drinking it, I understood why the Sufis use wine as a metaphor for divine nectar; why they speak of drinking "the wine of God." The desserts had played their part in an opening of the space of the heart among us. One sip of this wine was an arrow that pierced into the very center of the heart itself, into the hidden jewel of love that shimmered beneath all the spoken exchange and vulnerability in the room. The desserts, the wine, the conversation, and the permeating presence of the teachers opened the door into the mystical territory in which the Beloved can be found. It was the consummate answer to my question about what it was that awaited me beyond the lonely mountaintop: the piercing possibility of human relationship as the doorway into direct encounter with that reality which I had glimpsed on a spring afternoon in Georgia years ago.

LA FERME DE JUTREAU

During his trip to France in 1995, Lee had made final arrangements for a property where we would establish our first European ashram. Previously the community had tried to purchase land in India next to the ashram of Yogi Ramsuratkumar, and we had expected to establish an ashram there. However, the land had become entangled in an endless bureaucratic morass, fueled by the Indian government's fear of outside groups gaining power in their country. Unable to build on our Indian property, eventually we let the land go to wait for a more propitious circumstance. In the meantime, we acquired, with unexpected ease, a property in central France about two hundred miles south of Paris—a land of rolling hills, meandering rivers, and lush farmland filled with feed corn and classic fields of sunflowers. In ancient times the kings of France had called this area of France "la douce France," "the sweet France," for its mild and welcoming climate and its green and flowering terrain.

As Lee was arranging the community purchase of the French property, a couple from the Arizona *sangha* had just completed building a lovely house within a few minutes' walk from the Prescott ashram. It was a pioneering construction of their own design, built of rammed earth, with a curved green copper roof reminiscent of their sojourn in Japan. Yet when Lee asked for volunteers to go to France, this couple was willing to relinquish their new house, lucrative jobs, and physical proximity to the guru and the Arizona *sangha* to answer his call and manage the new ashram.

The new French property, La Ferme de Jutreau, had originally been the farm and dairy adjacent to a medieval castle that was still inhabited. Over the years the farm had fallen idle and the buildings had been abandoned. We heard from those who accompanied Lee on his initial inspection of the property that in order to enter the main house and investigate the rooms they had to pull overgrown ivy off the shutters and then pry them open to let in light. Lee spent perhaps five minutes walking briskly, almost running, through the rooms. The energy was right, the physical structures were essentially sound, there was electricity and plumbing. That was all he needed to know.

The plan was for a large group from the Arizona ashram, including the members of LGB and Shri, to accompany Lee and spend the following summer at the new ashram. In order for that to happen, its new managers would spend an intense winter with a few helpers who had moved from Germany. The small group's tasks ranged from making the abandoned buildings habitable again to scheduling a busy summer of seminars and public talks.

In addition to the main house, which contained a large kitchen and a main room that would become the "salon" for teaching meetings, study, festive gatherings, and a place of warmth around the fire for winter residents, there was a smaller guest house and a huge old barn. With almost no money to pay for improvements, the new residents were limited to what they could create mainly out of their own physical labor.

By the time we arrived the next summer, the transformation was astonishing. Flowers bloomed around a great maple tree at the center of the farm. Ripe cherries sparkled among the leaves of trees by the barn. Hazelnut bushes were laden with nuts slowly maturing for the fall. Grapevines scaling the walls of the outbuildings hinted that the touch of Bacchus had blessed this place. A large *darshan* hall graced one end of the barn, next to a rough but serviceable dining hall that could seat one hundred people at skillfully homemade, varnished wooden tables.

The end of the barn opposite the dining area had been divided with hanging sheets into tiny rooms for couples and families, while bunks had been built into the walls to make a dormitory for women and another for men. The accommodations were exceedingly rough, with animal troughs converted into shelves for the tiny rooms and dorms. The hanging sheets provided more of an illusion of privacy than any real enclosure of space. Sounds traveled from one end of the barn to the other, uninterrupted by the thin sheets. During the first weeks of summer it was so cold that many people wore knitted hats as they huddled in their sleeping bags, seeking protection from the ever-present drafts in the uninsulated barn. Yet, in spite of the rough conditions, there was great excitement about and appreciation for the opportunity that Lee was offering us to participate in this new chapter in his work.

During seminars and Celebrations at La Ferme de Jutreau, we housed in these "sheet rooms" not only members of our own *sangha*, seasoned in Lee's radical and renegade activities, but French guests accustomed to comfortable and elegant accommodations at European seminar houses. Not only were people sleeping in sheet rooms in a barn, but because the small septic system could not handle the number of visitors attending these events, we asked everyone to use outhouses which had been newly constructed at the edge of the meadow. This meant guests as well as residents had to walk through the cold nights, or sometimes the pouring rain, to use crude facilities for toilets. Outdoor sinks and showers had been constructed by the garden, where people brushed their teeth and washed. Even our guests showed continual and cheerful good will about accepting and even embracing these conditions, so unusual for Western civilized cultures, in order to participate in the opportunities to hear and live the teaching that Lee was offering.

However unconventional, Lee's singular way of establishing an ashram in France proved to have work value and reliable longevity. An older French woman who visited the ashram with her grandchildren found great delight in telling us about her early years in a boarding school outside Paris where the walls had been similarly made of sheets. Lee's methods might be outrageous, but they also revealed themselves to have unexpected roots in the culture into which he had begun to bring his signature brand of the teaching.

During our first summer at the French ashram we visited Hauteville, the new ashram of Arnaud Desjardins, where Lee gave a week-long seminar. The day after we arrived, it stormed off and on all day—rare for that dry time of year. Lightning streaked across the distant mountains, and thunder rolled among the hills. During one of Lee's teaching sessions that day I was one of two caretakers with the children. Near the end of the two-hour period the children were contentedly occupied, and the other caretaker suggested that I go to the last part of the teaching session. I hesitated, thinking that by the time I got my shawl and walked to the seminar space there would only be about twenty minutes left in the session. It occurred to me that to walk in so near the end and hear such a short segment might be both rude and unproductive. Most likely I would not even hear enough to comprehend the point of the teaching. But my inner sense told me to accept my friend's offer nonetheless. I could slip into the back without interrupting or disturbing others, and in twenty minutes of focused attention I might absorb as much of the teaching as in two hours with less intention.

I walked into the space and sat down. Lee was just launching into one of the most brilliant and memorable transmissions of the teaching I have ever heard him give. He spoke of the storm so fiercely and beautifully breaking across the hills outside; yet, he said, the external storm was only a reflection and the merest hint of the storm of grace that can flood and transform our entire lives. The intimacy with which he spoke of God's grace, God's movement within our hearts, and the cataclysmic effects this grace can have upon our ordinary existence could arise only out of a living relationship with God. It was not so much the words that he spoke, eloquent as they were, but the communication of this living relationship that touched and inspired me. That twenty minutes ignited with fiery brilliance a possibility that I would have missed had I not heeded the inner sense that brought me to the space.

REAL LIFE

> *"Real life is meeting."*
> —C. S. Lewis, *That Hideous Strength*

As time moved on, I began to participate more actively in Lee's travels and visits with other teachers. I recorded in detail one such meeting both for the power of its particular gift and as an example of the multidimensional spaces in which the teachers move and meet.

On a sunny afternoon in the summer of 1996, I accompanied Lee on a visit to the home of another teacher—a man who seeks no publicity for himself, who simply works with quiet integrity with those who can recognize what he has to offer. I was grateful to sit in the presence of his penetrating wisdom; yet I was even more grateful for the way in which this meeting revealed my own teacher in a deeper light. To sit with the two teachers as they talked together was to experience the electric current of this Work with the wires momentarily bared. The power of that current both feeds and shocks. I have felt that sense of bared wires humming at other meetings between teachers; for example, sitting in the presence of Lee and Arnaud Desjardins. Such teachers meet in so many more dimensions than I can perceive. It is as if I journey underwater, while they meet in the air above, filled simultaneously with sun and thunder and lightning. Their meeting is so packed with charge that the reverberations carry into the deep water where my resistances hide.

Prior to our visit to this teacher, Lee looked carefully at a large wall map of the subway system, making brief notes as a friend pointed out where we would change trains for a different line. Then we set out into the underground labyrinth. Although the modern turnstiles looked different from the mythical Gates of Hades guarded by the two-headed dog Cerberus, sentinel of the underworld, I had no doubt that demons and disguised angels lurked in the dark corners of this subterranean world.

Ancient wisdom taught that we must descend into the underworld to confront, challenge and conquer its demons in order to release the treasures of heaven. Lee has said that we must not only conquer our demons, we must make friends with them—come into full relationship with them—in order to meet the angels as well and use all available resources for our work. It is through the descent into the underworld that we find our way to the deities of the upperworld and learn to use both worlds in our work in the middleworld, along the middle path.

Our physical journey that day took us into the dark depths and through the labyrinth, where we looked out the window as the train stopped at station after station. At one station, a man was replacing an old poster ad with a new one. The ad was perhaps ten feet high, made up of smaller squares that he pasted onto the backboard so as to make one large image. The man worked with rapidity and precision, putting glue on the back of each square with a roller; then, with a few skilled motions, placing each square in exact right relation to the next so that the picture appeared as one unbroken whole. There were no gaps, no overlapping edges. Lee watched him with appreciation.

"Pretty good," he said, laconically.

Watching this apparently useless task—erecting an ad for sparkling water or expensive perfume—I felt the value of what to my rational mind often appear to be "useless" Work exercises. As far as I could tell, Lee was appreciating the effectiveness of the man's attention: awareness of detail, precision in action, ability to hold a vision and to employ skillful means to make it manifest.

In our work, it is often attention or inattention to detail (based on awareness of the larger context that orders the details) that makes the difference between manifestation or loss of possibility in a space. This is especially evident when Lee is in the space, holding an intention that we either resist or serve. In or out of Lee's presence, however, the possibility of our work in each moment lives or dies as a result of the quality and direction of our attention. In a moment that real attention is given to the children, the innocence in them flares into full manifestation and nourishes all of us. At the same time, attention to the children is one of the basic requirements that Lee has said must be met so that he can be free to work. Those who attend to the children free other adults to attend to Lee's specific work direction. The same is true of every element of our lives together. Often (if not always), the greater possibilities of our work rest on the foundation of attention to detail in regard to food, finances, spaces, relationships, and the most simple jobs that come our way.

There is a story told about Yogi Ramsuratkumar that dramatically illustrates this point. He had invited a number of people to have tea with him. The teacups were set at each place by Yogi Ramsuratkumar himself. Out of habit and in unconscious manifestation, one of the Westerners moved his teacup to a slightly different position. "It's ruined! My work is ruined!" Yogi Ramsuratkumar shouted, jumping up and not completing the work that his specific conjuration was designed to produce.

Back in the subway tunnels, Lee and I climbed the stairs, leaving the underworld for a sunny June afternoon. According to myth, if we had "eaten seeds" in the underworld we would be forced to return in six months, as was Persephone, bringing the end of summer with the tears of Mother Demeter. To enter and leave the underworld without "traces" is a great skill. It involves the tantric practice of being able to encounter the darkest or most fascinating substances without becoming either fascinated or entangled so that we can use their power for higher work, rather than being used by them.

During travels with Lee, I have repeatedly found that what looked like the middle- or upperworld was in fact a fast track to the underworld. My attachment to the idea that there might be "vacation" or "treats" somewhere on our journey became an open trapdoor through which I fell into my personal underworld and into the collective unconscious desire for personal aggrandizement. As one falls through that door, a piece of chocolate turns to mud in the hand, a cup of coffee becomes poison as one drinks, a dance among flowers turns to a dance among Kali's skulls as she sharpens her knife by one's head. This is the opposite of the tantric use of substances as a way to open the door to the divine. In these instances the substances use us, and we are eaten—chewed bite by bite—by the entities that enter through the substances. The reference here is not just to substances we physically eat, but even more to the substances of emotional and mental fascination and sentimentality. To eat pomegranate seeds in the underworld is to connect to and eat these substances from a position of greed and selfishness, rather than from the detached position of service and the clear intention of sacred use.

As we emerged onto the city streets, we had almost two hours till our meeting. Apparently our host had not given a specific time, but Lee said, as we climbed the subway stairs, "About 4 o'clock will be a good time, time for tea."

My own habitual mode would have been to "do something" somewhere else in the city for those two hours and then rush out of the subway; with luck, barely arriving on time. Lee's approach was totally different. He set the momentum of time and space moving toward the meeting by his physical approach. Then he looked around for what to do in the vicinity while inwardly waiting.

Lee's relation to time and space provides a great lesson in waiting. He is not waiting for the Beloved just in those "romantic moments" when the full moon rises over the mountains, or in the moments of his short visits to Tiruvannamalai. He is waiting always, in each moment, for the movement of divine will, for the touch of the Beloved; and out of the spaciousness of waiting, he responds with total attention and alacrity. Whether he sits at a table preparing the space two hours before liars, gods and beggars performs at a club, or shouts instructions at a devotee who has suffered a lapse of attention, there is that essential stance of waiting. He is waiting not only as a gentle Lover waits, but as a Tiger waits to spring. He waits to seize the Work at the precise moment when Something can happen, when one correct motion can ignite alchemical action. So we had two hours till our meeting, and we waited.

"Would you rather walk or sit?" Lee asked.

"I'd rather walk," I said.

We walked first to a couple of street corners until Lee satisfied himself that he knew the way to the apartment. Then we strolled down streets filled with small expensive shops selling everything from chocolate to children's clothes. Although I was ready to be entranced and distracted by every window, I did not expect the displays to be of any interest to Lee, especially since I knew he would not be buying anything. To my surprise he gazed carefully at each successive shop window; he seemed to be almost studying the contents of each display. In contrast to my own preference for windows filled with pastries and chocolate, he gave the same thorough attention to the displays of ties (which I've never seen him wear) or soaps as he did to those of desserts. It seemed that he was extracting something—some usable substance—from each display simply through the focused attention of his eyes.

Again I was struck by how he seemed to make use of what I would have ignored or discarded as insignificant. Outside of his company I would have been blind to any possible usefulness in silk ties observed through a glass window. If I mentioned this to Lee, he might laugh and say that he was doing nothing, it was just entertainment while waiting. Whatever the case, I was reminded that the tantric practitioner uses the mundane substances of everyday life in the grand process of alchemy. Discrimination, which is essential, is different from judgmental tunnel vision. In our commitment to the life of a beggar we can get caught in a kind of prudery, a refusal to touch the rich cloths and perfumes of this world. Lee once commented that we sometimes swing from indulgence to Puritanism, and neither one is the point.

There is an attitude of spiritual pride and disdain for the world that can separate us from the arena in which we are called to work and that can be just as much an obstacle to our work as fascination with the world. Jesus taught his followers to be "in the world but not of it." Lee offered a small example, as he strolled the city streets that day, of what this means. He was in discriminating relationship with the world around him. He neither ignored the shops nor rushed in to buy their wares. He simply extracted something he could use even out of these humble (if expensive!) material forms.

We stopped at a window full of luscious pastries, chocolates, and elegant dessert creations. Lee looked carefully at each one. At other times that summer I had felt angry and disappointed that he had not offered opulent desserts at any time when I had been with him. But this day, although I knew that he would not buy anything from that window, I did not feel that horrible grasping disappointment or anger. As though I were feeling through Lee more than through myself, I felt his pure enjoyment of the sweets as they were, sitting in the window, and understood his unsentimental choice that it would serve no purpose (of the Work) in that moment to eat one. As we stepped away I realized to my surprise that I felt as if I had eaten not just one but every individual dessert in the window. It was as though my desire for the desserts had been fully satiated, neither through indulgence nor through rejection but through a mood in which appreciation, enjoyment, discipline, and renunciation joined in an unlikely union that hints at tantric work. Later, on our return along the same streets, Lee did not look at any of the windows. From a place of fascination I am endlessly interested in looking in windows and coveting items—even the same items over and over. Again it was clear that Lee was doing something different, with a different purpose. Having looked once, he did not need to look again.

When we had finished looking at the window displays, there was half an hour or so still to wait.

"Ready to sit?" Lee said, heading toward a cafe with outdoor tables near a small traffic circle with a fountain in the center. He ordered water and I ordered juice, and we sat watching the passers-by. Here I was, finally, at the elegant cafe I had imagined in moments of envious craving on the ashram, yet in Lee's presence it lost all sentiment and became just a pleasant cafe, no more, no less. It was simply a circumstance that had some use in the ritual of the afternoon. I went to the restroom, where an elderly, aristocratic woman was talking intimately to her elegantly coifed poodle, which she had brought into the restroom with her. I laughed. We are a tragic and comical race, we human beings.

I went back upstairs and we walked down the street again. When we were two blocks from our host's apartment, Lee stopped, leaned against a wall, and said, "Tell me when it's a quarter till four." There was a park full of green trees and flowers a block away. I thought, We could wait there instead of leaning against a wall next to parked cars. But it was clear that the park at that moment would be a distraction, even an obstacle. Lee was turned toward the meeting, and the environment was nothing to him. All his attention was gathered into waiting, into that inner preparation of space and time.

At a quarter to four we walked the two blocks to the apartment building. Lee rang the doorbell, spoke his own name into the intercom, and the door opened. Eschewing the elevator, he climbed the stairs, physically as well as energetically ascending into the higher realms to reach the door to this meeting.

As the two teachers greeted one another, I found myself stunned by the shared quality of commitment to the space. It was a commitment to the service of reality, yet mediated through a quality of the heart—perhaps one could say through Love. In their presence it felt impossible to want something other than to enter more deeply into the space that they knew—the space of the committed heart.

As I watched the teachers greeting, I thought of my first meeting with Lee almost ten years earlier. At the time I had a vague impression of a man whose presence was elegant, even courtly— "courtly" in the sense of being respectful of and precise about inner protocols; of being obedient to the royal, or the divine. There was an orderliness about him that was rooted far below the surface, in an expression of and alignment with the proper Order of all things. That courtly elegance and essential order were evident that afternoon in Lee's presence as he accepted hospitality. He was respectful, receptive, following his host's lead, and at the same time actively, vividly present. I remember no difference in the attire of the two teachers, although it's likely that Lee was wearing a T-shirt and his host an expensive suit coat. I remember only the burning presence of each, and of their meeting.

"What would you like to drink?" our host asked Lee.

"I'll have whatever you're having," Lee replied. Almost immediately a silver tray and coffeepot appeared along with demitasse cups and cookies.

The coffee was strong and black. The two teachers began to talk, leaving their cups in front of them, untouched. I waited. After awhile, our host drank, but still Lee did not. It seemed I could not drink until Lee did, but even if he had, the energetic food that was being offered and consumed in the space was so strong that I could not yet mix it with physical food.

Finally, Lee motioned to me to feel free to drink. Obediently, I drank, and found the physical food blended with the subtle food, and somehow each made the other stronger. What I remember most distinctly about that moment is the intensity of subtle substance in the space and the feeling of waiting until the door was opened to mix the physical coffee with the food of those other dimensions. It seems that this small incident holds a hint about how food, or any substance, becomes sacred. There was no grasping desire for the coffee in that space, and no rejection of it. There was simply embracing and using it as one element in the growing momentum of communion.

Each of the teachers had a gift for the other. Lee offered a copy of our new two-volume, red-bound study course, the *Hohm Sahaj Mandir Study Manual*. Our host looked through it appreciatively and said with a smile, "It's a long Path!" He offered Lee a book in return, and they began to discuss written teachings they particularly liked. There was in the other man a sense of the same humility I have seen in Lee, where there is no desire (or no quarter for such desire, if it exists) for personal aggrandizement, no taking personal advantage of one's relation to others in the Work or one's position of influence. Their conversation was focused wholly on the work to be done and their appreciation of others' contributions. There was no jockeying for position, no small power plays, no interest or even concern with whether their own names were recognized in this great Work to which they had devoted their lives. Their sole focus of attention was on what could best serve the Work.

The conversation turned to the busy schedules and travels of both teachers, then to our bands—liars, gods and beggars and Shri, Lee's new blues band—and then to the pervasive fear in Western culture of spiritual cults. Lee commented that our basic approach is to be honest and cooperative when confronted with cult investigators. He described how two investigators attended the morning session of one of his seminars, interviewed him afterward, and took his picture. The investigators were appreciative of his cooperation and told Lee that some spiritual leaders refuse to talk with them or allow pictures. But, Lee said to our host, "Ordinary people will never understand what we are doing; why anyone would even want to do this."

The other teacher agreed, saying, "Ordinary people will never understand—and if you break it down far enough for them to have any understanding at all, it is so far from Reality. And yet if people have no understanding . . ." He paused, and his eyes seemed to look over the distances of his own life and the great Life of the Work. "If one stands back and looks," he continued, "one can see that people are moved by influences of which they have no idea. They feel a profound need to move in this direction but they don't know why, what it is. There are people who will never recognize Reality; yet their opinions play into the movement of things and they are also part of a larger movement of energies of which they know nothing." A hint of poignant and compassionate sorrow tinged his voice. "Then there are all these interpretations, so many people's opinions, that cover and veil Reality." As he spoke I had an image of Reality as a clear energy field covered with the dense waves of people's opinions and emotions, and I felt his sorrow at the obscuring of that clear field in which we have the chance to live.

The teachers spoke about La Ferme de Jutreau, our community's new French ashram. Lee described how La Ferme was small, crowded with residents and guests, with living conditions that could irritate those accustomed to physical comforts, and with a great amount of physical work. The lack of accustomed comforts and the intensity of life in community with a focus on much physical labor created a strong environment for work on self and with others. Our host's receptive understanding of the purpose and practical mechanics of this experiment contrasted strongly with the intermittent reactivity and doubt I have seen in myself and in others as we have been presented with this opportunity.

Repeatedly throughout the conversation I was struck by the exactitude of the two teachers' use of language. The precise meanings of their words rippled through dimensions I could sense, yet not see. I have seen frustration in Lee because his students do not register and use the subtlety of his teaching. To hold creations that delicately and powerfully extend through many dimensions and to see students crack and break them through lack of attention even in the domains we can see must be excruciating. Even after years in Lee's company I only begin at times to see a few vague outlines of what he is holding in a space. The Reality to which our host was committed colored his every move and word. The clarity of that Reality threw my own teacher into sharp relief, cutting through the veil of familiarity which often obscures my view of him to reveal the spiritual slavery in which Lee lives and the precision of action that results.

Throughout the conversation I felt that a great meal was in process, not just between the two teachers but through them and beyond. Something was being fed that was larger than either of them, larger than any individual teacher or even the meeting of the teachers, something that moved through and around both of them in different ways. For a moment I saw this "something" (as earlier I had seen Lee himself) as a Tiger crouching to spring—not to spring toward anyone individually but to spring deeper "into Life," rich and raw with its powerful and uncompromising energy. It was clear that these teachers had the same Lover, and that Lover was drawing them into alignment and intimacy with each other regardless of the content of their conversation, regardless even of their physical meeting or distance. The beat of that Lover's Heart filled the space.

During the weeks before that meeting, I had been in and out of reactivity, doubt, fear, and pain in relation to Lee. In the upheaval of our move to France for the summer my resistances were kicked to the surface like mud being stirred from the bottom of a pond. Sometimes Lee looked to me like simply a crazy man, rather than the crazy man of crazy wisdom. I was frightened by his handling of the car, of the people around him, and of our entire situation in France. In the brilliant light of that afternoon, all those fears and reactions dissolved like chimera, as if they had never existed. (In mythology, the Chimaera is a monster with a lion's head, a goat's body, and a serpent's tail. A fitting image for the monster of egoic resistance that lurks within us!)

Our host commented that the next year he might have a larger space available, where he could invite Lee to bring more students to their meeting. Again I was struck by the differences in form, even while the essential Work both teachers serve is the same. As Baul beggars, we would have crowded perhaps thirty people into that spacious room, most sitting crammed together on the floor. In contrast, the room's elegant furnishings were clearly designed for an intimate gathering of four or five at the most. In either case, the spaciousness and purposeful order of the room held an energy in which subtle realities could work.

There were cookies on the table, along with the coffee. Here at last were the treats I had craved, and under the circumstances I could hardly pay them any attention. At one point our host went out of the room for something, and with the energy temporarily turned down a notch, I seized the moment to grab and eat a few cookies. I wanted to eat more, but the energy field stopped me. In that space greed could not live. When we left, the remaining cookies sat on the table untasted. In a tiny way, they symbolized the deeper fact of the visit itself. While much was exchanged, still more was left implicit, possible but untasted. What was left, finally, was longing.

As we walked toward the subway, the space was still so suffused with the power of the Heart that had been beating in that meeting that talk seemed almost irrelevant. "Short but very sweet," Lee said.

I felt as if my heart had been crying throughout the visit and felt it still as we walked. Though I didn't understand why, it seemed to have something to do with the presence of our wise, compassionate, and gracious host, whose greatest gift to me had been what he had shown me of my own teacher. Was it that he still had innocence that we rarely see undisguised, unveiled? Was it that he himself was wounded by his own teacher with that wound that Lee has said is Yogi Ramsuratkumar's gift to him, the most essential gift of one's master—the wound that only the divine can heal? Was it that he and Lee were in touch with Something that opens and breaks the heart—Something that was breaking my heart more and more deeply as I sat in their presence? There was a sense of opening the way to a glimpse of true feeling, or real Love. I wanted to ask Lee what it was that I felt—why my heart was crying in the presence of this man. But I hesitated, wondering if this was the kind of question that should not even be asked—that was up to me to answer or simply hold.

"Ask now. This is the moment, or the door will close," said an inner voice.

"I'll ask when we get on the subway train and are sitting still," I said to myself as we walked rapidly down the subway corridors.

The train door opened, and we stepped in. The car was crowded, and I held onto the center pole for balance as the train started. As I looked around I found myself, unbelievably, looking into the eyes of *sangha* friends who were in Paris independently of us. Of all the subway trains in that huge city, we had found ourselves in the same car.

In that instant, one space closed and another opened. All spaces are connected; yet I saw clearly at that moment that particular kinds of work can happen in each particular kind of space. We eat in the dining room. We cleanse in the bathroom. If we try to cook in the bathroom, the results may be confused (though Lee has made some great salads, so I hear, washing the veggies in the bathtub of a two-bit motel). It is again a question of attention. When the subway door closed, the demand for attention shifted. The door to the room where the teachers met was closed. I had hesitated at the last step in that room, and the chance was gone.

Yet, though I entered a different workspace when I entered that subway door, the food from each space permeates others. Walking through the dark subway tunnels and through the streets of the city afterward, I found everything was intensified and changed. The details of ordinary life had, paradoxically, both less hold on me and more Presence. I felt the essential Divine moving through all things so that I had no need to try to hold onto it in one form. I had appreciation for that Presence and movement in all forms. At dinner I found taste was intensified—there was a sharp enjoyment of each specific food—and at the same time I was wholly content with whatever was given to me. I was simply grateful for each gift. What a contrast to my recent state of being! What a much better place to live! Reality was made momentarily more visible to me in the light of the shared Presence of the teachers and the Work they serve, still irradiating the space in which I walked.

During that summer in France we made another memorable visit. It was the single meeting I would have in person with Yvan Amar, a teacher I had been hearing about for years. We left La Ferme de Jutreau in the early hours before dawn to drive south in our heavily loaded vans through the wine country to the Mediterranean coast and then north again high into the Maritime Alps. The trip took about fourteen hours. Finally we arrived at a traditional mountain chalet, in which, we later learned, grandparents had hidden Jews from the Nazis, inspiring the whole village to similar courageous resistance. On a sofa in the dim living room, filled with a quiet reverence, Yvan waited for us. Because of a degenerating physical condition, he could hardly walk upstairs and often had to be carried. His conversation throughout our visit was interrupted by coughing and labored efforts to breathe. Yet his attention remained steadfastly, brilliantly, and joyously focused on the teaching.

At breakfast the next morning we gathered on the outdoor patio around a circular table shaded by an umbrella. As Yvan's wife, Nadège, served us with her peerless warm hospitality, the space softened and opened into a profound exchange about the principles of the teaching as lived in daily life. Somehow the topic of politics arose. Without my having spoken a word that revealed my entrenched attachment to a political view, Yvan began to address my conflicts through his own clear perspective. It was the work of a teacher skilled in the sly approach which slips in the teaching without directly addressing the individual student—an example, like the many I have observed Lee demonstrate, of an intuitive response to the space which speaks with uncanny exactitude and clarity to the particular lessons that students in the space need to learn.

We were talking about the terror of spiritual cults common in French culture and the regular surveillance and investigation of any spiritual group by French police and other government authorities. Someone mentioned that in the recent French elections a leader whose views tended to the political left had been elected, and that under his leadership it seemed we could expect some relaxation around the issue of cults.

Yvan agreed, then made an observation based in a deeper principle. "In some ways it makes things easier for us [for spiritual groups] when parties that tend to the left have more power," he said. "Yet essentially, right or left, it doesn't make a difference. The real issue is commitment to spiritual authority; the decision to live a life based in spiritual reality. Short of that, right or left, it's all the same."

I knew as he spoke that he was correct. In the light of his clarity, I saw with acuity the qualitative difference between a life based in the limitations of human opinion and a life based in attention to ultimate verities beyond and infusing the human. Yet this incisive dismissal of the fervent struggle between right and left, of a political framework that had defined and impassioned my early years, struck at the remaining roots of my political world view with a full-body shock.

From this foundational principle, the commitment to spiritual reality, Yvan began to speak about the possibility of adoration. He spoke about the relationship of man and woman and the relationship of student and teacher as two complementary arenas in which an experience of love could arise that carried us beyond grasping for self-gratification to a discovery of our own essential selves through service and adoration of the other. It was an articulation, in his own terms, of the possibility of discovery of a unique quality of relationship to the divine in an approach as lover to Beloved, the quintessential possibility which Lee has articulated as "the only Grace" of loving God.

The discussion turned to relationship to children. "One can only truly love and serve one's own child if one sees all children as one's own children," Yvan observed, continuing his rigorous demand for bringing spiritual principles into the most intimate daily relationships. "If there is favoritism or special treatment of a child because this is *my* child, this child is connected to *me*, then that attitude skews our decisions and blinds us to the objective principles that should underlie our relationships to all children. We can most truly serve the child only if we are equally committed to the good of all children."

That afternoon, seated again in the living room that felt almost like a shrine, Yvan continued his teaching with us, giving each person present specific and penetrating lessons without ever confronting us directly, but using himself as a frequent example. Someone asked him about visiting the cave in southern France where the bones of Mary Magdalene are said to be preserved. The questioner was one of Lee's students whom Lee had repeatedly addressed about fascination with temples and artifacts outside her own tradition; about how a passionate interest in spiritual traditions could be used as a distraction from focused attention on her path and work in Lee's school.

Without being told any of this history, Yvan responded to the woman's questions by telling a story about himself. He said that at an earlier point in his spiritual *sadhana* he had been tremendously interested in the Christian tradition, particularly in the legends about the transmission of the lineage of Christ's teaching into France. A number of legends, some now recorded in popular accounts of research findings, tell of a journey by Mary Magdalene, Mary the Mother of Jesus, and others such as Joseph of Arimathea from Israel to France after Jesus' death. Some of these stories say that Mary Magdalene was pregnant with the child of Jesus, and that the bloodline of Jesus has continued unbroken, though hidden, from that day to the present.

Yvan said that he had begun to investigate these stories, to make great efforts to find various legendary artifacts, and to move more deeply into communication with others concerned with this investigation. At the same time, he was continuing his commitment as a disciple to his own master, Chandra Swami. Suddenly, in the midst of his mounting fascination, he realized that his entire investigation of these legends and artifacts of the Christian tradition was a dangerous distraction from his own lineage. He had an overwhelming sense that if he took one step further along the lines he was uncovering he would create a kind of short-circuit of energy between the tradition he was investigating and his own. He could not make real use of secret information about another tradition because he was not bonded into and committed to that tradition. He could only pursue a fascination that could ultimately be deadly to his own work. With this realization, he immediately and absolutely ceased all investigation and involvement in the legends of the French Christians and turned his attention wholly to his own tradition, where his work could bear fruit. The lesson for the student who had questioned him was left obvious but unspoken.

Another student asked Yvan about happiness. She said she wanted happiness, and she did not find herself frequently happy in spiritual life. The result was that she sometimes doubted whether spiritual life was really what she wanted, or whether she was making a mistake in this basic choice about her life. Yvan responded with great gentleness, acceptance, and understanding. He said that at one stage of development, the human being seeks simply for pleasure, for happiness. This is a normal and natural impulse, placed in us by the divine Creator. It is through pursuit of this initial impulse that we reach out to the world, that we grow. Yet as we grow, a deeper impulse begins to emerge. There is something we want more than happiness. This is the desire to serve and to know what is Real. The more we know the reality of the divine, the more we naturally seek to serve it. Finally, in our search for the Real, divine reality begins to emerge and consciously live in us. The ultimate possibility of the human is to come to know and live the Real so that we become God, and in or through us, God meets God. Perhaps, he continued, God created the human simply for the possibility of relationship, or love.

In his gentle acceptance of this student's desire for happiness, and his simultaneous recognition of a deeper impulse emerging in her which she herself (although she already deeply lived from it) had not yet named, Yvan gave her space to respect the first impulse, while nourishing the emergence of the deeper desire.

After a day overflowing with the richness of the teaching that Yvan had given us both through his words and through his living example, we left the next day for another feast of the teaching, a week-long seminar Lee would present at Hauteville—a week replete with the spoken and unspoken teaching lessons that flow constantly from Lee and Arnaud's relationship.

KINDRED SPIRITS

Another meeting of kindred spirits took place in the spring of 1997, when we had the privilege of hosting Judy Lief, one of the *acharyas*, or empowered teachers, in the lineage of Chögyam Trungpa Rinpoche. Judy presented a two-day seminar rich with classic *dharma*, practical application in daily life, and inspiring stories about her teacher and his work with her and other students. Sometime during this seminar, one of us asked how Trungpa's students could possibly complete the exhaustive requirements for full initiation into Vajrayana Buddhist practice, especially the requirement of doing many thousands of full prostrations, ritual observances, and mantras. The questioner wondered how practitioners who were parents, professionals with full-time jobs, and participants in the extensive activities of Trungpa's community could find the time for hours of formal practice every day over a period of years.

Judy looked at the questioner with a silence that spoke loudly. Implicit in that silence was the same message Lee has given us over and over: You just have to do it. Not talk about it, not consider it, not agonize over it, just do it. Her answer cut through all levels of excuse. "Well," she responded, with a poignant blend of compassion and asperity, "you have to set some priorities."

In her response there was compassion for the intensity of the demand that faces anyone who seeks to move out of ordinary habits into real engagement of spiritual work, but there was also the slight asperity of someone who has faced that demand and made the necessary choices and who knows that these choices are wholly possible for others as well.

Judy's response to that question was the single moment of the seminar that Lee has recalled most often, repeating it in talks and seminars in Europe and the U.S. It is the answer to my own difficulties with time management; the answer to Lee's students' struggles with attachments and habitual desires; the answer to complaints about the overwhelming demands of community life, work, and practices that often confront serious students.

The moment that Judy Lief had walked in our door, there was again that feeling of meeting a kindred spirit. We welcomed her with a Buddhist ritual gesture, handing her a white scarf which she then returned to us with a generous, embracing motion. She sat at the dinner table talking easily about movies and her children, yet her entire presence communicated a foundation of rigorous and impassioned spiritual practice. Her stories about her teacher cast new light upon our struggles with the unconventional and sometimes apparently inexplicable behavior of our own teacher.

In Judy's presence I found myself recalling the hours spent with my Buddhist friend when I first arrived, alone and a stranger, in Boulder. The currents of our two schools seemed to keep crossing—the Tibetan Buddhist path, with its classical tradition and crazy-wise teacher, and the renegade sect of Western Bauls with a radical Western leader. I first experienced this crossing of currents in my own period of transition when students from the schools of Chögyam Trungpa Rinpoche and Lee Lozowick, with their commitment to a life founded in reality, were the only ones who commanded my inner attention. Later there were the two conferences on crazy wisdom which our schools shared in producing: the first sponsored by our school with assistance from Dr.

Reginald Ray and Naropa Institute; the second sponsored by Naropa with assistance offered by students in our community. Now there was another meeting point as Judy Lief brought the power and inspiration of that lineage into our *darshan* hall with her memorable talks and her vivification of the teaching through her life and presence.

These periodic interactions which Lee facilitates with other teachers may eventually serve in unexpected ways, as cross-pollination can serve and make possible the blossoming of particular flowers. It seems that this kind of cross-pollination is one of the functions that Lee and this school are increasingly fulfilling as Lee weaves threads of interconnection between different schools through his own relationships with a variety of teachers.

AT THE BEACH

That summer a friend offered Lee the use of his beach house on the French coast of the Atlantic Ocean. Lee has often said that he has no interest in sightseeing, or vacations, or time to rest. "I want to be *working*," he has declared emphatically when people have asked him what kind of schedule he wanted during seminars or teaching visits. However, in this case he was willing to take a trip to the beach.

Our traveling group crowded into the beach house for three days, making ourselves at home in our usual gypsy style. During the day we swam and played on the beach, and in the evenings we gathered for dinner and games of bridge or walks in town. While the rest of us raced for the showers after spending the day on the sandy beach, Lee never used them. He commented that our constant use of the showers cost our host expensive payments to the water company and suggested that we might consider expressing our gratitude for his hospitality by not burdening his generosity further. We could use this as an opportunity to choose something other than our own comfort. Setting us an example, he simply accepted the gritty feeling of salt and sand on his body for the entire visit.

As usual, the chance to travel with Lee brought with it daily teaching lessons. One evening we were playing bridge, which Lee presented to the community as a practice many years ago and which we usually play at least once a week. I was learning the rudiments of the game. I was dealing the cards when someone came up and asked me a question. Attempting to answer and deal at the same time, I found myself confused, and ended up with a misdeal.

"I can't deal and answer questions at the same time," I said to Lee in rueful excuse.

Lee was taking no prisoners. "You should be able to deal, answer questions, cook dinner, and talk on the phone, all at the same time!" he responded.

There was in his tone a quality of fierce demand for what is to most of us an uncommon breadth and depth of attention. It involves precise attention to every detail and, at the same time, an awareness of the entire field in which these details are taking place. Lee has been sharply critical of my own and others' tendency to what he calls "tunnel vision," seeing only one element and missing the matrix that gives appropriate direction and context to that element. Lee himself is an example of the ability to split attention without losing precision of awareness. He often plays bridge, answers students' questions with profound *dharmic* considerations, and interrupts himself to answer the phone and handle practical details, all without losing the thread of the game or the dialogue.

Food, Reprise

Another lesson for me that summer in France involved a further consideration of my relationship to food. It was a reprise of an event that had occurred several months earlier in Arizona. On that occasion we had had a celebratory meal and there were two lemon meringue pies left over. Having finally learned not to casually consume the leftovers that remained in the kitchen as my self-indulgent right, I still hoped that Lee might offer some to us adults rather than just passing them on, as he often does, to the children.

"What are you going to do with those lemon meringue pies?" I asked him as he passed me in the kitchen the next morning.

"You can have one yourself," he replied in a challenging tone, "if you will eat the *whole thing* yourself, all at once."

I had not yet eaten breakfast, and I was voraciously hungry. A whole pie was normally too much for me to eat all at once, but that morning I thought perhaps I could manage it.

Someone else in the kitchen, who was obviously also coveting the pie, asked Lee, "What about serving the pie at lunch?" Lee didn't answer, acting as if he hadn't heard. This is a man who picks up whispered conversations in another room, so I knew he had heard. His response was a clear cue that he did not want to offer any option other than the one he had already given: that I could eat the whole pie myself.

While on the level of my food addiction the option was attractive, I knew that if I accepted it I would be devouring an entire pie in the face of at least one other person's craving for it, and probably a number of others as well. What Lee has called my tendency to "rescue" flared up, along with my terror of facing someone else's jealousy and rejection of me if I took the whole thing for myself. The situation was a direct confrontation of my ingrained habit, imprinted in childhood, that everything must be shared.

"We could serve it at lunch," I echoed, capitulating totally and abjectly to habit and attachment.

Instantly, Lee's mood of generosity and friendly challenge dissolved in a subtle air of defeat that has pierced my heart many times when we refuse the gift of his instruction and choose instead the prisons of our encrusted, habitual lives. I could have said yes or no to his offer, and either answer would have been an adult response. Instead, I sold his gift for the price of approval and superficial harmony with another student.

"Whatever," Lee replied, in a tone that was an amalgamation of disinterest and despair.

Even at that moment I could have chosen to align with the choice my teacher had offered. Instead I allowed the force of my emotional habits to rule. At lunch we divided the pie evenly among the ten people at the table. The pie had been delicious the night before, but at lunch, at least for me, it was tasteless. What began as Lee's gift had been robbed of its life. Even sugar, without life, loses its sweetness.

During this sojourn at the beach in France, I had another chance to face my desperate compulsion to share any food (and everything it represented), rather than receive exactly what my teacher gave me, trusting that I was being given what I could effectively use and that others would receive what they could effectively use.

That afternoon at the beach Lee had a box of cookies, and he was giving them out to the children. As I passed by him, he handed two to me.

"Eat it all!" he said with a smile.

Just then another adult noticed the cookies in my hand. Lee had not given any to the other adults.

"Oh, could I have a bite?" she asked. "I didn't get to taste them."

Once again I stood trapped between my teacher's clear and direct instruction and my habitual emotional relationship to my friend. To give her the cookie was an expression of disrespect to my teacher, to myself, and to her. It assumed that her desire for the cookie was stronger than her desire to respect the teaching lesson I was being given (which she had not heard). Yet, once again I let my ingrained habits rule. I gave her the cookie. Then I went behind the beach house and cried at my own betrayal.

It may seem such a small thing, to give away a cookie, but the principle was not a small one. If I cannot receive even a cookie without giving it away at the first hint of someone else's envy or emptiness, how can I receive greater gifts that I am responsible for using for self-transformation rather than passing on to others, denying their intended function?

Lee's tone of voice when he said to me, "Eat it all," was echoed later, during our trip to India, when Yogi Ramsuratkumar said to us in *darshan*, as he handed us *prasad*, "Eat it, here and now." Lee was handing me *prasad* in those small cookies, yet they remained *prasad* only as long as I received and used them in alignment with him and his intention. To give one away, altruistic and generous as that might look to a casual observer, was to throw divine blessing in the trash. It was not usable as blessing to my friend, because it was not intended for her. As I handed it to her, it became mere physical flour and sugar again. Worse, it became the divine degraded and entrapped in physical form rather than the physical form blessed and uplifted through the touch of the divine.

This event exemplifies the entire challenge and opportunity that we face in human incarnation. We have the choice to degrade and entrap the divine in the habitual forms of our daily lives, or in each moment to create a form which expresses the divine reality immanent within all forms—a form through which the divine itself, already perfect, can also evolve. These choices are not anchored and made real in a few great moments of inspiration and commitment, although such moments can infuse and transform our entire lives. These choices are made by the small—even tiny—choices we make each day: the tone with which we speak to a child, the mood with which we prepare a meal, the welcome which we offer to a stranger.

That moment in which I betrayed my teacher's gift for the second time, even in so small a way, caused me pain that began to penetrate through the layers of my emotional confusion to a bedrock where I could find a commitment to begin to act differently in spite of the weight of habit. The changes that resulted were not instantaneous, but in spite of errors and stumbles I began to build a different habit. I began to choose to receive what my teacher offered me instead of wantonly giving it away, and I began to respect his choices to give to others without inwardly demanding that he give the same things to me.

THE BURIED MACHINE

When one of the old toilets on the ashram was finally replaced with a newer model, someone asked Lee what to do with the old fixture. Lee commanded, "Put it in the garden in front of the *darshan* hall!" When I saw the toilet sitting among the coreiopsis and lavender bushes, I couldn't believe it had been placed there intentionally, and made the assumption that someone must have set it down on the way to the trash station when called away by some emergency.

Isn't this just how denial works? Unable to digest the shock or dissonance of some event, we make an interpretation that has no basis in fact—that could not be supported by the actual, evident relationship of things. It was obvious that the toilet was in the middle of the garden for a reason and that it created an intentional dissonance. I did not want to feel that dissonance, so I made up an explanation to try to create consonance where there was none. I devised a totally absurd explanation in the thinly-veiled hope of manipulating things to fit my own personal preference, which was that the *darshan* hall garden look elegant and be in harmony with my preconceptions and preferences.

I asked Lee if he wanted the toilet moved to wherever it was going to stay.

"That is where it is going to stay!" he announced. "That's where I want it—in the *darshan* hall garden!" His tone was acerbic. "After untold reminders about *prasad* wrappers and used tissues dropped on the ground all over the ashram—and not just by children—I've decided the ashram could use a toilet bowl in front of the *darshan* hall as a reminder!"

He continued his tirade. "Seeing the wrappers on what is supposed to be sacred ground is as dissonant to me as it's going to be to many people to see this toilet in front of the *darshan* hall!" He added decisively that he did not want the toilet explained to people; he did not want his comment repeated so as to shame people; if anyone asked, he wanted it left to each person to decipher whatever teaching lesson might be found in it.

The toilet remained in the *darshan* hall garden, and Lee directed the ashram landscaper to plant flowers in it. Soon honeysuckle vines and variegated pansies filled the porcelain frame.

Lee's teaching often involves these apparently contradictory, yet interwoven levels of communication. The toilet in front of the *darshan* hall sets in motion vibrations of response. It can evoke a consideration of the relation of underworld to upperworld, similar to some of the experiences that emerge through attending a performance by a community band at a roadside bar. It can suggest the esoteric possibilities of tantric use of our most physical and "lowest" human aspects in a transformative process opening into realms of the divine. It can simply shock us into stopping for a moment to actually look at and receive the entire present reality that lies around and within us: the toilet, the honeysuckle trailing out of it, the entryway to the *darshan* hall, the energies flowing out of that hall, invisible yet as tangible at times as the porcelain toilet. And it can be just what it is: a toilet used as a planter in the midst of trees and flowers. To explain or elucidate the lesson of the toilet can rob it of its aliveness. To investigate the subtleties of Lee's teaching can allow us to receive some of the hidden lessons and energies implicit in his communication.

The toilet is not the only mundane fixture Lee has used as the focus of a teaching lesson. After many years of producing meals for over a hundred people at Celebrations on a four-burner stove designed for a small nuclear family, the ashram finally sprang for an impressive stove with convection oven designed for a restaurant or industrial kitchen. A few weeks later Lee noticed the old stove sitting out exposed to the elements, next to our storage sheds at the back of the ashram. The plan had been for the old stove to be stored and used as an adjunct during large-scale cooking.

Lee was irate at seeing it so casually abandoned to the sun and rain. He sent an emphatic message to one of the ashram managers. "If that stove is not moved and taken care of completely by this afternoon, I want it put in my bedroom!"

It was clear that if the stove once migrated into Lee's bedroom, it would remain there, like the toilet in the *darshan* hall garden, as a permanent reminder of our inattention, disobedience, and dissonance in relation to his teaching. Lee would be walking around that stove to get to his dresser and bookshelves for years to come.

He rolled on like a train hitting the straightaway where it can build momentum. "The instructions were that that stove be kept covered and usable for Celebrations and all our ashram needs—and that's just the way we do everything on this ashram—leaving it sitting out in the weather!"

Needless to say, the issue of the stove was handled almost instantaneously. The ashram manager personally loaded it into his own truck, since there was at that time no place to store it, and carried the stove around for days until a place could be prepared for its permanent storage.

Like the toilet, one of the ashram cars also became an enigmatic reminding factor. On an ashram of thirty people, we have on the average five vehicles available for general use. In addition, there are two large vans for use on community trips, and vans specifically designed for use by the bands. We live on a dirt road minimally maintained, and the vehicles show the wear of high mileage, a variety of drivers with varying levels of attention, and harsh road conditions.

One of our vehicles, a small Hyundai, had been driven for so many miles that in the end we literally "drove it into the ground." The car was so old and worn out that we could not sell it, except to a junkyard dealer. And in order to sell it even to him, we needed ownership papers, which had been lost somewhere along the way. To replace them would cost fifty dollars, and we would receive perhaps a hundred dollars from the junkyard. Lee declared that it was not worth the hassle for that small amount of money. He decided to do something totally different with the car.

At the next Celebration, the schedule included a mysterious slot for "performance art." As the time approached, a number of us looking curiously out the front window of the main building saw a regiment of community men armed with shovels approaching the small circle of grass in front of the ashram office. They began to dig—and dig—and dig. Soon they had created a hole big enough for a small elephant.

At the appointed hour, everyone gathered expectantly in front of the main building, excitedly discussing various rumors about the hole and the upcoming mystery event. Around the corner of the building appeared the group of men once again, this time pushing the old blue Hyundai inexorably toward its final destination. They carefully lined the car up and maneuvered it backward into the hole. Then we all shared in shoveling the dirt over it until only the windshield and front hood remained, peering out of the earth. Later Lee instructed the ashram landscaper to plant flowers and bushes around the car. The half-buried car remains as part of the first impression offered any new visitor to the ashram.

One day, after the car was ensconced in its new location and surrounded by plantings, Lee looked at it with evident satisfaction. "It's great!" he remarked, without explanation (although he has been heard telling curiosity seekers who refuse to let it be without an explanation, "It is *ART!*").

The automobile in the midst of lawn and flowers offers a great metaphor: we do not have to be ruled by the machine or trapped in conventional assumptions about its role; we can choose how to use it and what its relation will be to the surrounding universe. This automobile that was helping to pollute our earth, that we so often drove to town out of the desperate need to escape the living moment, can instead take a place in the sacred earth, a place from which it serves in a completely different way from what we might ever have expected, a place from which green grass and flowers grow. Even after seeing the half-buried machine daily for years, I find it a continual reminder to look with fresh eyes at the mechanical body of habits in which I live, and at the relationship of the human machine that I inhabit to the world around me.

Desire is Endless

One day in 1997 Lee was strolling with some students along the streets of Boulder. They passed an outdoor stand where someone was selling silver bracelets, earrings, and other hand-crafted jewelry. Several women in the party began to peruse the lovely bracelets and earrings, twittering like birds at a full feeder. Lee stood back, his attention resting not on the stand but on his students. The fact that he was totally unaffected by any magnetic pull from these jeweled treasures was in sharp contrast with the kind of automatic, almost mesmerized attraction that is so common for many of us. He made no motion to interrupt his students' covetous attention on the silver and jewels. He simply stood at a slight but noticeably neutral distance, observing.

"Desire is endless," he commented quietly, echoing a line from the Bodhisattva Vow. "I vow to conquer it all."

OPENING DOORS

At one of Lee's summer seminars, given in 1998 at Le Rozet, a beautiful Swiss chalet reworked into a seminar house in the midst of the lush mountains at the border of France and Switzerland, he began with a challenging consideration of the demand to develop not just outer obedience but inner consonance with the master. He said that in twenty-five years of hearing and observing his teaching almost none of his students had learned to follow even the simplest of his examples in terms of practice. The challenge of external obedience, let alone the challenge of a sensitivity and consonance that does not need specific example and instruction, seemed to be more than even the most committed students could or would embrace.

The second day, he moved from telling bawdy jokes to giving a graphic description of various sexual dynamics and tensions that men and women typically experience. Through some labyrinthine path he began to talk about how we would feel if we went home with a hot date and found a turd lying in the person's bed. He suggested that most of us would probably react with shock and disgust and lose our interest in pursuing any sexual encounter, although a few people with a particular fetish might find this unexpected addition to the scene provocative and titillating. Lee laughed uproariously as he considered the various looks on people's faces in this particular situation. Some people in the room were laughing with him; others were staring at him in a kind of disbelief at the turn he had taken from sublime *dharmic* considerations. The pockets of shocked silence in various parts of the room seemed only to increase his sense of the humor of the situation.

I found myself experiencing that paradoxical and poignant mixture of emotions that I often find arising in the uncomfortable situations Lee creates in order to trigger and confront various aspects of the human condition. While I thoroughly enjoyed watching Lee's merriment, I was also inwardly cringing at his choice of subject matter in the midst of this gathering of proper French people, many of whom were accustomed to the elegant and aristocratic lineage of Arnaud Desjardins.

Having wrung the last confrontive image out of the scenario, Lee went on to ask for questions. A young Frenchman raised his hand. He was clean cut and nicely dressed. His appearance suggested just the kind of person I was afraid would be mortally offended by Lee's graphic considerations. Yet there was a brightness in his eyes and a softness in his face that presaged his words.

"I want to thank you," he said to Lee with great sincerity and obviously heartfelt appreciation. "In my family nobody talks about any of these things. Nobody talks about sex, and for sure nobody can laugh. I feel as if you have just released me from a prison. I realize, listening to you talk and hearing you laugh, that there is nothing wrong with me. I want to break out of the silence and hypocrisy that are my family's pattern. I want an openness around sexuality, and the space to explore sexuality as something good and healthy. Somehow you have just unlocked the whole prison of my family's approach, and I feel as if I have just stepped free."

Time and again I find that Lee will speak something shocking, or particularly vulnerable, or he will launch unexpectedly into a consideration that has no linear relation to his previous discussion. Although his topic or mood seems inappropriate to the space from a rational and conventional point of view, that consideration or that shock or that space of vulnerability will prove to be just the piece that was required for some individual in the room who has real need. That person may not be a student of Lee's—may be someone he will never even see again. Or it may be a long-term student who he has guided through many prior confrontations and breakthroughs. The amazing thing is how he intuitively responds to this need, this call, that exists in the space, and opens a door that the person can walk through to receive his help and become consciously able to work, whether with Lee or with another teacher. In this case Lee's abrupt and shocking departure from conventional *dharma*, from his earlier sublime presentation, opened a door that could make a lifelong difference for this young man.

PART III

AT THE FEET OF THE MASTER

CHAPTER 7

INDIA

*F*or over ten years I had been hearing stories of Yogi Ramsuratkumar and Lee's trips with his students to India. In November of 1998 I was about to have the opportunity to participate in one of these mythical trips. We would stay on the ashram of Yogi Ramsuratkumar for two weeks, attending his *darshan* twice a day. After that we would travel for two weeks visiting sacred places such as the burning *ghats* of Benares and the Ganges in Rishikesh as it flows out of the mountains. This trip was in a way the acme of all my years in Lee's company and, at the same time, a launching point for a deepening phase of *sadhana*.

In Yogi Ramsuratkumar I met the point toward which Lee's work is moving; a point of blossoming. Yogi Ramsuratkumar was visible as the blossoming of the divine into these ordinary human planes. He was the divine present without veil. He was a living saint, in a world that I had believed had no saints.

Two weeks before we stepped on the plane for India, it felt to me that the trip had already begun. Physically we were approaching Yogi Ramsuratkumar, but the sensation I had was that he was approaching us. I felt his Presence as an approaching wave, as a physical force against my body.

Prior to our trip, we practiced songs and chants to sing if Yogi Ramsuratkumar asked. Someone asked Lee if we should collate the pages on which the music was written into a booklet for each person.

"No!" he said. "Just leave the pages loose."

"So you want us to have the pages falling out all over the floor?" the woman responded, smiling. She was acquiescing, but with a clear expectation—a prognosis—of disorder when we began to sing.

Lee snapped his fingers crisply. "Be alert, be on the ball; I want you to show up." The unspoken demand was to pay attention. "I want you to show up the way you do here." It seemed to me that he was both complimenting us for how we do show up at home, and challenging us about how we don't, leaving it up to us how deeply we wanted to look into the window he opened with a snap of his fingers.

Later we were talking about our anticipation and our fears of seeing Yogi Ramsuratkumar. I had never been to India, never seen Yogi Ramsuratkumar, and I was excited, grateful, and terrified. I said to Lee, "I feel as if he is going to kill me. And I want this [for him to destroy the separate self, my resistances to this Work], yet at the same time I am terrified." Other people were also speaking about their fears and their experiences with Yogi Ramsuratkumar— about finding themselves inwardly in turmoil. Lee looked around at us and said, "Everything he does will be an empowerment."

On Monday, November 23, at 4:30 A.M., we entered the tunnel of birth that this trip represented. As we walked in darkness toward the van, the bright, sharp stars of Arizona seared the sky while the warm, vague shapes of the *sangha* surrounded and shepherded us. Suddenly division was complete. Those of us traveling to India were seated in the waiting vehicle, while those remaining behind were standing outside waving, chanting, and throwing rose petals.

The van passengers were almost buried under mounds of luggage, although Lee had directed each of us to bring only one backpack for the four-week trip. Somehow the seemingly tiny extensions and additions that many of us had made—the small extra bag here and there—added up to a sum of excess weight that created a visible, physical interference with the lightness and quick responsiveness with which Lee always wishes to travel. The metaphor for the ways in which our small indulgences in other arenas also interfere with his intended movement was inescapable. Nevertheless, regardless of the extra weight that somehow Lee would carry for us, regardless of how unwieldy our initial flight might be, the trip had begun. We drove through the ashram gate, through the tunnel of trees at the entrance to the ashram, and on into the dark night, following the beacon of our own headlights.

Lee began the trip with practical instruction. He had already told us that we would be drinking only bottled water in India, since the tap water was unreliable, and that we would buy a limited amount of water. He was not about to spend money on making his students "water fat," a term the inhabitants of the fictitious desert planet Dune called untrained city dwellers who had never learned the disciplines necessary to survive in the planet's native climate. While we were still within the magical circle of the trees that guard the ashram entrance, Lee told the driver to stop the van and he turned to us.

"It's two hours to Phoenix," he announced, "and this van does not make stops. We're going to India and we won't be drinking a lot of water there. When we went in 1986 we didn't drink water for ten weeks—just soda and coffee! So it would be a good idea to start now. Don't drink water or tea or juice so you don't need to stop for a bathroom, because this van is not making stops! All right, let's go!"

Lee was setting a tone of practice, attention, and simple sacrifices of comfort, using the moment of genesis, the initial moment of enthusiastic entry into adventure, as a chance to build momentum and define parameters that could affect the entire journey and its possibilities.

In Los Angeles, we boarded the plane for Kuala Lumpur. The plane lifted into the air, bent briefly over the stunning coastline, still unspoiled, of the Pacific Ocean, then turned west and headed into the unknown mystery of India and the world of Yogi Ramsuratkumar.

Kuala Lumpur

As we approached Kuala Lumpur, we received broadcast warnings from the cockpit that possession of even a small amount of drugs carries a mandatory death penalty in Malaysia. Later we heard that to spit on the ground is an offense for which one can be jailed. Clearly this pretty country was ruled with iron hands. Lee announced that people could do as they chose, but that he would stay on the hotel property during our eighteen-hour layover. I sensed Lee's decision was an example of conservation of energy. If entering the streets of Malaysia served a work purpose, we would enter them with attention and sensitivity, according to that purpose. If there was no work purpose, then it was a potentially costly indulgence to wander exploratively in a fundamentalist Muslim country where there are so many ways in which one could unwittingly commit a small but consequential offense. Lee would not risk that cost, even if the risk was small.

At 3 A.M. local time, we landed in Kuala Lumpur, where we would stay at a local hotel during our layover. I had heard much about the 1986 trip to India, when Lee was accompanied by a group of twenty people, including four children, traveling as the Indians do in crowded trains and buses and staying in the cheapest, dirty Indian hotels, with bedbugs and without working bathrooms. I had heard they slept with ten people in one double bed, just so they wouldn't have to pay a few more rupees for the night. Perhaps it was only six people in the bed, but the story had grown in my mind to mythical proportions. I was now beginning my own initiation into traveling in India with Lee, and I was ready for anything. However dirty or cramped our quarters might be for this layover, I was prepared to rest in gratitude, without complaint.

The airline bus took us through the quiet city, past closed shops and streets so empty and safe they felt scary. Surely, I thought, there must be a curfew and the threat of maiming and execution behind streets that are so "safe" for Western businessmen. We turned onto a superhighway and breezed past trees and fields so lush we could feel the green even in the darkness of the night.

To my utter amazement, the bus entered a spacious drive lined with flowering trees whose fragrance filled the night air. In the depths of darkness this perfume was a presence so strong it was almost tactile. The bus delivered us to the wide doors of a luxury hotel. Apparently this was where the airline would lodge us for the night. Beyond the protected entrance we were treated to luxurious suites with balconies overlooking gardens and an immense swimming pool—unaccustomed accommodations for gypsy Bauls used to traveling in crowded vans and sleeping on floors!

At 6:30 A.M., after filling our plates at the bounteous buffet, we sat down together at a long table that accommodated our whole group. The waiter asked if we wanted coffee. Lee had already said, while previewing the trip in Arizona, that coffee was served twice daily at Yogi Ramsuratkumar's ashram, and that during the trip we would be making exceptions to our usual strict avoidance of caf-

feine. I really enjoy coffee and we had been traveling for over twenty hours. I wondered if the period of exceptions had begun.
Someone sitting near me who had been in the school many more
years than I had was saying, "Yes, coffee," to the waiter. I wanted to
use this as an excuse to go ahead and say yes myself. If a senior student thought it was okay, it must be. But the truth was that I had to
find resonance to Lee and to this Work within myself. I thought,
"We'll be having coffee twice a day at Yogi's ashram, starting
tomorrow. It doesn't seem necessary to push things. I'd rather wait
till it's given." I realized that taking the coffee would be like opening a gift before it was intended to be given, robbing it of some of
the energy that is gathered in waiting until the appropriate time.
"No thanks," I said to the waiter.

This small incident revealed to me an important principle
about resonance to one's teacher. I often try to find resonance by
looking to Lee, reading his unspoken preferences and subtle gestures, or, on a more gross level, by questioning him directly.
Although this attention to the teacher can be a route toward resonance, it can all too easily become itself a distraction. If we tune to
the principles of the Work, we will come into resonance with the
teacher because we are in resonance to That which moves him. The
teacher is a tuning fork that brings us into resonance with That
which Is. Both modes of attention can be useful. On this particular morning, by tuning to the principles of the field—that the
timing for coffee was not yet—I found myself spontaneously in resonance with Lee.

We swam all morning, and I floated not just in the warm,
flower-strewn water, but in gratitude for the blissful luxury of the
day, the spacious embrace of the water, the gifts of relationship that
arise in Lee's company. At the same time I was acutely aware that I
could embrace these gifts wholly only if I was willing to also
embrace the opposite gifts—those of poverty, emptiness, and

aloneness. The same One who gives such wealth is also the One who gives poverty. These seeming opposites are the same blessing. Lee and his students had paid for the luxury we were currently experiencing when they were willing to embrace the gifts of poverty on the 1986 trip to India, when Lee was willing to walk from one poor, dirty Indian hotel to another, saving a few rupees—less than a few cents—to live as the Indians did. And Lee's students were willing to follow him in this begging, however many tears and complaints they may have had. Those moments were intimately related to the moments where we floated among flowers and feasted together at the buffet. If we refuse either gift—poverty or wealth—we reject half of the Giver, either the Beggar or the King. Then the flow of energy is blocked, as if we deaden one pole of an electrical circuit. If we accept both extremes as they emerge in our work, we free an energy flow that lifts us above both poles to something unseen and previously unknown.

We gathered at 1:30 P.M. for the lunch buffet. Two of our group were missing, and Lee sent someone to check on them. The messenger returned saying their alarm had not gone off and they would be down shortly. Lee mumbled, "They already used that excuse this morning at breakfast!" I was reminded of Lee quoting Gurdjieff, who said, "Everybody makes a mistake—once."

Lee's expectation is that if we make a mistake, we learn from it the first time. I have seen him exemplify this level of learning in his own practice. When he realizes he made a mistake, he says, "It won't happen again"—and it doesn't. I have questioned him about where he goes in himself to make such an effective decision. Where does he find such clarity of awareness and intention that he can make such a statement and be reliable? The closest answer he has given to me (or that I have heard) is that he is willing to look at himself. He has clarity of self-observation. He has also said that he knows others—he knows the dynamics of the human being—because he is willing to know himself. When I thought about this principle of learning from the first time we make a mistake, I realized that after the first time the repetition of an error is no longer a mistake, it's the beginning of a habit.

Before embarking on the final phase of our flight to India we dressed in traditional Indian garb: saris for the women, *kirtas* and pyjamas for the men. As I struggled with the folds of my sari in the airport restroom before boarding, an Indian woman and her adult daughter came to my rescue and deftly wrapped the yards of material into an elegantly draped costume.

"It's wonderful you're wearing the traditional Indian saris," observed the mother appreciatively. "I wish more Indian women still did."

Even in this momentary meeting, the women's response offered confirmation of the value of Lee's instruction that we honor and embrace the culture by wearing traditional dress while traveling in India. The sari is merely an outer form, yet it carries an energy developed over thousands of years of use, a hint of the spiritual feminine of Mother India from which we Western women have much to learn. I remember once watching a graceful Western woman perform, in the tradition of Bharatnatyam, traditional sacred temple dances of India. She was highly trained and also resonant to the emotional mood of the pieces. Afterward, Lee commented, "There is something in the eyes of Eastern women when they dance these dances that I have never seen in the eyes of a Western dancer." I had observed the same thing, without ever having articulated it before.

I slept while the ocean passed beneath us and we flew steadily deeper into the darkness, the feminine, the womb of mystery and spirit that was India, from which ancient spiritual wisdom and traditions have been born and flourished over thousands of years. The goddess Kali danced among the clouds, and already, in my

246

dreams, the mood was beginning to shift from idyllic gestation into the stark reality of confrontation with self and God in the field of the divine that is Yogi Ramsuratkumar. The many heads of ego were beginning to roll as Kali danced on the wings of the plane and her knife flashed in the moonlight, her necklace of skulls aglow. The plane, like the van in which we had begun, did not make stops, and we flew inexorably forward in the darkness toward a waiting island of light—the light of Yogi Ramsuratkumar and his ashram.

I had no idea what day it was when we arrived in Madras (now Chennai), but it was about 10 P.M. Although it was night, for us it was not time to sleep. We would be traveling in a small bus for the next five hours to arrive at the ashram in time to see Yogi Ramsuratkumar drive by as he entered the ashram gates for breakfast; in time to attend morning *darshan*.

We drove through the outskirts of Chennai. It was past midnight, yet lights and noise and activities continued unabated along the streets. Bodies lay in the dirt under thin cloths or tattered saris as homeless men and women slept where they were, looking like dead bodies left lying for scavengers to eat. Those with the good fortune to have a small cart for a stall, to sell bananas or bangles in the day, slept on their carts, curled defenselessly on the wooden boards. There was nothing green between the bodies on the ground and the carts. The land at the edge of the city was totally destroyed; there was nothing but trash and garbage and packed dirt in the empty spaces. If we want to graphically observe what we humans are doing to the planet that sustains our life, we could take a hard look at a few square feet of the ravaged earth at the edges of Chennai.

TIRUVANNAMALAI

As we pulled up to the gates of the ashram of Yogi Ramsuratkumar, the driver stopped. In the dark I couldn't see much, but I later realized that someone must have been opening the gates so the bus could drive in. Lee was not waiting for the gates or for anything else.

"Let me out!" he called, his voice full of energy but not loud. No one moved. Sitting right behind him, I heard him clearly and wondered why there was no response. Maybe I could hear him because no response was demanded of me from where I was sitting. It is much harder to hear him when hearing means we have to do something, to act, to change our position.

"Let me out!" he said again, more loudly. No one moved.

"Let me out!" he exclaimed a third time, and as someone finally began to move a pack or two and people ponderously shifted positions to make space for him to get out, he clambered over people and bags to make his exit from the van. So this is how we begin our visit to Yogi Ramsuratkumar, I thought: with Lee commanding and almost begging us to let him out, while we sit stolidly around him, imprisoning him with our bodies, our baggage, and our self-absorption.

As Lee climbed out of the van, someone asked him, "Do we wear shoes on the ashram?" Lee was barefoot, focused on stepping with his bare feet onto the sacred ground of Yogi Ramsuratkumar's ashram. "I don't," he replied briefly. Then he was gone, disappearing from the van like a butterfly climbing out of a cocoon that can no longer hold it encased. Yogi Ramsuratkumar was not physically present; he was perhaps asleep a few blocks away at Sudama House. It was 4:30 in the morning. But his energy enfolded Lee like the sky in which the butterfly takes wing: limitless, all-encompassing, full of the gift of grace.

Between unpacking, settling into our cottages, and resting a little, two hours flew by. Suddenly it was time to walk to the ashram gates for our first sighting of Yogi Ramsuratkumar, when he would drive by the waiting line of devotees on his way to breakfast in a thatched hut. During most days of the year, this "drive-by" is one of the few moments when devotees can receive his glance and physical presence, but while Lee is visiting, Yogi Ramsuratkumar attends morning and afternoon *darshans* daily. During the rest of the year he sits each day in the temple, allowing people only to circumambulate his statue and bow to him briefly before they are expected to go on to *darshan* in another hall, without his physical presence.

I was appalled to realize that it was time for my first physical sighting of Yogi Ramsuratkumar, my teacher's master, and I was not prepared. I was still in the midst of yards of material, the unfamiliar sari billowing around me like endless waves. Obviously habits do not dissolve just from being in the force field of a saint. Here I was, so determined to be different in this long-awaited approach into the physical presence of Yogi Ramsuratkumar, yet I found myself unprepared and about to be late once again.

I finished wrapping the sari and raced to the ashram gates to join the others. By great blessing I was granted a reprieve from the consequences of my habits. Yogi Ramsuratkumar had not yet arrived. People were just lining up. I would be able to participate in the first drive-by—the first physical sight of Yogi Ramsuratkumar—with our group.

We stood waiting in the fresh morning light. The ashram looked lovely, graced with green palms and bushes with bright red and white flowers. Jasmine perfumed the air. Mount Arunachala, the holy mountain, loomed beyond the ashram gates, massive with the masculine energy of Shiva (legend recounts that the mountain is an incarnation of Shiva), yet softened by a green and fertile feminine energy of gestating creation. There was a light wind; birds were singing. It was as if we had left the desert and crossed the parted waters of the Red Sea and come into the Promised Land, a holy land. There was the faint sound of a motor that I recognized from

videos that I had seen of earlier trips—the sound of the Indian-
made sedan that was carrying Yogi Ramsuratkumar toward us. We
began to chant as the car approached the gates. Then, suddenly, he
was there; he was driving slowly past the line of devotees.

As when I had met Lee, all I could really see were his eyes.
What flowed through them touched me in a way that was both
miraculous and of the utmost ordinariness. In the light of those
eyes I found myself faced with the primordial fact—the most obvious and incontrovertible truth: God is real.

All this, this momentary revelation of reality, took place in an
instant, and he had passed by. We stood stunned in the aftermath
of his physical presence, this instantaneous *darshan* of the Godchild
of Tiruvannamalai, the saint called Yogi Ramsuratkumar. I had
never thought much about saints. Whoever they might be, they
seemed to live in a state too far beyond my muddled human existence to come close to me. If they existed, which I rather doubted,
they existed only as some distant inspiration. But this being that
had passed within a few feet of me was unquestionably a saint. He
lived from a foundation and among parameters wholly released
from the human desires that sway and concern me; it was instantaneously self-evident that he lived founded in his Father; yet he had
passed so close that I could almost touch him, and the effects of
this one moment were left rippling through my body and soul.

At 9:30 A.M. we prepared for the second drive-by, to be followed by morning *darshan*, usually held from 10 A.M. until noon.
We stood in line for drive-by, then entered the temple to bow and
walk around the statue of Yogi Ramsuratkumar. Finally, we bowed
to Yogi Ramsuratkumar himself, seated on a simple chair to the
side of the statue. He was intensely present; I felt that he saw each
one of us, as we bowed, in our entirety. In a way, for me, the visit
felt complete in that moment. I had seen him; he had seen me.

Nothing else was needed. Everything else that might happen would be only an extension of that moment.

Yogi Ramsuratkumar entered the *darshan* hall leaning on the arm of his assistant, Selvaraj, a young man of great gentleness and sensitive responsiveness to Yogi Ramsuratkumar's every gesture. Although they lived with Yogi Ramsuratkumar, served him constantly, and sat with him on the dais at the front of the hall every day, Ma Devaki and Vijaya Laksmi waited for his gesture of invitation before they sat themselves at the edge of the dais, while Yogi Ramsuratkumar sat on a pillow in the center. After a bit Yogi Ramsuratkumar reached for a cigarette—one of his legendary "Charimars" in a small orange box. He struck a match to light it and the glow illuminated his face as if the sun had just broken through clouds. It was as if the halo of light that emanated from the holy ones had become acutely visible in that instant, glowing from within and around his face. I was looking through a window directly into the face of the divine. His body was the window, and within it was both emptiness and richness beyond imagining.

Once during our visit, Yogi Ramsuratkumar shook the match to put it out and laid it on the ashtray, but the match somehow rekindled. The flame remained burning, a small bright fire in the ashtray, very near the robes around his legs. He did nothing about it. He looked straight at the fire but did not move, all his attention gathered into the act of smoking. It is often said that Yogi Ramsuratkumar is burning away people's karma as he smokes; whatever his intention, his action was totally focused. The fire in the ashtray was not his business. It was clear that if his Father did not move him to put out the fire, he would not move, even if the flames began to burn him. Ma Devaki, wholly attentive from the first instant he reached for the cigarette (as she is attentive to all his movements, as well as to his silence and stillness) leaned over and put out the flame. She is a living example of what it is to "attend" to a master, to this Godchild who does nothing for himself unless his Father moves him. One can attend in this way only by letting go of all distraction, all attention to oneself and to the ordinary world. One must turn wholly to the flame of the divine as it burns in the master whom one serves.

We were seated in rows on the floor in front of Yogi Ramsuratkumar. While some of the women led chanting, Yogi Ramsuratkumar gestured ever so slightly to Lee. Lee leapt up and almost ran to the dais. He bowed, and Yogi Ramsuratkumar held his hands in a gesture of blessing and affection that was repeated every day, at every *darshan*. Yogi Ramsuratkumar's relationship to Lee and to most or all of his devotees seems to have become increasingly formal. He did not invite Lee or anyone else to breakfast as he consistently did in earlier years. There was no conversation over chai, sitting on a porch, as in the early days. Lee's only contact with Yogi Ramsuratkumar throughout the visit was through the formal ritual of *darshan*. Yet what was given and communicated within the protocol of that formal space was tremendously intimate and personal as well as formal and impersonal.

Lee had been, at various times, embraced with the fullness given to a young child; sent away as a father may send away a son as part of initiation into manhood; welcomed as a son is welcomed as he returns to his home in the new relationship of adulthood. Now he was clearly expected to carry responsibility independently yet responsively, to engage formal duties that served the work of his master. Yet the personal caring and affection between Father and son were not lost but transmuted as they were shared in the present form. In Yogi Ramsuratkumar's blessing, the personal and the impersonal live as one.

Lee presented Yogi Ramsuratkumar with a newsletter, *Om Sri Ram*, which included an article about Yogi Ramsuratkumar written by one of Lee's students. Yogi Ramsuratkumar asked that student to read the article. As she sat down after her reading, Yogi Ramsuratkumar called Lee up and asked him to read the same article. Undoubtedly, there were various levels of meaning and reasons for this. To me it said that whatever work and service we do, it is essentially Lee's doing; it is Lee working through us, as Lee's work is Yogi Ramsuratkumar working through him.

A second aspect of Lee's reading was that it put the communication of the article clearly and strongly into the concrete dimensions of time and space. He read loudly and with great clarity. Any word that had been lost in his student's quieter reading was, through Lee's reading, imprinted into the time/space continuum.

That afternoon we made a trip into the town of Tiruvannamalai, where we perused the shops for Indian clothes for those who needed them. The shops were filled with every color and variety of sari and *punjabi*, yet, after having looked forward tremendously to this chance to choose a sari, I found myself strangely disinterested. The chance to choose a sari in my favorite shade of blue was an opportunity that was limited to satisfaction of a personal desire, and I suddenly realized that satisfaction of personal desire, which has in my psyche been a great driving force, actually didn't interest me very much. I didn't realize this quite fully enough to forego buying a sari, however, and afterward wished that I had not bought it. I told myself that I needed one more sari, even though Lee had previously told me that the two saris I already owned were enough. I bought one mainly out of old habit still driving my actions while new realization was percolating underneath.

The sari was of shades of blue like the sky; however, when I later understood more about fabrics, I realized that it was wholly polyester, rather than the traditional cotton cloth Lee prefers, which is hand-loomed by the Indian people. Polyester saris, in contrast, make the Indian culture dependent on Western-style fac-

tories and fabrics and insidiously invade the Indian traditions
while appearing to support them.

Riding back to the ashram, crowded into a small auto-rick-
shaw, someone commented to Lee that Yogi Ramsuratkumar
seemed to continue *darshan* longer than usual—well past noon.

"Yes," Lee replied, "He held *darshan* till almost one o'clock.
He likes us." There was an innocent, childlike delight in Lee's
face. It was an exact mirroring of the delight in Yogi
Ramsuratkumar's face as he received the poetry book, *Death of a
Dishonest Man*. Each was willing to receive the other without
defense, in complete innocence.

Back at the ashram, at about 3:30 Lee headed for the gate to
wait for Yogi Ramsuratkumar's afternoon drive-by. It was almost
half an hour until the car would approach the gate, but again Lee
put his energy into preparation and waiting with an air of alacrity.
A space of waiting can be sluggish, spaced-out, inattentive: Okay,
I'm here, wake me up when something's ready to happen. Lee's
waiting, on the contrary, was attentive and alert, feeding the space
in which Yogi Ramsuratkumar's entry would take place. Lee's
waiting, sitting still under the thatched roof by the gate or standing in line quietly talking, had the same energy of intention and
responsiveness as when he ran to the dais at Yogi's slightest gesture
in *darshan*.

The next day one of the men asked what he could have done
differently the day before. Lee replied, "You couldn't have done
anything about yesterday. You weren't on the firing line." Lee had
already given some specific feedback to those of us who had led
chants. He'd said, "Don't keep looking over at me! Look at the
audience, at the people who are chanting. You can glance over at
me every so often just to see if I'm giving an instruction [to change
chants or to stop chanting]. And you don't need to look at Yogi
Ramsuratkumar either," he added. "What he's doing with people

he invites up—to give *prasad* or whatever—is his private business. That was disgusting, how some people who were supposed to be leading chants were peering over at Yogi Ramsuratkumar, ogling him. When you're leading chants, that's your job: to lead chants. Just do your job. Look at the audience and lead the chants. Keep your attention on your job." Lee had given this commentary with great emphasis during our trip to town the previous day. He had been speaking to me, who happened to be one of the "some people" who had turned to stare at Yogi Ramsuratkumar's activity.

Later I spoke to Lee about the frustrating predictability of my machine—my body of habits, my personal egoic structure. I am predictably late, predictably in scarcity around food or his attention, predictably desperate for approval that I mistakenly equate with love. How could I develop a machine that is usable rather than predictably unusable and unresponsive, I asked.

Lee answered, "Take what people offer you. Don't defend yourself against people's feedback or tell them how they're wrong. Just take what people give you."

I heard him give a similar instruction to another student who asked him for help with her dynamics and resistance. "Don't shoot people in the leg when they try to help you," he told her. He was making a strong point that help does not come just from him; it comes from those around us. To accept this requires humility and a willingness to live in relationship with others.

I had the experience that on Yogi Ramsuratkumar's ashram we were an island of sanity in the midst of a world of insane war and greed and suffering. This island was sending out a continuous healing sound that, although it may not have been consciously heard by the suffering millions, had profound—even infinite—effects. As we chanted the Name of Yogi Ramsuratkumar, I felt the absolute reality of this healing possibility.

Before my involvement in the Hohm community, I was a political activist. I marched on Washington and demonstrated in city streets and organized alternative institutions. Although I believed in God, I saw him as a distant power who gave us responsibility for our human affairs. I would have thought that to sing together, though inspiring, would not bring real change. To believe that chanting the Names of God could overturn the ancient human politics of greed and personal power would have been to me a fantasy resulting in abdication of personal responsibility. Now I am quite certain of the opposite. To chant the Names of God is to set ringing within our human planes a Sound that is at the source of all things. It is one of the deepest healing actions we can take. And from this action, all other actions and forms flow in right relationship and right timing.

The following afternoon Lee took us to Sanadhi Street, to the small house where Yogi Ramsuratkumar used to live, at the edge of the brass market. Metal bars enclosed a dark, shaded porch at the front of the house. This was where Yogi Ramsuratkumar would often sit with his visitors, drinking chai and talking. Across the street from this house was where Lee sat in the Indian sun all day, waiting for glimpses of his master after Yogi Ramsuratkumar sent him away. The darkened porch was so full of history, so imbued with the power and living myth of Yogi Ramsuratkumar, that shapes and sounds of these moments from the past seemed to pour out of the shaded darkness into the present moment. I had the sensation that the tiny demarcations we call past and present and future dissolve in this living Presence; that time is a puny illusion that we throw over Reality in an attempt to control, order and understand a living Unity far beyond our grasp.

Across the street, wide stairs led up to a flat roof that looked out over the crowds and markets of Tiruvannamalai. The roof itself was a quiet, shaded oasis. We climbed the stairs, looking for

Perumal, the man who for many years was Yogi Ramsuratkumar's attendant at the Sanadhi Street house. After Yogi Ramsuratkumar left the Sanadi Street house to live at Sudama House, Perumal remained, still attending to Yogi's space there.

At the top of the stairs we found that Perumal was not there, but that his son was carrying on the work of attending the space. This young man was a small boy when Lee first visited, and he grew up helping his father attend to Yogi Ramsuratkumar, obeying his instructions and running out for cups of chai from the chai stall for Yogi's guests. His father was a successful businessman with two shops when he met Yogi Ramsuratkumar and left everything to serve him. Now Perumal's son, in turn, spent the entire day, every day, caring for Yogi Ramsuratkumar's space. He lifted a large tarp at the edge of the roof and showed us stacks of burlap bags in which Yogi Ramsuratkumar for years collected trash, rags, and unknown treasures. Poems that Lee had sent to Yogi Ramsuratkumar over many years may have been stuffed into similar bags. Perhaps some early poems still remained there, hidden like time capsules or crystals of radioactive rock, emitting the call to surrender into the unsuspecting, sleeping world.

A week later Lee visited Perumal at his home, where he was warmly welcomed. He told us that Perumal and his entire extended family lived in the poorest section of Tiruvannamalai in one small house. The whole family accepted living in poverty and simplicity in order to support first Perumal and then his son in service to Yogi Ramsuratkumar. What makes their sacrifice even more striking is that they make this choice so as to serve Yogi Ramsuratkumar and yet do not even see him. He does not come to Sanadhi Street, and Perumal and his family rarely if ever go to the ashram. They simply attend to Yogi Ramsuratkumar's space and to his Work.

Accustomed to a level of material ease and relative wealth, we Westerners often find that letting go of familiar riches and comforts is a challenge too hard to embrace. The contrast between the level of sacrifice Perumal's whole family was making and our commitment to material accumulation would become even more stark when our group was set loose on the markets of India after we left the ashram of Yogi Ramsuratkumar.

After the trip to Sanadhi Street, we returned to Yogi Ramsuratkumar's ashram in time for afternoon coffee. As we sat on the cottage porch drinking our coffee, someone commented that Purna's group would arrive the following day.

"Yes," Lee commented. "When we got here we were weak, undisciplined, and sloppy; but when Purna's group gets here, they'll make us look like *practitioners!*"

Purna was one of Lee's most senior students, recently empowered by Lee to teach on his own and establish his own community. His was a new group not yet trained in working together, nor trained even as individuals in the protocols related to Yogi Ramsuratkumar's ashram or in practices of attention on a spiritual path. Lee did not expect the same level of attention from them that he did from us; what he did expect was that they give attention to learning. Our group, on the other hand, was made up of students who had been with Lee from five to almost twenty-five years. From us he expected practice and attention, sacrifice gladly given without reactivity, awareness of the needs of the group as a whole and of each space in which we found ourselves, and mature responsibility. So far we had not been demonstrating this kind of attention. The fact that it took a group of brand new students to make us look, by comparison, like practitioners was not a compliment.

During afternoon *darshan* Yogi Ramsuratkumar asked Lee to "say something useful." Lee spoke about the title of the poetry book, *Death of a Dishonest Man,* a collection of hundreds of poems written by Lee to Yogi Ramsuratkumar, plus a number of essays and commentaries by other teachers and by Lee's students. Lee said that everything that is based in a belief in separation from God is dishonest. He said that Yogi Ramsuratkumar is wholly honest because there is nothing left in him that is separate from God, nothing that believes in separation from his Father. Lee said that the title of the book named a process that was still going on in himself. Yogi Ramsuratkumar was gradually bringing about the death of everything in Lee that is dishonest, that is based in the illusion of separation.

Listening to Lee I had a glimpse of what he means when he says real self-observation is without judgment. He is able to see himself clearly because he does not cloud the view with guilt or shame or any kind of reactivity. He simply sees what is, as it is in the moment, which releases the present to become something new.

Often Yogi Ramsuratkumar left about half an hour before the end of *darshan*. Before he left, he asked Lee to sit in his seat on the dais and to "conduct these affairs." Sometimes I looked at Lee's eyes as he sat there, and his eyes had in them the same infinite wildness I have glimpsed in the eyes of Yogi Ramsuratkumar: a madness to this world because they are focused wholly in the world of the Father. That wildness has at the same time infinite gentleness; these are eyes that are sometimes washed with tears just looking at the world as seen in the face of a devotee or of a child. Sometimes it seemed to me that as he sat in that seat Lee had become transparent, and looking through him I saw Yogi Ramsuratkumar sitting there.

Purna's group was due to arrive about 5 A.M. the following day. Lee rose early so he would be present to greet them upon their arrival. He made this choice as if it were the most ordinary thing to do, the only natural response to Purna's arrival. Yet, the fact is that he could easily have slept another hour or two and then greeted

Purna. Purna's group had to get settled anyway, and they didn't need Lee's help for that. Lee could offer generous hospitality and welcome after getting a full night's sleep.

To be in Yogi Ramsuratkumar's presence is both energizing and tiring; there are many levels on which we were working very hard, or being worked. This inner working must have been even stronger for Lee than it was for the rest of us, given the position of responsibility in which he stands, in direct relationship to Yogi Ramsuratkumar as his master and at the same time responsible for his own students. I knew from looking at Lee's face and from how early he was going to bed that he was deeply tired. Yet there was no conflict, no drag, no struggle with resistance in his choice to wake a couple of hours early to meet Purna. It was the correct action, and it was what he wanted to do. He gives to Purna, who works for him, the same respect and precise attention that he gives to Yogi Ramsuratkumar, for whom he works.

Something about true hierarchy can be glimpsed in Lee's action. The hierarchy of the Work is based on mutuality and equality of respect, concomitant with vast differences in levels of responsibility. Lee was demonstrating this hierarchical model in which greater power is used to teach those with lesser power, and power at every level is used to serve. Lee was supporting and honoring Purna and his work by meeting him and his group when they arrived. Purna did not ask for Lee's support, but Lee gave it because Purna's work had created a matrix, a magnet, that drew Lee's attention and response.

As I sat watching Yogi Ramsuratkumar's work with Lee day after day, it seemed that Lee's arrogance and presumptuousness (which Lee freely admits he brought to his first visits with Yogi Ramsuratkumar) are vitally useful to a master such as Yogi Ramsuratkumar. To Yogi Ramsuratkumar, what we consider our foibles, our weaknesses, even our positive characteristics, are simply elements that he can use. Lee does not obscure those characteristics through shame, but clarifies them through self-observation. This fact, combined with his intentional alignment and the degree of his surrender to Yogi Ramsuratkumar, makes all of his characteristics available for use. Lee's arrogance and presumptuousness, as well as his active creativity and Western ability to initiate forcefully and effectively—in a sense, his Western independence—are gradually being blended with instruction and experience in obedience, resonance and devotion as inherent and developed in the East. In Lee, it seems to me, Yogi Ramsuratkumar is blending masculine and feminine, East and West, so as to carry out the teaching in a contemporary yet traditionally rooted form.

On December 1, the celebration of Yogi Ramsuratkumar's birthday—his Jayanthi—began with a *puja* ceremony at 3 A.M. and continued with ritual dancing and chanting around his statue in the temple until dawn. Then there was a pause for chai before the traditional Vedic fire ceremony performed by several Brahmin priests. As we sat drinking chai, Mani, the ashram manager, paused for a rare moment to speak with us. Someone asked him if there was a plan to cover the dirt floor of the huge temple with a marble floor like the one in the temple's dining hall.

Mani replied that he didn't know. "I'm kept here," he said, "because I don't ask questions. I don't ask why or what for. I just say yes to whatever he wants. I've learned in four-and-a-half years here that it's better to listen than to talk. Each of us comes here only because Yogi Ramsuratkumar chooses us," Mani continued. "He's very possessive of those he chooses. If he sees me talking to somebody, he'll call me over and want to know why I'm talking, what's the topic. Then he'll say, 'Mani doesn't need to talk. Mani must need more work to do. Mani doesn't need to talk. Mani just needs to do his work.'

"Yogi Ramsuratkumar asks the impossible," Mani went on. "But if I don't say it's impossible, if I don't question him but just go ahead and do it, then the impossible happens. I'm not the one who does these impossible things," he added. "It's Yogi Ramsuratkumar who does them. When he chooses you, then he creates in you what is needed so you can do what he's asking, what he needs. We can only do these things from faith, and he is the one that makes faith in us. He changes us, from inside. He grows in us what is needed. He gives us the faith. And he is unpredictable, totally unpredictable. You never know what he will do. If he sits in the temple and never goes into the *darshan* hall, and you think you can count on that, then suddenly he will go in the *darshan* hall. If he tells Lee to sit on the dais when he leaves *darshan* every day, so you think you know what he will do today, then this day he will not do that. You can never predict what he will do.

"It is not easy living with a saint," Mani commented, a little ruefully. "But it is not difficult either—because he is really doing it all. He is doing it through us. I can't do all this—but Yogi Ramsuratkumar does it through me."

Mani looked around at the temple. The structural skeleton is complete, and still visible, because Yogi Ramsuratkumar suddenly stopped construction work some time ago. Metal rods of rebar stick out of the cement walls all around the outside of the temple, framing sacred sculptures built into the walls. Mani told us that when Yogi Ramsuratkumar said to stop construction on the temple and on other parts of the ashram, all work stopped immediately. Within fifteen minutes there was no construction going on, and it has been left just as it was at that point. Yet, in fact, Mani continued, the temple is already complete. And this is why any impossible task that Yogi Ramsuratkumar asks in building it can be accomplished.

"We look around," Mani said, "and to us it looks as if the temple is not finished. But Yogi Ramsuratkumar has already completed the temple. He sees it as it really is. We just don't see it yet. It is that which makes everything possible, because Yogi Ramsuratkumar has already completed it."

Listening to Mani, I was thinking that the same principle applies to us as human beings. The temple of the divine is already complete in us, but we do not yet see it and so we do not yet act in accordance with that reality. Yogi Ramsuratkumar sees that temple in us, already complete, and so it is possible, and in fact inevitable, that this completeness will finally manifest—that what he sees will become visible to our human eyes. To rely on that fact is to have faith, and to act with faith is to open the door to that reality, that completion. From his own experience, in his own words, Mani was voicing the principle that Lee gives us when he speaks of "already present enlightenment." That teaching, like all of Lee's teaching, comes subtly but directly from Yogi Ramsuratkumar, and here at dawn of Yogi Ramsuratkumar's Jayanthi in India I was hearing this teaching presented with living understanding by another of Yogi Ramsuratkumar's devotees.

When we walked to the gates for drive-by, we saw lines of people waiting in the roped aisles and packed masses outside the gate. We walked around the statue in the temple, and then bowed to Yogi Ramsuratkumar. Finally, we went into the *darshan* hall. Yogi Ramsuratkumar remained in the temple as line after line of people entered and bowed to him. His seat in *darshan* remained empty as the first hour passed. Yet that seat was charged with his presence. He had asked Lee to have people from our group lead chanting. So we chanted his name in the *darshan* hall while hundreds or thousands of people passed before him in the temple.

I was sitting on the aisle seat on the women's side, and Lee sat on the aisle seat on the men's side. The two women next to me were leading the chanting. As the chanting stretched on toward noon, the woman next to me whispered, "Ask Lee if we should stop chanting at noon." I asked Lee and he answered forcefully, "Tell them, 'I want you to keep singing till I tell you to stop! It could be one o'clock, two, three, or nine o'clock at night. Keep singing till I tell you to stop!'" Once again Lee wanted the chant leaders to have their attention solely on the chants; not on the clock, not on whether Yogi Ramsuratkumar was still on the ashram. He wanted the chanting itself to be "Just This."

Lee continued the chanting until after noon, until someone came to tell him that Yogi Ramsuratkumar had completed giving blessings in the temple and had left the ashram for lunch. Then we broke into "Mangalam," the ending chant, and morning *darshan* was over.

At sunset our group gathered in the women's cottage to share our usual simple supper. Most people had been up since 3 A.M. As soon as supper was over, we headed immediately for bed. It was the end of Jayanthi, the formal celebration of the appearance of Yogi Ramsuratkumar in the world; yet, if we remember, this is something we celebrate every day.

One year there was a birthday cake for Yogi Ramsuratkumar, but he did not want his devotees to do this again. It seems that his emphasis is not on rituals that honor him but on rituals that honor the traditions, such as the Vedic fire ceremony, and on efforts that serve and bless the people, such as the ashram meals. (The ashram serves free meals to thousands of people on days of celebration such as Jayanthi.) I was reminded of Lee's disinterest in new rugs or furniture for his living room or even a new vacuum for the ashram, versus his great enthusiasm about spending money for Celebration feasts or for CD recordings by Shri or LGB, which feed people in another way.

Each day at Yogi Ramsuratkumar's ashram felt like a jewel strung on a thread. The thread was continuous, yet each jewel was unique. Together they made up a mala, a string of prayer beads, shining around the neck of God, around the heart of Yogi Ramsuratkumar, beating in the midst of all of us, in the midst of "All, All." As he so often says: "My Father blesses all, All!"

For me each jewel was hard and bright. These were not easy days. Yet as Mani said about living with a saint, they were not difficult either. They simply did not fit into the "normal" categories of "either/or." To be in his Presence—not just the physical presence but the pervading Life of Yogi Ramsuratkumar that flows through his ashram—is to have everything revealed. For me, what was most visible were the layers of darkness, the dimensions of underworld in myself that I can in ordinary times and spaces more easily ignore or pretend don't exist: anger, impatience, jealousy, inattention (which is actually attention to self in some way that overrides or distracts from attention to the world around me and what is needed), selfish grasping, greed, a heart closed to the ceaseless gifts of the compassionate divine.

I found myself remembering again the words of Irina Tweedie about the teaching she received from her master: "I hoped to get instructions in Yoga, expected wonderful teachings, but what the Teacher did was mainly to force me to face the darkness within myself, and it almost killed me." (Tweedie, I. *Daughter of Fire: A Diary of a Spiritual Teaching With a Sufi Master*, Nevada City, Calif.: Blue Dolphin Press, 1986, p. x)

Yet at the same time—how incomprehensibly paradoxical—I felt great gratitude for the priceless opportunity to be in the physical presence of Yogi Ramsuratkumar, to see Lee with his spiritual Father and to perhaps glimpse the barest hints of the relationship of Yogi Ramsuratkumar to his Father in Heaven. I felt appreciation, gift, the waves of this Life flowing over and through me in a

way that no human dimensions, no aspects of underworld or distortions of upperworld, could possibly stop or even hinder in the
slightest way.

Two days after the Jayanthai celebration, during morning
darshan, as we sat chanting under Yogi Ramsuratkumar's gaze while
he smoked cigarettes, a space opened within or around me. It was
like feeling the tectonic plates of the earth shift so that everything—
land, water, fire—stood in a new relationship. It was as if for days
I had been slogging through dark swamps within myself while
longing for the warmth and purity of the sun somewhere far distant. Suddenly I felt—I *knew*—that there was no separation between
these caverns of darkness and the light of the sun, no separation
between the underworld and the upperworld, between Hades and
heaven. A space was flowing from the heart of Yogi
Ramsuratkumar that included all of it. And in being included,
instead of divided and excluded, the wounds in the darkness began
to heal. I could *feel* this happening, as if the stately speed of time-
lapse photography were taking place within me. Not that I was
healed in a moment; not that the human condition was erased;
and yet, just as the temple is already complete because Yogi
Ramsuratkumar has seen it in its completion, in that moment I
could feel my own wholeness, which did not escape but embraced
and transmuted all the inner horrors that had previously overwhelmed me. Like the temple, I was complete because Yogi
Ramsuratkumar had seen my completion; and not just mine, but
the objective completion of every human soul, as one. I looked up
and Yogi Ramsuratkumar was smiling. It was the first time in days
that I had seen him smile. I'm sure he did smile during those days,
but I was not able to see it until that moment.

No sooner was this moment of epiphany complete than Lee
asked another woman and me to lead chants. I had made no outer
indication of what had just happened to me; the whole room had

simply been chanting together in the presence of Yogi Ramsuratkumar. Yet with his typical instinctive reading of the field, Lee was responding to the moment when I was inwardly present and giving me the chance to bring the inner energy into outer action. To lead the chants is to take responsibility for one aspect of Lee's gift to his master. At the same time, it was for me an unfamiliar task. Though I had ample opportunity to practice the chants back in the U.S., I had not practiced enough to be sure of all the melodies and rhythms. In Yogi Ramsuratkumar's presence, I was appalled at my lack of impeccable preparation. The other woman also was not an experienced chant leader, so I could not hide behind her.

In spite of our stumbles, Lee had the two of us continue to lead the chanting without reprieve as the *darshan* stretched on into eternity. After what seemed an aeon, Yogi Ramsuratkumar moved down the aisle toward his car; the clock hands moved toward noon, and Lee indicated that it was time to sing "Mangalam," the ending chant. We had been leading chanting for over an hour and we were drenched with sweat.

As we walked outside the hall, someone raced up to us and said, "You know you weren't supposed to sing that chant, and it was the wrong melody!" We were already at a point of hysteria, and this was the last straw. This was hardly information we were lacking or that we needed to know at that moment. I dissolved in laughter and the other woman dissolved in tears. The pressure we had been experiencing had to find release.

As we walked to the soda stall after lunch, I questioned Lee about how to make use of what happened. How do I learn not to go blank, not to let my fear rule? How do I learn to carry correctly the responsibility of leading chants?

I was prepared for Lee to yell at me for my imperfection, to be highly critical of our performance before his master. But once again he surprised me. "If you're going to take on a major assignment," he said gently, "you can't expect to get a hundred the first time." This response just stopped me in my tracks. It was the last thing I expected, and it spoke to a number of my unconscious assumptions and dynamics. When I was in third grade, I cried because I got only a 99 instead of 100 on my first spelling test. Here I was, forty years later, enacting the same dynamic in regard to spiritual life. Once again I saw that life is not interested in whether we are perfect; life is interested in whether we learn.

While there were many things we did not do well on this trip, there were also many things we did do well. One of the latter, in my perception, is that we were willing to recognize our areas of weakness; to hear both Lee's feedback and the voice of our own conscience, our own inner attention. This is what made it possible for us to learn from whatever happened. To recognize weakness and to persevere in the face of it is a prerequisite for growth.

In afternoon *darshan* that day, Yogi Ramsuratkumar surprised our group. He opened the poetry book, *Death of a Dishonest Man*, to the collection of Lee's lyrics, written for our bands, at the back of the book.

"I would like someone to sing some of these," he told Lee. Lee asked two of the women to choose some songs they knew and sing them. They chose several that on one level are haunting love songs, yet can also be taken as mystical poems to the divine Beloved. As they sang "Blind Devotion," "Driftin'" and "Make a Little Room for Grace," Yogi Ramsuratkumar moved his head in rhythm to their singing. I certainly never expected to see this great yogi keeping time to blues and rock 'n' roll! It struck me that Lee and his Father are not so different after all, even though his Father sits in a temple in India while Lee dances around the stage of a Phoenix bar with a mike in his hand, belting out a gravelly rendition of the blues.

The lines of the songs lingered in the space, reverberating with their layered levels of meaning and the moods they evoked.

> She blows in off the mountain
> Like a human hurricane
> She opens all your windows
> And laughs like she's truly sane
> She's not all that attached
> To clothes or to prejudice
> You got no place to stand
> And you're so grateful for this
>
> Make a little room for Grace
> She's a woman
> Make a little room for Grace
> Don't you love her?
> Make a little room for Grace
> But if you play her game
> When she's had her way with you
> You'll never . . . ever be the same

❧

> Now I am driftin', lost in the mood
> Floating from your love
> Oh, how you moved me
> How you turned me around
> Pulled me from the bottom
> To the heavens above

❧

Ask me to do anything
Your wish is my command
I will fly up to the sun for you
Bring it to your hand
I will conquer armies
You know what I mean
Allow me to adore you
Be your slave, not your queen

Got a question for you honey
Please forgive my great emotion
Is it dangerous to love you
With such blind devotion?

When the women finished singing, Yogi Ramsuratkumar called Lee up and asked him to sing some of the lyrics himself. Lee explained that his first choice was a song about life without love, and he sang a song about an old man that begins, "Can you see the old man cryin'?" The next song he described as being about life lived without the sacred, and he sang, "Can You Trust?" Finally he sang a song, "Refused to Die," about the commitment of the Native Americans to their intrinsically sacred culture.

Singing a cappella, without any instrumental backup, Lee was not always totally on key, but this did not detract and perhaps even added to the power of his communication. After sweating in front of the room myself while leading chanting for over an hour that morning, I was especially inspired by the way Lee simply gave himself completely to Yogi Ramsuratkumar's request; he offered what he has and what he is for Yogi Ramsuratkumar to use as he chooses, with nothing held back. The suffering of the entire world is encapsulated in the story of that one old man. And the possibility, the challenge, to commit everything to what is true rolled through the room as Lee sang, "Refused to Die."

When we came into morning *darshan* the next day, Yogi Ramsuratkumar was already seated on the dais, and Vijaya Laksmi was reciting the opening prayer. Yogi Ramsuratkumar was almost laughing out loud even before the prayer was finished. It occurred to me that he must have something in mind to surprise us once again.

He called Lee up and gave his instructions. He wanted the two women who had sung the day before to sing *all* the lyrics collected at the end of the poetry book. Some of these lyrics did not yet have a melody written for them. Others had complex melodies that few people except the lead singers in the bands knew well enough to sing, especially without any instrumental support. Only one of the women was in the hall at the time, and when Lee gave her Yogi Ramsuratkumar's instructions, she looked at him aghast.

"Just start!" Lee ordered her. "Start at the beginning of the lyrics, and go straight through. Make it up if you have to. Just start!"

Within minutes the other woman entered the hall and joined her. As they sang, Yogi Ramsuratkumar listened intently. Once again I realized that perfection is really not relevant. I was sure these two women were sweating at least as much as I had been the previous day. They were experienced chant leaders, but they had been asked to offer something at which they were not experienced, which they had not practiced and could not have foreseen. Yet although the singing was mostly unpracticed and much of it was made up on the spot, it had an aliveness, a freshness, that seemed much more useful than practiced professionalism.

I had a sore throat that day, and it had been getting worse since the night before. As I sat in afternoon *darshan*, fighting the sore throat and feeling it worsen regardless, I was thinking that people came to the ashram with life-threatening illnesses, and they had the faith to let Yogi Ramsuratkumar heal them. Yet I did not seem to have the faith even to allow a sore throat to heal. I remembered a story that someone had told us about a man whose mother had cancer in her intestines. The man brought his mother to Yogi Ramsuratkumar's *darshan*, but Yogi never spoke to her or even looked at her. He just sat there during the entire *darshan* untwisting a tangled rope or mala.

"Imagine how the man and his mother felt," the storyteller said. "Yogi never even looked at them, and here she was likely to die of cancer."

The next day the mother went to the hospital for her checkup prior to surgery. The doctor found no trace of cancer. Yogi Ramsuratkumar had released it from her body as he released the tangled knots of the mala.

As I sat remembering this story, it occurred to me that faith does not mean expecting Yogi Ramsuratkumar to do what I want, to carry out my goals. Faith involves accepting whatever is as his gift. Perhaps the sore throat was meant to be there; perhaps the sore throat itself, rather than its healing, was his gift. As acceptance of whatever Yogi Ramsuratkumar gives expanded within me, I stopped fighting the sore throat, and simultaneously it began to clear. I remembered having once had a similar experience in the night, when I woke with a sore throat and suddenly saw it as a habit of thought, a habit of relationship, rather than as a real thing. In that instant it began to dissipate. Not that every illness is a habit of thought, or that every illness is to be dissolved in such a way, but in accepting the fact that illness as well as health might be a part of divine purpose, something unlocks that allows relationship to the illness to change. Then whether the sore throat or illness remains or dissolves becomes a side issue, not the main point.

Two days later, after the ashram server had come to our cottage and filled our cups with the usual milk-coffee, Lee made a caustic comment about how some of us, out of our greed, were using our own big metal cups for coffee rather than the small plastic cups the ashram provided. I had been consciously and self-righteously using the metal cup to avoid adding to the plastic that literally blankets India, filling her creek beds and strewing her fields. Traditionally, Indians used small clay cups for chai and threw the cups down on the ground to return to the earth when they were done to avoid dishwashing and considerations of transmission of disease through used cups. Now they throw down the plastic cups, which accumulate as eternal monuments to technological "advances." While I had been self-righteously aware of my environmentally correct choice, I had been strategically unaware that I was using the large metal cup to get more coffee along with being politically correct.

Here was a precise example of the weakness in political efforts aimed at social change without a strong element of self-observation. I was intent on saving the environment in India by eschewing the plastic cup, but I was blind to the greed in myself that is the same driving force underlying planetary environmental destruction. Greed destroys, by its nature; and if we do not face the greed in ourselves, then we will, as a race, continue to destroy our environment no matter how many environmental protection laws we pass.

Lee said to me simply, "We get coffee twice a day, every day. We don't have to grasp for a little bit more. We can be content with what we have."

Such tiny incidents and choices contribute to the mood and direction of our lives. If we discern and eradicate the weeds of competitiveness, grasping, jealousy, greed, and cruelty within ourselves, then the natural qualities of kindness, generosity, and compassion can flower. If we ignore these small weeds, they can take over the garden—especially because, like many weeds, they have a stubborn system of interlinking, hidden roots, which are exposed only by pulling up the small visible shoots. There is an old and instructive story that says if you want to catch a donkey, begin by catching its tail. Then all you have to do is follow the tail to catch the whole beast. The tail may look small, but it is connected to a much larger thing, a larger pattern.

In morning *darshan* the next day, Lee recounted that Yogi Ramsuratkumar once said, "My Father will give Lee whatever he wants." Then Yogi Ramsuratkumar looked up for a moment, looked back at Lee, and said, "My Father will give Lee whatever he *needs*." Lee added, "His Father must have said to Yogi Ramsuratkumar, 'Wait a minute—Lee's not ready for that yet!'"

Yogi Ramsuratkumar laughed with great delight as Lee told this story. Lee went on to say that sometimes he comes to a choice-point and he may go a little way down the wrong road, but he can't go far wrong because there will be stronger and stronger signs that it is the wrong direction. He recalled the old Rolling Stones song, "Under My Thumb."

"Yogi Ramsuratkumar has Lee under his thumb," Lee said gratefully, "so Lee can't go far off course." Yogi Ramsuratkumar laughed again, delighting in the image of Lee under his thumb.

It is strongly evident that Lee feels appreciation and gratitude for being under the thumb of Yogi Ramsuratkumar and for being given only the responsibility and power he can rightly handle. His example provides such a contrast to the struggle I often see in myself and in others when lust for power and control wrestle against our deeper desire for obedience and responsible service. And Yogi Ramsuratkumar is clearly glad for this example that Lee provides. Yogi Ramsuratkumar laughs for many unknown reasons, but one reason seems to be that Lee *is* under his thumb, and there is joy in this, for both of them. This is such a strikingly different attitude toward obedience from the Western fear that obedience will create lifeless robots lost in cults. In the relationship between Lee and Yogi Ramsuratkumar, it is clear that obedience brings deepening life and joy.

During afternoon *darshan* Yogi Ramsuratkumar again asked Lee to speak. In the midst of Lee's talk, Yogi Ramsuratkumar interrupted him just as he had during morning *darshan*. Yogi Ramsuratkumar carried on some other business, then told Lee he could continue. Lee followed Yogi Ramsuratkumar like a dancer following the lead of her partner. He stopped immediately when Yogi Ramsuratkumar asked it, then continued with whole-hearted enthusiasm when he was asked to resume speaking. Yogi Ramsuratkumar seemed to thoroughly enjoy this process: poking a bit at Lee to see if there was any arrogance or attachment to continuity and control of his talk; leading Lee in some unexpected fancy steps in the dance and seeing him follow responsively.

On the last day of our visit, morning *darshan* had a feeling of great ordinariness. Just as Lee demands that his students meet and express the divine in ordinary life, so Yogi Ramsuratkumar was showing us the numinous as it is found in the ordinary. But at the same time that his presence among us had a sense of great ordinariness, it was also miraculous. Many small and large events, both in his company and in his physical absence, reminded us of the respect and awe that are due to him—which he engenders.

One of Yogi Ramsuratkumar's Indian devotees told us that she had gone on a retreat with a small group high in the Himalayas. They began the descent from the retreat house late in the day. She was riding a pony that walked more and more slowly until finally she lost sight of the others. There was hardly any path to follow, and soon she was lost—alone in the midst of the snow and the high mountains, with night approaching. In terror, she called out the Name of Yogi Ramsuratkumar. Within a few minutes, in the midst of this totally uninhabited territory, a man appeared riding on a white horse. He led her down the mountain to safety, then disappeared.

A few weeks later, when the woman visited Yogi Ramsuratkumar, he asked her, "Did you call this Beggar's Name when you were in the Himalayas?"

"Yes, I did," she replied. She told us it was clear to her that the man who guided her to safety was an emanation of Yogi Ramsuratkumar, responding to her call.

Yogi Ramsuratkumar asked Alain to speak again, which he did, briefly, before lowering his large body to kneel before Yogi Ramsuratkumar. Alain came to Yogi Ramsuratkumar in a wheelchair the first year he visited. Yogi Ramsuratkumar laid his hands on Alain's knees repeatedly during that visit, and since then Alain has walked freely, with only the occasional help of a cane. In seeing Alain bend his knees in front of Yogi Ramsuratkumar we were seeing woundedness offered as part of a gift to the master rather than used as an excuse for withholding oneself. It could not have been comfortable for this large man—who is so tall he has to have a *kirta* specially made for him, as there are none so large in the Indian markets—to put his weight on his knees. Yet he knelt and did a full *pranam*, lying full-length on the floor in front of Yogi Ramsuratkumar.

Alain's act was a reminder of the depth of the help that the masters give us. This man came to Yogi Ramsuratkumar almost unable to walk on his own; and through the grace of Yogi Ramsuratkumar, he now not only walks but is able to kneel and bow. The masters teach us both to stand in our own work and to deliver that work into a larger work in which it is subsumed. They teach us to discover ourselves—our own potential—in discovering that which is larger than ourselves, to which we bow.

In the afternoon we lined the roadway by the ashram gate for the last drive-by. There is a way to hold these moments of closing as moments of opening as well: a way to use the acuity of perception they can engender as food for our work as we walk forward, rather than as sentimental, nostalgic tranquilizers. It is the difference between personal sentiment and the objective poignancy of longing.

Yogi Ramsuratkumar's deep eyes penetrated and held each of us in turn, and all of us together, as he drove by. He went straight to the *darshan* hall, while we circumambulated the statue in the temple, then entered the hall to sit in the familiar rows before him.

When Yogi Ramsuratkumar asked Lee to speak, Lee described how that night we would appear to climb into a bus, leave the ashram, and drive to the airport. Yet in truth, he said, we would still and always be sitting at the feet of Yogi Ramsuratkumar. This was the reality, and everything else was just the play of phenomena. I felt the truth of what he said as I sat there: that we could not possibly leave that place, but rather that place, sitting at the feet of Yogi Ramsuratkumar, underlies and is the foundation for all that we do and become.

Lee spoke further about this view of reality. He said that all the tasks we carry out, all our activities and the forms of our lives, are just the play of phenomena. That being the case, in one sense what we do is not that important. Yet at the same time, what we do has real effects; it has consequences and is therefore consequential. In this play of phenomena we can embrace the part that is choreographed for us or we can aggressively intrude upon the pattern of the divine dance. Lee said that through his relationship to Yogi Ramsuratkumar and through speaking about his master in far parts of the world, he has helped to increase the flow of Westerners who come to see Yogi Ramsuratkumar and to visit the ashram. Westerners can be insensitive and aggressive in their approach to a master, and since he has some responsibility for their increased presence, Lee said that he feels compelled to make a plea for responsiveness to the movement of the dance, to the movement of Yogi Ramsuratkumar.

"Never be a burden to the Teacher," he implored passionately. "Never be a burden to the teaching, to the Work."

As the Sudama sisters walked out the door of the *darshan* hall, Yogi Ramsuratkumar rose and leaned on his attendant's arm. He walked down the aisle and out to the waiting car. We watched him with our palms pressed together in the traditional Indian mudra, imprinting in our hearts this last sight. I turned to look at Lee, and as the sound of the car engine disappeared into the distance, Lee made a gesture to Tom, who was operating the video camera.

"Wrap it up," Lee gestured with his hands. Tom turned off the camera. Lee gave him a sign of approval: thumbs up. Then, with a beatific smile, he turned his hands palms down in a gesture of finality: *C'est fini.*

VARANASI

At midnight, almost blown out of the ashram by the winds of a nearby cyclone that drenched us with a driving rain, we began the long drive to the airport in Chennai. From there we would fly to the great holy city on the Ganges, Benares, called by the Indians Varanasi or Kashi. Our bus bounced through pools and puddles as the rain streamed relentlessly across the darkened land. I was grateful for the rain. After days of sun and heat blazing through both our inner and outer worlds, the rain washed away the ash and impurities to reveal what had been created and tempered in that fire. It was not a gentle rain. It was a fierce, pounding, cyclonic rain whirling around and through us like the storm of Yogi Ramsuratkumar ripping away our disguises and pretenses, laying bare the outlines of the land within us, our inner territory. Yet the rain washed us with a tenderness inherent in the soft touch of water. This rain was also Yogi Ramsurakmular's gift to us as he shepherded us on our way.

As we plowed our way through the rain and the night, I remembered a moment in *darshan* one day when a woman from Professor Rangarajan's group brought a gift of shawls and offered it directly to Ma Devaki as she sat on the dais. Ma Devaki made no gesture to receive or decline the gift. She simply looked toward Yogi Ramsuratkumar for his direction. It seemed to me that she was shocked that someone would offer a gift directly to her rather than offer it to Yogi Ramsuratkumar in respect of his authority to decide what should be given and how. In any case, she turned wholly to him. He gave one glance toward her and the woman with the shawls, and waved the gift away.

Apparently, in Yogi Ramsurakumar's estimation, Ma Devaki and Vijayalakshmi did not need the gift, and that was the end of it. They made no ripple around his decision. Not only did they not argue or discuss it with him, they made not the smallest motion to interfere or express personal preference. They did not take the shawls first and then look to Yogi Ramsuratkumar for whether to keep them. They did not try to soften the moment for the woman who had brought the shawls. I noticed this because if I were in a similar situation, even if I wholly accepted Lee's decision for myself, my tendency would be to try to "rescue" the woman and take care of her possible feelings of rejection by smiling or reaching out to her energetically. Ma Devaki and Vijayalakshmi stayed entirely out of the interaction, so that the relationship was only between the woman with the gift and Yogi Ramsuratkumar.

How would Lee's movement, and our movement as a school, accelerate if we moved in this synchronous obedience to him; this smooth, frictionless alignment? I wondered. In the following two weeks this incident, and this question, would return to haunt me as we stumbled through the minefield of the war between our personal preferences and Lee's guidance on our journey through the holy motherland of India.

After our arrival in Varanasi, and following a bounteous dinner at a restaurant known for its excellence in traditional Indian dishes, we gathered on one of the city's main streets, crowded with people, cows, water buffalo, bicycle rickshaws packed with living bodies, and carts carrying dead bodies wrapped in red and gold. Lee wanted to walk through the streets among the nighttime crowds to feel the energy of the city and to visit the burning *ghats* by the river, the sacred Ganges. In earlier trips he swam in the Ganges like the Indians, braving sewage and dead bodies of animals or humans. He told us that tests have shown that no matter what filth or dead carcasses are dumped into the Ganges, the water is pure of disease or bacteria. It is holy water, and even modern scientific testing bows to this fact.

The next day I was up at 5 A.M., grumbling to myself about Lee's arrangement of the day but determined to be on time nevertheless. This was our first sleep in a bed in two nights, and he wanted us to leave the hotel for a boat ride before dawn! Doesn't he ever stop pushing? I asked myself. At 5:15 there was a knock on the door. Lee was sending around a message that we were checking out of the hotel and should bring all our baggage with us. The hotel was so dirty that I hadn't unpacked anything, so I didn't have my usual packrat's nest to clean up. I assumed we would be carrying our baggage on the boat ride and thought what a sight that would be! Westerners floating down the sacred Ganges carrying more belongings on a boat ride than some Indians see in a lifetime.

We met in front of the hotel. For once, I was on time. Someone else was thinking the same thing I was and was more vocal about it. She said to Lee, in a tone of incredulous exasperation at what she perceived to be the absurdity of his behavior, "So we're going to carry all our baggage all over town, everywhere we go today?"

"It'll be fine," was Lee's placid reply.

The other student withdrew with a muttered grumble. Lee directed her and the rest of us to fit three people and all their luggage into each jitney. Well, I thought, that really proved it would be fine! Three adults and all their baggage in one jitney!

At that point I had given up fighting him. I knew there was no way he could fit three adults and all their luggage into a jitney that was a little larger than a bicycle built for two with a motor. But I also knew he was going to do it. I had dragged my baggage through the airports of the U.S. and India; if I had to drag it through the streets of Varanasi maybe I would finally learn to really pack light the next trip.

As I stopped inwardly grousing and looked around at the dawning light, I remembered that as I had awakened I'd heard the Muslim call to prayer. What a riveting sound! The call to prayer resounding through and beyond our sleep and all our daily activities, reminding us that the divine reverberates through all our ordinary life, that its Note can be heard always, if we listen, through and beyond all sounds of earth.

We crammed ourselves and our luggage into the jitneys, which took off at their usual breakneck speed through the streets of Varanasi. When they stopped in a dirt parking lot, we piled out, and I looked around. We were not at the river, though I glimpsed it flowing through the mists not far away. We were in front of a hotel called Temple on the Ganges. Walking in, we heard a rumor that we might have breakfast there at some point.

One look around showed it to be a place so much nicer than the one where we had stayed the previous night as to be of a different species altogether. This place was clean and fresh; the owner, in the yellow robes of a spiritual practitioner, bowed and greeted us with a "*Namaste*." In the bathroom, which was sparkling clean, there were peach-colored bars of soap. Such niceties, which we take for granted in an American motel, are non-existent in the kind of place we had stayed in the night before. Lee's top price would hardly pay for the toilet paper in these rooms.

Just having breakfast there sounded great. We were told to stack our baggage in a downstairs room, as full of bags as Rumpelstiltskin's room of gold. Then we gathered in front of the hotel and walked to the river in the soft dawn light.

As we approached the river, Lee looked up and down the rows of boats. He chose a boatman and began to bargain. The man had a shaved head and a round, friendly face. There was a sense of spiritual practice in him, as there was in the hotel owner, that was quite different from many of the boatmen who looked simply poor and hungry and consumed with the task of daily survival. Lee offered a price that the man refused.

"I have to feed my family," he said.

They continued to bargain. A price was set. Lee paid half then and said he would pay the rest upon our return. The boatman started to decline being paid beforehand. "I trust you," he said to Lee.

Lee shook his head, insisting, and handed him the money. It seemed to me that even with this boatman he might never see again, Lee was teaching. He respected the man's right to a good faith payment, even while he honored the man's trust. This boatman had real goodness about him, and while Lee knew that he himself could be trusted, he would not set a precedent that could encourage the man to let his trust be abused and betrayed in another situation.

We stepped into the boat and settled onto the wooden benches. The boatman pushed us away from the shore, and we were afloat on holy water, surrounded by dim mists, the only sound the creaking of the oars. I thought of how ancient myths described the crossing of the river into Hades, when Demeter braved the underworld to seek her daughter Persephone.

As we floated down the river, the sun—a smooth red disk suspended in a world of gray—began to emerge from the mists behind us. On the riverbank people were walking down long flights of stairs that led straight into the river. Men, women and children took off their clothes and plunged into the cold water. Ahead of us, outlines of temples, trees, towers, markets and funeral pyres began to emerge. Varanasi/Benares/Kashi. The mythical holy city rising out of the morning mist. The ancient transit point between life and death. The holy cliff from which souls leap from the flames of this world into the mysteries of the world of spirit unfettered by body. We were seeing this city, meeting this ancient guiding power, at the moment of transit from night to day, from formless darkness to blazing sun. Varanasi was being born out of the mists as the sun is born each day out of darkness, with the power of original creation. That moment was Lee's gift to us. We were there to receive it because once again he had chosen action over sleep, because he would not stop pushing. And we were there because, regardless of inner complaint, we had followed his instruction instead of fighting with him over a few hours' sleep. I wondered if I would be able to remember that moment the next time I wanted to haggle with him and refuse his gift.

Soon the market boats began to swarm like sharks around us, eager for tourist blood in the form of rupees. Lee's lack of attachment to buying does not make him an easy mark. Soon the boatmen were shouting to each other in Hindi and they were all giving us a wide berth.

"They're telling each other, 'Don't bother. He's a cheap bastard!'" Lee interpreted with a laugh.

We did buy from one boat before they started ignoring us—a boat selling dewali lamps: small clay bowls holding *ghee* or oil and a wick and decorated with fresh flowers. Traditionally, these candles are lit and sent floating down the Ganges with a prayer. The boatman wanted something like twenty rupees for each candle: about fifty cents; not much to pay for a prayer! Lee said he would pay only five rupees (about twelve cents). The man tried to bargain, but Lee was adamant. After Lee refused his offer of seven or eight rupees, the boatman rowed away. Lee let him go without comment.

A few minutes later the boat pulled up beside us again. Rowing away was just a test to see if Lee really meant it. Lee nodded his head in a satisfied manner as he saw the boat pulling alongside us.

"Let people learn from that!" he exclaimed. "If people don't get that lesson . . .!"

To me it seemed the lesson was more than a practical example of how to bargain in the Indian culture—of sticking to a Baul beggar's price rather than paying tourist prices just because we could. As the boatman came near, Lee muttered, "I could have gotten them for three rupees, but I didn't want to push him that hard." He was demonstrating the principle of non-attachment. He was ruled neither by greed for the lowest possible price, nor by grasping for the candles regardless of cost. He was willing to pay a certain price—a reasonable Indian price, but not a tourist price. If we couldn't have the candles at that price, we would make our prayers without them. At the same time, he was illustrating something about standing by our principles. If we work with integrity to spiritual principles, the things that are rightfully part of our work eventually come to us, just as the boat with the candles swung around in the current and returned to us. Lee simply sat there doing nothing but holding a clear intention about what he was willing to pay.

These *dewali* lamps were the only thing we saw in the market boats that had a strong meaning for me—a sense of direct relationship to our voyage on the Ganges, of rightness that they should come to us that morning. And that boatman was the only one who returned to Lee.

Once the price had been set, the lamps practically leapt out of the seller's boat into our hands. Soon nearly all the women had lamps ready to sail. Lee looked around.

"Don't any of the men want one?" he asked.

This was permission for anyone who was still wondering if Lee was just indulging the women. In seconds almost everyone in our boat had a lamp, and the second boat was busy buying. The boatman lit our lamps as he gave them to us, and we set them afloat on the sacred Ganges, each with a silent prayer. I heard later that someone asked Lee if he wanted one, and he answered, "I don't need one. My prayers are already taken care of."

One of the party had not yet set his lamp into the river. "I can't decide what to wish," he said. "Can I make more than one wish?" He had a flower mala also ready to throw into the river. "I could make lots of wishes, one on each flower," he added.

"If you get greedy," Lee replied, "you don't get any of your wishes. Make one wish with total intention and concentration, and that's all you need."

We floated on down the river, where colorful saris were being washed and laid out on the bank to dry. Sadhus were meditating in temples and towers as we passed. We were nearing the burning *ghats* where we could see smoke rising from a pyre.

Over and over in traveling with Lee I have seen the value of following his intuitive sense of direction and timing. If we allow him to move without interruption or distortion of his direction, we suddenly discover he is entering the gate of a hidden garden or revealing to us possibilities we never imagined. That morning he had captured for us the single moment at which the heart of that holy river could be seen unveiled.

When we arrived back at the hotel, Purna sat at a long table with the hotel owner, and they began to make a list of everyone in our group. They moved patiently through some arduous arrangements, taking account of various individuals' requirements, from one woman's need for a ground floor room because of her broken foot to someone else's request for an Indian toilet. Gradually it dawned on me that we were not just pausing at the hotel for breakfast, we were staying there! This seemed miraculous. I had never heard of Lee staying in such a place in all his trips to India. Of course we had stayed in lovely accommodations at Yogi Ramsuratkumar's ashram, but that was Yogi's gift to us and to all who come to stay there. I hadn't expected his gift to be so lavish once we were on the road.

Just before we'd left his ashram, Yogi Ramsuratkumar had asked Lee the details of our journey: the departure and arrival times of our plane flights, our lodgings in each city, and the date and time of our return to the United States. Lee gave him all the information he asked for and told him that we did not yet know where we would stay in Varanasi. Yogi Ramsuratkumar closed his eyes in silence for a moment and then remarked with assurance, "My Father says all will be arranged [in Varanasi]." Clearly, Yogi Ramsuratkumar had not just meant we would have a roof in the rain. He had meant we would be royally cared for. Somehow we were being given this place at a price Lee was willing to pay.

We ate breakfast on the rooftop of the hotel, surrounded by flowering plants and looking out over the Ganges. At this breakfast, and at most or all of the subsequent meals, Lee called continuously on Ted, one of his students, to handle everything at Lee's direction. My recollection is that it was Ted who had handled the boarding passes in Chennai and failed to get mine, prompting Lee to declare that he himself would "handle *everything* from now on." Ted's perseverance in the face of failure quickly regained the master's trust.

At this first breakfast at the hotel, Lee sent Ted for various items. When, after we had waited longer than we had anticipated for the food, someone suggested to Lee that Ted could check when the food would be ready, Lee refused. "No!" he said. "We can just wait."

The principle of hospitality dictates that we make no demands, even from a restaurant chef, and Lee was being pristinely obedient to this principle. He let Ted get us our drinks, but beyond that he would not allow any pressure to be placed on the kitchen and hotel staff. We would eat whenever the food arrived.

Finally everyone was served. The food was delicious, and Ted also sat to eat. Watching Ted, who seldom got to eat with the rest of us because of the heavy demands Lee was making on him, I saw the different level of food that is created between master and student when the student begins to show reliability.

After intensive negotiations, Lee hired bicycle rickshaws to take us from the hotel into town. The rickshaw drivers wanted twenty rupees, but Lee was adamant about paying only fifteen; if no one would take us for that amount, we would walk. Many of the drivers refused his price, but five were willing to accept it and we piled into their carts. The road took us up a long slow hill, and the rickshaw drivers were working hard pedaling. Sometimes they would get off and push the bicycles that pulled the carts. I thought what a lot of work it was for fifteen rupees.

The road leveled off and we were in the center of town, in the midst of the markets. As we clambered out, Lee handed the first driver twenty rupees—the amount the drivers had originally wanted—instead of the fifteen for which he had stubbornly fought. The driver looked at him questioningly. Did he want change?

"It was a long way," Lee said, slapping the driver affectionately on the arm, and he turned to pay twenty rupees to the others as well.

Every moment in our daily life is a hologram of a larger life; a slice of the Real in dimensions we can see, with all the further dimensions implicit. The lesson in that small interaction burned its imprint into me. The drivers who refused to surrender to Lee in the small matter of five rupees received nothing. The drivers who, knowing nothing of him as a teacher, simply meeting him on the street, were willing to surrender in this tiny way received not only the fifteen rupees they were promised but the original twenty as gift. When we obey and practice surrender even in the smallest way, we receive back as gift far more than what we lost. This, of course, is not the reason to obey and sacrifice; to do so for this reason is not really letting go. Nevertheless, it is one of the incontrovertible laws of a compassionate universe, and we saw it in action among the rickshaw drivers on the streets of Varanasi that morning.

I had never seen a dead body before, let alone a burning body. When we stood at the burning *ghats*, what struck me was the ordinariness of death. The body that burns is in one way no different from the pieces of wood that make up its flaming pyre. What makes the difference between the matter of wood and the matter of a human body is the degree of the divine which is able to enter this matter—the degree of conscious receiving and expression of divine energy. Once the spirit has departed, the atoms of bone and the atoms of wood both return to the same state, moving from solid form to vapor and ash. It is the spirit that is extraordinary; the body of matter by itself is inert and holds nothing of interest. All the distractions of this world are only trickery, because what attracts us is the glimpse, through all them, of the living Lord. It is only the ruse of the veil of illusion that makes us believe we will find Him in separative indulgence rather than in the sacrifice and service through which He is revealed to us as omnipresent, radiating through all things, yet trapped and limited by none.

It was not the blackened, burning skulls or the feet sticking out of the pyre at fierce, sharp angles that I found most revelatory. This seemed most ordinary—the natural expression of the ending of a cycle. It was the sense of souls and spirit moving, releasing, and recombining in the air just above and beyond the burning pyres that held my attention. I had never felt a clearer confirmation that death as we Westerners conceive of it, as a tragic ending, does not exist. On the contrary, death is an ecstatic leap of life into the next octave, beyond our sight. I realized that the burning pyres are not a center of mourning but of celebration, in the deepest sense, as life in the human realm lifts into the dimensions just beyond our grasp and begins anew. This is the gift of the burning *ghats*: this fiery illumination of what is most real.

The next day we were hosted by old friends of Lee's, the Mehtas, a family of silk merchants who use a portion of their wealth to support village organizations first established by Mahatma Gandhi to educate and empower the Indian people. After touring the silk factory, we crowded into taxis and drove off into the countryside. Mr. Mehta was taking us to an agricultural village to see something of traditional Indian village life. We stopped along the way and Mr. Mehta got out for something. Someone in our group asked Lee why we were stopping.

"I don't know. Mr. Mehta's in charge," Lee answered. "For today, he's my guru. The way I am with him today, that's how I want people to be with me. I do what he says. No questions, no complaining, no grumbling, no recommendations, no opinions. Just follow [what he says]. Just follow."

It sounded so simple. Yet, as Lee spoke, I thought of the barrage of reactions and opinions that he was constantly receiving from all of us: about the length of the boat ride, the plan of the day, the choice of breakfast menu, the number of people in the taxi, the amount to pay the rickshaw driver, how long to stay at the market, when to go to dinner. It was endless! I realized that if we could follow the simple advice he had just given, the trip would be transformed. It would shift from a continual and obvious source of irritation for our spiritual master to an exercise in obedience that would flower in ways we couldn't imagine or discover except by acting, by carrying out his direction with consistency.

Our entire trip to India was in one sense simply the backdrop for Lee's communication of the teaching. Even our relationship to Yogi Ramsuratkumar was mediated through Lee as our teacher. Each day and moment was a chance to use the shock of a foreign culture and the upheaval of our daily routines as a way to open ourselves to hear his teaching in a new way. In another sense, India itself was the teaching that Lee offered us; and Yogi Ramsuratkumar was the culmination of this offering.

The next day Lee went into another tirade—this time about our greed, addictive relationship to caffeine, and attachment to comfort. On previous mornings we had shared a group breakfast at a highly reduced rate, but this day the chef was sick. Hearing that the hotel owner was struggling to handle his guests' breakfast demands, Lee cancelled our usual arrangement and told people there would be no group meal planned until dinner. Later in the day he reported, "One third of the people in our group bought breakfast, and it cost more than a meal for the whole group. We are with a bunch of babies!" He was irate.

People had paid for their breakfasts with their personal money, and it would seem from a conventional point of view that the decision to have breakfast was their personal choice and none of Lee's business. But from the perspective of the guru principle, it was Lee's job to lead us and teach us to function as one coherent, living organism. Eating together as one body is part of the method by which we build this unified creation. When he had chosen to eliminate the day's breakfast for the group, he was creating an opportunity for the group as a whole to deal with hunger as a part of *sadhana*, as a method of building a different level of shared energy than sharing physical food. He did not purposely take food from us when it was available; he simply accepted the movement of the universe—the fact that the chef was sick—and aligned with that movement to create a different opportunity. For some people to choose to eat independently created holes in the matrix of the group activity, the group's *sadhana*. In addition, Lee was paying energetically for the entire trip, for all of us, as the spiritual master. Although people may have taken the rupees out of their own wallets, the cost to Lee when there was fragmentation in the group was far more than the rupees.

We were in a city and a nation where many people, including children, were constantly hungry or starving. Lee was giving us a chance to taste this hunger; to participate in the realities of India rather than to view Indian culture from the outside as a tourist. He was giving us the chance to glimpse the culture's heights and depths—from sublime spiritual traditions to the claws of hunger. Giving up a meal was one more way in which he delivered us deeper into the culture, as he had done by lodging his group in cheap Indian hotels, by wearing Indian dress, and by riding close to the sounds, smells and pace of the street in bicycle rickshaws. Through entering the matrix of the culture in that way we ate something that Westerners cannot touch, let alone ingest, by riding only in auto-jitneys and cars, eating in fine restaurants, and sitting in first-class seats.

The following night we were invited to a private performance by a *tabla* player who once gave concerts around the world, but who withdrew from the world of fame and fortune when he felt it was

291

robbing his playing of the original spiritual focus. When the *tabla* player arrived, the Mehtas gestured unobtrusively to us to move from our seats on platforms to the floor. The performer would play sitting on the floor, and in respect for the master we would not sit higher than he did. Some of us were slow to recognize this request. We had a kind of stolid self-centeredness that made us dense and insensitive to shifts in the space around us. This was particularly irritating to Lee, it seemed, as we ignored the demand for acute attention and group awareness and breached the laws of hospitality at the same time.

Once we were all seated, the concert began. The *tabla* player played as if the drums were alive, as if he were making love with them. He caressed them, pounded them, drew a myriad of unexpected sounds and rhythms out of them. The first piece, he said, was about fundamental rights; the next about the moods between man and woman as they worked and talked together. His playing evoked moods of silence, of sharing, of dissonance, of love. Finally he moved into the last piece, about a hunting lion. In this piece his drumming seemed to draw a direct line of connection between our spiritual nature and our animal existence. In the rhythms and passion of his drumming these polar realities were intimately linked; they became not separate, but one. Through a totally different medium than our own he was making a statement about—evoking the reality of—the tantric foundation of life: that spirit lives and expresses not divorced from the body but through the body. As he evoked this mood of the royal lion hunting, he opened a space that invited energies from a higher plane. He was transported, shifted into other frames of reference from those we can normally see; but through his playing we glimpsed these realms. Then suddenly he stopped, and the journey was over. The energies or deities that had brushed by us returned to other planes. We went into the next room, where the Mehtas welcomed us to a dinner of traditional Indian dishes.

At breakfast the next morning, the day we were scheduled to travel to Delhi on our way to Rishikesh, Lee mentioned that he wanted to stop in the shop of an expert stone carver to look for a Hanuman statue he wanted to give to Purna. "But don't let everybody find out and follow me!" he said. "There'll be thirty people buying whatever I buy! Don't let anybody follow me and get in my way!"

Bryan, one of Lee's younger students, said with some diffidence that he had been thinking of going to the stone carver's shop also. "But I guess I'll go someplace else instead," he added with a smile, "so as not to get in your way."

"Bryan never gets in my way," Lee declared emphatically to the whole table. "Bryan, you can go with me anytime. You never get in my way."

As I thought back, I realized I had never heard Bryan give an opinion or make a complaint to Lee during the entire trip. It is not just what he said, but his energy that was alert, sensitive and responsive. He was neither following Lee blindly nor interrupting Lee's activity. Using Bryan as an example, Lee was giving us another hint about obedience. Obedience is not the same as following indiscriminately. It does not mean trying to be clones of the spiritual master. It involves being wholly ourselves—our true selves—and learning from and actively serving the master and the Work he serves.

RISHIKESH

We arrived in Rishikesh the following day in time to settle into rooms at a local ashram and go out to a restaurant for a traditional Indian dinner. As we walked back to the ashram I said to Lee, "I am so grateful for the opportunity to go on this trip to

India. And yet I see that my unconsciousness gets in the way. How can I express my gratitude? How can I pay back something for what I have been given?"

"Just learn something and take it back with you," Lee replied.

From all our mistakes, we have the chance to learn. And what we learn, we have the opportunity and obligation to bring back to share.

Before I was even dressed the next morning I got a message that Lee wanted to meet with several of us. As we gathered, the air was pulsing with energy. It was clear that he had some strong communication to make. But he didn't begin by roaring at us, as I had expected. He said, with calm irony, yet almost pleading, "Imagine that I'm your spiritual master. Indulge me in that fantasy for a moment. Imagine that I'm your guru instead of just some guy you are traveling with. I want to ask something from each of you." He turned to me. "Would you stop being a Good Samaritan? Stop offering suggestions; stop trying to fix things; stop trying to take care of everybody on the trip. It's doing more harm than good and it's getting in the way of what I am trying to do."

Chögyam Trungpa Rinpoche once said, "Sometimes help is no help." What appears on the surface as altruistic behavior can be just as much in the way as outright rebellion when the behavior is motivated by compulsive and manipulative dynamics rather than by resonance to the teacher's purpose and direction.

Although I sensed the principle Lee was addressing, I was bewildered as to how I had been enacting this dynamic when I had been consciously trying to follow his lead. Later in the day I asked him for an example.

"Like the time at the airport when you tried to go find the doll's shoe," he reminded me. "The energy is moving onward—and you won't just let it go. You interrupt the flow to 'help.' It doesn't help; it gets in the way and starts the upset all over again."

294

He was referring to an unforgettable incident that I had nonetheless managed to erase from memory until he painfully recalled it for me. We were at the small airport in Varanasi, in line for a security check before entering the boarding area for our plane to Delhi. When we got to the checkpoint, each adult went into a tiny booth where a guard of the same sex did a quick body check. Then we waited in line again to put our luggage through the x-ray machine. This was the only airport check we had been through in all our travels where the guards and airport personnel were rigidly authoritarian and unfriendly. They barked at us if we moved too fast or too slow. They pushed us back if a toe inched over the white line where we waited our turn for the x-ray. The airport was small, and my sense was that they were not used to such a large group and were angry at us for overloading their system with too many people at once.

Finally we had all passed through the checkpoint and sat down to wait for our plane. One of the women had bought a doll to take home to her child. She noticed that one of the doll's shoes had fallen out of her pack. When she mentioned it to me and I heard the disappointment in her voice, against my better judgment I tried to help.

"I'll look for the shoe," I told her magnanimously. "Do you know where you had it last?"

"In the line," she replied.

I rushed back toward the guards, who were visibly at their limit with these hordes of unwieldy Americans overrunning their quiet routine. I leaned over the x-ray machine, scouring the floor for the shoe. There was no sign of it. My energy body was already barreling toward the guards to ask to go back through the checkpoint to look for the shoe, but my physical body was resisting.

I was already thinking it wasn't a good idea when I heard Lee call my name in a muted, focused shout that reached me yet slid through the space so that other people hardly heard it. Instantly I knew that annoying the guards with *any* special request, let alone trying to go through their precious system in reverse, was definitely not a good idea. As I disengaged from high gear I saw that the woman who had lost the shoe had already moved through her own annoyance. She had accepted her loss and gone on to something else, while I was about to bring the wrath of the entire airport staff to a full boil and draw it toward our whole group. I sat down meekly, inwardly criticizing Lee because he thought I was actually going to carry out such an absurd idea as going back through the checkpoint. Within a few minutes I had conveniently forgotten the entire incident.

As Lee recalled this example of my constant attempts to "fix things," for an instant I glimpsed the entire scene from his point of view instead of mine. From this view I could see that my compulsion to fix, help, correct, and add to the flow of movement is chronic, if not incessant. His example was only one incident, so dramatic that I remembered it vividly once reminded. I knew there were numerous other such incidents, less striking but tremendously irritating and obstructive to the flow of Lee's movement, like sand particles between wheel bearings that can eventually block the wheels from rolling altogether. So that was what he meant by being a "Good Samaritan"—being "generous" in a way that truly isn't.

After breakfast Lee wanted to walk along the Ganges. "I want to put my feet in the Ganges," were his words. We walked with him through the markets until we reached the sandy beach that ran along the edge of the river. We scrambled over and around large rocks that were scattered across the sand. By many of them sadhus were cooking breakfast over a small fire or drying clothes after a dip in the Ganges. It was true, as we had heard, that the river was dramatically different here—clean and clear, its blue-green waters carrying the snowy cold and the vitality of the high mountains from which it flowed. Lee took off his sandals and walked barefoot along the beach. Many of the rest of us did the same. It was a lovely morning, permeated with the sacred gift of the holy water flowing past us. However, some of our party decided to go shopping in the markets rather than to continue following Lee along the beach.

After they had left, Lee was highly critical of their decision to separate. "It's impatience," he commented. "People can't stand an instant of self-reflection; a moment that isn't filled with self-centered activity, greed, and grasping."

After walking for some time, Lee told us that he was looking for the cave where a particular spiritual teacher had lived, whom he had visited twelve years ago. That teacher had died, but the cave was still there, and his devotees still lived or gathered near it. Someone in our group had seen just such a cave as Lee was describing, and most of the adults set out with Lee to find it. It was the cave of Mastram Baba, a little known but very highly considered tantric guru. Lee found the cave and sat there for quite a while, conversing with one of the sadhus and accepting a bowl of steaming sweet rice *prasad*. His cranky mood dissolved like mist in the morning sun. After some time we left to reconnect with the others.

On Friday afternoon Lee gave a public talk in a large conference room at the ashram where we were staying. The room was full: a mixture of Western travelers and spiritual seekers and a few Indians. In answer to a question about obedience, Lee made a distinction of crucial importance. He said there is a great difference between saying no to the guru's direction because we don't want to do it—we don't feel like it—and saying no based in integrity to our essential being. If the guru directs us to do something that is in dissonance with our core being, our integrity in refusing to do it is a gift we offer the guru. The guru's response to such a decision can help us discern power hungry false gurus from real teachers. A real teacher will respect such a decision and honor the integrity of the student's essential being, while someone hungry for power will try to force or manipulate compliance. Again Lee was deepening the distinction between blind following and living obedience.

Lee complained repeatedly on this trip that we were not working as a group. We were all so absorbed in self-reference and selfish attention that we didn't notice what was needed for the movement and harmony of the group. Our attachments and desires interrupted our responsiveness to the teacher's direction so he could not build the momentum needed to lift our work into a place of higher possibility. The basic principle that we had not embraced was "radical reliance on the guru." We Westerners are so terrified of the idea that we might lose our individual identity that we are almost oblivious to the possibility that participation in committed relationship and group work might be the avenue through which we discover and live our deepest essence.

Toward the end of our trip, someone asked Lee what he most wanted covered in the report of the India trip in *Tawagoto*, the community journal. I couldn't hear the exact words of his answer from where I was sitting, but his energy was electrifying. People near him were practically brushing sparks out of their hair. The communication I sensed rather than actually heard was: "Write about failure to practice! Write about adults who think they are spiritual students having to cater to every little demand for comfort that the animal makes. If the body has the least little desire, people have to leap to fill it. And if it isn't filled, they are whining and complaining. Write about being oblivious to the most basic protocol and principles of our work. Write about the refusal to sacrifice even our most petty desires so we could build some energy for work. We think we're going to die if we don't have drinking water for an hour or we don't get lunch. And we think we're spiritual warriors! Ha!"

His communication complete, Lee looked peacefully out the window or turned to make a joke. I remembered once seeing Arnaud Desjardins shout at a student with such fierce anger that Arnaud's face was glowing red and he was almost leaping out of his seat, yet a moment later was looking utterly serene. The anger and fierceness of the teachers seems to be of a qualitatively different character from ordinary human anger. It lives in the realm of love. The quality of rejection that often colors anger is absent. Their anger seems to be a focused sword intended to pierce twisted defenses around essence—a sword intended to free rather than to harm—and they can release it and step into a state of calmness or laughter in an instant because they have no attachment to that anger.

TRANSMUTATION

We drove on toward Delhi, where we would board our flight for the United States. After about seven hours of traveling, as dusk was gathering, we reached the outskirts of the city. About a half-hour from the airport, traffic suddenly slowed, then came to a complete stop. Our bus was wedged between trucks and other buses crowded with Indian travelers on the regular routes. After a few moments the air in the bus began to thicken with exhaust from the surrounding vehicles. Soon we were all coughing. The bus couldn't move; the stalled vehicles fitted together as tightly as a jigsaw puzzle. We closed our windows, but the exhaust still seeped in rapidly and we no longer had outside air to dilute it. Coughs rippled through the bus as the fumes thickened. We could see the gray smokiness of the air we were breathing in the light from the street lamps. It was an intense confrontation with the foundational physical needs of our bodies.

As we complained in tones ranging from joking to panic, Lee leapt up. In the haranguing drawl of a classic southern Baptist preacher, he began a sermon about how five of Purna's uncles and some of his own relatives had died in gas chambers in the concentration camps. Now we knew a little of what that felt like, he said. If those people could face the gas chambers with dignity, we could show a little dignity in the face of some temporary vehicle exhaust. He didn't want to hear any more complaining. His speech was an odd, even poignant, combination of rude, dark humor and pristine principles of action in the face of the vicissitudes of human life.

The combination created in me a discomfort more disturbing than the choking exhaust. Stories of Gurdjieff tell about how he would create a situation where a student was caught between "the yes and the no"—where both the level of commitment and the level of resistance were deeply exposed and the student stood at the center point of the naked conflict between them. Gurdjieff called this "putting the student in galoshes."

What Lee was doing was somewhat different, but the flavor was reminiscent of these stories. As I had seen him do many times, he had, in a few words, touched such varied and even apparently contradictory dimensions that I didn't know whether to laugh or cry, whether to be repulsed at his partially comic allusion to death through genocide or to be penetrated and softened by the compassionate suggestion that we could let this moment of physical distress become a doorway into real feeling for human suffering— the suffering of both the executed and the executioners. In a few words he had linked us, mostly WASPs and affluent American Jews, with both those who died breathing gas instead of air and those who are so protected that they know nothing of such things—those who may participate in genocide if not by action then by inaction and the attachment to comfortable ignorance.

As the mood of complaint shifted, a new energy opened. Someone called from the back of the bus, "Ask Lee if we should chant the Name of Yogi Ramsuratkumar." Undoubtedly, many people had already been turning to Yogi Ramsuratkumar inwardly, as his presence permeated much of the trip, not just in moments of crisis but in all activity. Yet to chant his Name aloud as a unified body opens the door to an exponential increase in the power he is always generating and making available.

We began to chant, coughing as we sang, the fumes still pouring into the bus. But the chant was steady, even as the coughing continued. Yogi Ramsuratkumar's Name did not miraculously stop the fumes or start the traffic, but something that was more instructive than either took place. The fumes were still pouring in. I could see them and smell them. The traffic was still motionless, one vehicle wedged against the next, while currents of exhaust joined into an inescapable sea. Yet the effects of the fumes began to change. Gradually our coughing lessened. I could see that I was not breathing cleaner air, yet my lungs were experiencing an increase in oxygen. Chanting the Name of Yogi Ramsuratkumar as a group body was obviously changing our attitude, but it was changing more than our emotional relationship to the circumstance; it was changing the quality of breath. What entered our lungs as poison was being received in increasing proportion as life-giving air. This was transmutation—the process of alchemy.

As the trip to India ended, I knew that unless I fed the realizations of the trip through daily action they would fade and eventually would be lost. Even if I acted with consistent intention, there would inevitably be periods when the inspiration I felt so acutely at the time would dissolve like mist in my hands, like paths that slowly lose themselves in swampland.

At a seminar in Montpelier in France the previous summer, someone had asked Lee how to regain the experience of a state of grace when we feel we have lost touch with it. His answer was simple: "Follow the teachings of the master with integrity, regardless of the feeling or sensation." If we do this faithfully, eventually the experience of the state of grace will return. In that moment of shining inspiration, I knew that at some point such moments of emptiness would follow. All I could do at those times was remember and follow Lee's teaching.

CHAPTER 8

AT HOHM: LESSONS AND REFLECTIONS

~

I n 1999, shortly after the beginning of the new year, we traveled to San Francisco for a week-long teaching visit hosted by
a group of Lee's students. We drove west in one of our big fif-
teen-person vans, packed with people and luggage. It was a two-day
journey, with Lee driving the entire way.

When we reached the community household in San
Francisco, we were met by an ashram resident who had come by
plane from Arizona. She was a long-term practitioner who had
been through cancer surgery several months earlier. Just before
leaving for California, she had received news from her doctor that
new lesions had been found, this time in her lungs. When she met
us at the door, she was visibly shaken, her face pale from shock,
even while she was clearly and courageously facing this new challenge. Lee gave her a warm hug, yet treated her with an absolute
absence of sentimentality. Later he told her, "You have to live as if
you are already dead. If you had been doing that since the first
diagnosis, you would not be feeling this kind of shock now. You
have to let go of all attachment, even your attachment to being

alive. You have to live as if you are already dead," he repeated. "Then whatever life brings you, you can be grateful, without grasping or attachment."

~

In March of 1999, Andrew Cohen and several of his students visited our Arizona ashram. The highlight of Andrew's visit was a pristine explication of the *dharma*, which he presented as an After Dinner Talk. His passionate call to practice echoed the call of the teacher in every culture and in every age, reminding us that the impossible is possible. Near the end of his talk, someone asked if he had any feedback for us as a community—any observations that might be useful to our work.

"My observation is that you are too casual," Andrew responded. "I think I won't say more than that at this time."

We were left to extrapolate from his comment, to use it to sharpen our own self-observation as individuals and as a community. There were certainly many instances in which we could see the validity of his observation: the tendency to slouch in the *darshan* hall when we gathered for talks rather than for formal meditation; the excessive familiarity with which we sometimes treated Lee; an air of carelessness about the property that contrasted strongly with the meticulous attention to physical detail on Andrew's own ashram.

Andrew's observation reminded me of Judy Lief's comment in relation to the heavy demands of spiritual work: "You have to set some priorities." In a similar way, she was also confronting whatever it is in us, as individuals and as a community, that is caught in a casual sloth, a lack of precise and rigorous choices about the moments and spaces we create in our spiritual life.

The opportunity to receive feedback and commentary from outside observers is always highly useful to a spiritual community as a whole, as well as to individual practitioners, as we continually seek ways to look into our own blind spots.

~

In the spring of 1999 the Baul Theater Company gave a public performance of "The Magician," a play based on Isaac Bashevis Singer's well-known novel, *The Magician of Lublin*, to several hundred people at a local playhouse. "The Magician" is a story of transformation, of a man who in confronting tragedy and his own weaknesses moves from a life of selfish desire to a life of total service. Lee had allowed only a few months to prepare the production, which included elaborate sets complete with antiques loaned by local antique shops, a klezmer band composed of community members who had to learn traditional Jewish music, and chanting of traditional Jewish prayers in Hebrew, which required exacting training in precise pronunciations and particular harmonic relationships.

All of this was only the backdrop for the play itself, which involved complicated characterization and innumerable set changes. One of the women in the company created an evocative set using scaffolding as a matrix for some of the scenes, a screen and silhouettes for others, and a narrow raised ledge for the band, which was to be visible during certain scenes. After all this work, the final performance was, by Lee's choice, to be only one night.

The night arrived and the company's presentation was inspired to the point of becoming magical. The living world in which one man's transformation could take place was evoked upon the stage, and we in the audience became immersed in that transformative process. After the performance a man walked up to the leading actor and told him that the impact of the play was so deep that it had reconnected him to his original Jewish roots, and for the first time in years he intended to reengage religious life and practice.

From a rational point of view, it would seem that a play that was the product of such intense work might at least be offered for several days. Yet it was clear that Lee had specific and intensely important purposes in limiting the final performance to one night. It seemed he was not as concerned with having the greatest number of physical viewers as he was with making a communication whose focused power could emanate out into subtle realms, speaking truth into the ethers in which human life takes place and from which we draw impressions and perceptions.

Later I read that after asking his students to make immense efforts in preparing a complex presentation of "The Struggle of the Magicians," Gurdjieff ordered them to destroy the elaborate set into which they had put so much work. It seemed to me that Gurdjieff was demonstrating a similar principle of focusing effort into a concentrated presentation and then abruptly and absolutely closing and sealing the space in which that work and that transmission had taken place.

~

ME: One thing I've observed . . .

Lee [interrupts by singing gaily and gleefully in a Bob Dylan sound-alike, to the tune of Dylan's "Ballad of a Thin Man"]: Something is happening here and you don't know what it is, do you, Madame Rose? [Laughter]

ME: Well, one thing I've seen . . .

Lee [interrupts and continues singing]: You walk into the room, your liberal agenda in your hand. [Laughter] You see your spiritual master listening to Rush Limbaugh and you blanch! Something is happening here and you don't know what it is, do you, Madame Rose? [Much laughter]

❧

During the periods between seminars and band gigs, those of us living at La Ferme de Jutreau for the summer gathered for meals at the long dining tables in the barn. After the meal Lee would often spend a relaxed half-hour sharing jokes, gossip, and teaching lessons ranging in mood from fierce rapier attacks to the most gentle reminders, and even an occasional compliment. On one occasion, as he began to expound on over-permissive parenting and its consequences, blaming permissiveness for the increasingly destructive and violent actions of some youth in modern society, I launched into passionate debate.

"Alice Miller says that, in every case she investigated, the source of the individual's violence was in violent abuse suffered as an infant and child, in the state of primal vulnerability," I asserted with vehemence. "There's a strong body of research that supports her findings. Over-permissiveness is certainly an issue that parents have to face; but the cause of violence in youth is violent abuse of the child, which our society allows and denies is even happening."

Lee laughed and ceded victory graciously. "You're right, of course. You're always right." He turned to the others seated around him. "How can I fight Janet's facts?" he asked.

Something about winning a victory over my teacher did not feel comfortable to me, even while I fervently believed in my argument and wanted his agreement. "No, I'm not always right," I demurred, with some confusion.

Just then, when I was least expecting it, Lee proceeded to proclaim some further political viewpoint housed in the world view of the far right. Immediately I leapt again into passionate retort.

Lee laughed and gestured toward me like a circus ringleader calling attention to an entering act.

"Look at that," he commented, with an amused air. "It's like a mask she takes on and off. One minute she's relaxed, laughing, present in relationship—and the next minute, you just push that button, and this thing comes over her, like a cloud coming over the sun!" His enigmatic laugh rolled against the armor I donned so instantaneously at the first hint of political battle.

The entire incident left me with a memorable bodily impression of my political self that was startlingly different from my lifelong inner vision of that self as a kind of glowing Joan of Arc committed to principle and compassionately dedicated to the betterment of humanity. Lee had given me a tangible experience of that self as combative, highly armored, intent on warring with other points of view, and extremely rigid. The content of my argument might be based in exacting research, but the energetic entity that was using and controlling that argument had been exposed in its essentially divisive character. The contrast between the friendly and humorous relaxation I felt in one instant and the emotionally charged, separative rigidity that I felt when Lee triggered my political stance was inescapable. I found myself remembering Yvan Amar's teaching on this same subject two years before, when he had observed with quiet objectivity, "But essentially, left and right, it's all the same. The only real difference is a life dedicated to spiritual reality, to living the teaching."

Lessons repeat themselves from various angles and through various events until we begin to accept and use them and show ourselves ready for the next level of instruction.

Framed in the kitchen of the Arizona ashram is a saying: STUBBORN AND INDEPENDENT DOES NOT EQUAL STRONG AND CONFIDENT.

~

What is it to become a devotee? I say "become" because to be a devotee is something that we grow into, and this process is perhaps never complete. To be a devotee was never on my list of goals; however, I considered myself a radical thinker, open to possibilities and responsibilities not taught or even necessarily respected by the common Western culture. Idealist, political organizer, feminist—none of these included becoming a devotee. Why then had this goal which I would in fact have scorned earlier in my life become a focalizing principle?

It is as if we humans look out of a wounded eye. Much of what we see about ourselves and the world is through the distortions of this eye. In the company of a teacher, sometimes the field of the teacher's vision permeates our own so strongly that we see for a moment a truer vision of the world and ourselves within it. Sometimes the actions of the teacher, either intentionally or simply through the spontaneous synchronicity of the movement of the universe, bring us into sharp confrontation with those distortions. At times we have to choose between trust of our own view and trust of the teacher's. Yet at the core of each of us is the view of unwounded innocence, the vision of the eye of the divine seeded at the center of each being, each fragment of the universe, the parts of One Body. When Jesus said, "If thine eye be single, then shall thy whole body be full of light," perhaps he spoke of the singularity of vision that arises when we allow this unwounded core, this unitive reality, to penetrate us so deeply that there is an essential realignment—so that we see with that wholeness. Then we see not "through a glass dimly, but . . . face to face."

⁓

JANET: After all these years I am still struggling with the experience of scarcity—scarcity in relation to attention, or food, or love. How do you move beyond the illusion of scarcity?

LEE: You're asking the wrong person. I'm in scarcity all the time.

JANET: What do you do about it?

LEE: Nothing.

⁓

On January 9, 2000, Lee's mother died. She had been consciously approaching death for weeks, so it was not a surprise. She was in her mid-nineties and, finally, after a great deal of struggle with the desire to live, she was ready to die. Her home was thousands of miles from the ashram, and Lee sent a woman from the community to care for her night and day during the last months of her life. This woman said that in the last two days of her life Lee's mother was so full of love that she could not contain herself. Many times in previous days she had complained about pain, about being old, about fear of death. All that fell away in the last days. She would say only, "I'm so full of love, I don't know how to give it all, it's so much. I'm so full of love!"

Early that morning, just before dawn broke over the Arizona desert plains and mountains, we received the call that she had died. We went to the central *puja* in Lee's house, the *puja* with the *vigraha* (empowered statue) of Yogi Ramsuratkumar. We sang chants and read the death prayer. After three readings of the prayer, there was a vivid sense that her transition out of the body was complete; she was gone.

Lee responded to her death with an essential equanimity that demonstrated the reality of the principles he preaches. It was clear that he was strongly, infinitely, present to her in this transition. Yet there was no sentimentality, no mourning. How could there be mourning when he knew that she had been set free of a body she no longer needed, and that the time was right? Yet most of us mourned; we mourned out of convention or sentimentality or attention to our own loss rather than to the reality of passage for the one we loved.

When Lee returned from the memorial service on the East Coast, he said that someone close to his mother had asked him, "Tell me straight—what do you think about death?"

"There is no death," Lee replied. "Life doesn't end when the body dies."

The man looked at Lee with a huge, beatific smile. "That's what I thought," he said with great appreciation for Lee's confirmation.

A devotee of Papa Ramdas recounted that when someone brought Papa the news that his daughter had died his expression did not even change. He was talking with someone and smiling, and the smile never left his face. There was no reason for him to mourn or react to death, since he saw it as simply a change in state for the living spirit. Ever since I read it, this story has stayed with me as a dramatic contrast to our culture's usual view of death as a tragedy.

Lee's response to his mother's death or Papa Ramdas' to that of his daughter might seem to the conventional mind unfeeling; yet in fact it is based in deeper feeling, deeper respect, and deeper vision of the person's essential life and spiritual reality. To see Lee respond to his mother's death from the same point of view as Papa Ramdas had responded to the death of his daughter brought home to me that it is possible to actually live from that place of deep feeling without sentimentality rather than just to hold it as a theory that disintegrates in the face of the actual death of a loved one. These things that Lee teaches are not just ideas he is holding; they are living realities into which he is guiding us to the extent that we will respond, obey, practice, and learn.

~

In Zen, a sharp whack with a stick is used to bring meditators who are either falling asleep or going into ecstatic blisses back to a simple and acute state of clarity. In Lee's company, the reminder of reality comes not through the pain of the stick but through the unexpected shock of laughter. In *darshan* one evening in early 2000, two women were singing poems that Lee has written to Yogi Ramsuratkumar and which have been set into song using melodies from contemporary music, from soft folk ballads to hard core rock 'n' roll. The mood was ecstatic; some of us were in tears, dissolving into the bliss of divine love and longing. Lee interrupted the mood with a humorous comment that this was "English night" because the melodies were taken from songs by the Beatles and Elton John. He laughed, and we laughed with him, brought back from waves of sentimentality to raw and grounded reality. It seemed to me that Lee was showing us that real emotion is fluid and can move instantaneously from mystical bliss and open-hearted longing to joking and laughing and back again. Lower emotion, in contrast, is attached to itself, or we are attached to it. We demand pious respect for its "intensity," its supposed holiness, and we are insulted or offended by interruption of the mood, as if it is a brittle and fragile thing rather than a powerful and durable, though delicate, reality. Lower emotion has an exaggerated sense of itself. Lee pierces this inflated sense of self and the farce of false holiness with his jokes or apparent rudeness. Only that which is alive and can move fluidly can survive in his space.

～

Most spiritual schools produce written teaching that is unique to that particular school. Rarely is there mention of the writings and texts of other schools, except perhaps for some references to ancient scriptures. In contrast, in the literature of our school references and quotes abound from both contemporary and ancient teachings and from a wide variety of lineages. At the same time that we are held within a specific lineage, we venerate and make practical use of such diverse approaches as the written scriptures of Christ, of Buddha, and of Krishna; the Fourth Way teachings of Gurdjieff; the renegade examples of E. J. Gold or Werner Erhard; Zen and Tibetan Buddhism; Sufism; and the pristine and elegant *dharma* of Arnaud Desjardins. It is part of the Baul way to draw on whatever lines of the teaching can be useful and to weave them into our own unique evocation and expression of the divine in our daily lives. We draw from many sources, yet the living of these principles and the living teaching by our master is our own.

～

One morning in early 2000, Lee was in a mood that ranged from irascible ferocity to despairing depression to a glimpse of tenderness resting just beneath his painful discouragement with the level of practice among us, his students. He looked around at us and barked, with a tone of disbelief, "What a job! I'm consigned to put up with these people who have some faint trace of possibility that they'll probably never make use of, in this lifetime anyway—people with almost no real probability of ever reaching reliability, or any kind of real compassion or wisdom or enlightenment—and I am supposed to work with this!"

He was "on a roll," piercing our self-satisfaction with his ruthless observations about our actual state, not so much as individuals but as part of the entire field of spiritual students in the contemporary world, and in his world—the world of this school—in particular. I was reminded of a commentary written by Jeanne de Salzmann, one of Gurdjieff's closest students, in which she declared that in order to enter this Work, we must pay dearly—pay with ourselves, pay in advance. She said this payment is made through ruthless self-observation, which will bring us to the realization that our entire lives are based in a series of lies: "Your relations with others—lies . . . Your theories, your art—lies . . . And what you think of yourself—lies also." (*Gurdjieff: Essays and Reflections on the Man and His Teaching*, ed. by Jacob Needleman. N.Y.: Continuum, 1997, pp. 5-6)

In the moment that we see this, that in us which lives in truth can rise up from the place where it is buried, like a delicate new shoot of a plant just breaking through the ground. That delicate hint of something true in us is the "faint trace of possibility" with which Lee is asked to work. Yet the slightest untruth will bury that possibility once again. In the words of Gurdjieff, "the smallest lie kills it." (*Questions de Gurdjieff*, [No. 50], ed. Albin Michel, 1989, pp. 34-35) We are responsible for nourishing that faint possibility, that delicate shoot, so that we can make use in this lifetime of what Lee is offering us.

Lee made his commentary and went on with preparing a meal. It is uncanny to me how he can emanate a certain mood and at the same time stand quite clear of that mood, so that two vastly different currents wash through the space simultaneously. Perhaps this is what it means to feel passionately, yet with detachment. He has no attachment to his fierce and despairing frustration; he simply engages this mood as that which is, in this moment. In the next moment he may tell a joke or greet a child with affectionate tenderness. The mood of clarity underlies whatever he does, in contrast to the muddy wallowing in emotional reactions that I find so easy to engage.

As Lee proceeded with the meal preparation, someone opened a cupboard where foods such as nuts and raisins are stored to be served at our nightly community gatherings. In the cupboard was a small plate of wrapped candies, the remains of a gift that had been served several nights earlier. The candy should have been served each night after that until it was gone, but the servers responsible for the nightly space apparently had not realized this and had left it sitting in the cupboard, awaiting Lee's specific orders to serve it.

"Blind followers! People won't make the slightest decision for themselves! I've created a monster—and now I have to live with what I've created. It's a disaster!" Lee exclaimed with despairing frustration, as if continuing an unfinished conversation. "People are disrespectful, insolent, and insulting, and then they won't take a breath or make a move because they're afraid it's not what I want, it might not please me . . . It's the human condition."

I knew what he was referring to. We disregard his instructions in the simplest and most obvious of matters when it serves our personal preferences, then turn to him with obsequious deference when the circumstance calls for us to take responsibility for our own decisions.

The force of Lee's frustration seemed to catapult him into another area of dissatisfaction, without any linear connecting steps that I could see. Lee is acutely conscious of smells. When he receives a rose for *prasad* in *darshan*, he always smells it before placing it in a vase. If it has a rich perfume (which many hothouse roses no longer possess), he seems to drink in the fragrance for a long moment before setting it down. He frequently complains about the odors of garlic, of unbrushed teeth, and of unwashed bodies that sometimes fill the *darshan* hall when we gather to meditate in the mornings. This meditation space directed toward inner attentiveness and subtle and refined dimensions is clearly compromised for him by our disregard of the smells we bring into the room. The odor of garlic, at times endemic in the community because garlic is recommended by our healers for its health benefits, is one that Lee finds particularly offensive in its overpowering effects on the space. He finds it inexplicable that people cannot find a balanced relationship to this simple substance so that they use it wisely for its health properties without indulging its use to the point of rude insensitivity to others.

On this particular morning he flung himself into a tirade about people's blatant disregard of his requests and instruction around this simple thing. "People have been told about the use of garlic," he declared fiercely. "If they have to eat such quantities of garlic, then they can give up going to meditation that morning, or stay home from a gig instead of riding in an enclosed van where the entire group has to bear it." His mood was one of unmitigated criticism of people's disobedience in this matter, paralleling his despair at people's lack of responsible common sense a moment before.

"It's one thing when it's a blind spot, and you really don't know; and then someone tells you. It's another thing when people are fully conscious and fully aware, and they just go ahead and do what they want to do anyway—regardless of what's being asked, regardless of recommendations, regardless of the conditions of practice."

～

JANET: I'm doing a load of wash. Do you have anything you want thrown into a dark load?

LEE: How about desire, fear, greed, pride, shame, insecurity?

❧

When I walked into the kitchen one morning, Lee was busily fulfilling the role of short-order cook, turning out omelets made with homemade cheese that a Mexican friend had brought him as a gift. He was preparing literally to feed us all, a symbolic enactment of his role with us on deeper planes of nourishment. Although his abundant generosity filled the space, there was a tangible current of dissonance present as well. I was trying to sniff out what the problem was without asking, knowing he probably wouldn't answer anyway but would leave it to us to use our own powers of observation.

"I have a request," he declared gruffly. "Could everybody please leave the trash can lids *exactly* as I place them?"

We looked at the offending lids. He had placed the lid to the compost bucket at a rakish angle so that he could drop eggshells into the slight opening and had leaned the lid to the trash can so that it stood open and he could drop paper trash into it with one hand while managing the omelets with the other. One of us had unconsciously set the lids down in a proper fashion so that they sat tightly on their buckets—something Lee had commented on many dozens of times. He reset the lids and went on cooking.

"Where's the grapefruit juice?" someone at the table asked. "It was just here."

Lee looked at the table with incredulous exasperation. "I set it out so it would be there for breakfast," he said, obviously irritated that his intention for breakfast had once again been

317

interrupted—that we could not easefully accept even his most simple offering.

"I put it back in the refrigerator," someone else at the table confessed. "I'll get it."

"All right," Lee responded, without rancor, ready to go on the instant confession had been made and the error rectified.

Later I asked Lee what it was that had caused the dissonance in the space at breakfast. Was there some larger confrontation that had occurred earlier and was still impacting the space, or was it just all the little things in themselves?

"It was just all the little things," he replied, with somewhat uncharacteristic directness. "People kept changing the space that I was creating. They just could not leave things alone." I was reminded once again of the story about Yogi Ramsuratkumar and the Western devotee who moved a teacup that had been placed by Yogi Ramsuratkumar, prompting Yogi Ramsuratkumar's indignant response that his work had been ruined.

It seems to me that most Westerners are highly uneducated regarding the refinements of protocol in spiritual work. We cannot imagine that the placement of a teacup could have ramifications in profound interior spaces. We have no idea how the precise placement and interrelation of physical elements affects the subtle possibilities for work in a particular space. We often speak blithely about tantric work without realizing that much of tantric work is founded in the skilled use of ordinary, even mundane, elements to create a doorway into extraordinary realms of divine presence. Tantric work involves the capacity to discover the transcendent divine through the divine immanent in creation. This capacity depends on alchemical work of the utmost precision. Yet often we resent the inconvenience and discomfort of the demand for precision and disregard this demand, justifying our behavior with the idea that such minor details are really not worth all that attention and concern.

A close personal attendent of Chögyam Trungpa Rinpoche reported that the physical spaces around Trungpa Rinpoche always demonstrated the most pristine order and elegance. The attendant said it was clear that the order of the physical space was an expression of the inner order and clarity continuously emanating from Trungpa Rinpoche. Hearing this reminded me of the physical disorder that I still struggle to handle in my private space. Lee said once that this disorder is a function and expression of inner confusion—an outer demonstration of chaos and confusion of mind—in contrast to the clarity of mind that creates outer order as a natural consequence.

—⁓—

At the After-Dinner-Talk one night I asked Lee about moving deeper into intimacy, both in our human relations and with God. He had said once that in order to be intimate with anyone else, even with the divine, we first have to be intimate with ourselves. This requires penetrating and ruthless self-observation. It is this ruthless process of facing the truth about ourselves that enables the infinitely sensitive and delicate space of intimacy to open. In this space we naturally discover intimacy with others. From this point of view, we build our way toward a field in which intimacy is possible.

Recently I had been having the experience that intimacy exists, continuously, as a deep current of the life of the universe. We have only to let ourselves open to this current and we are *in* the fact of intimacy. It is not something we create; not something we build by doing or saying the right things; not a function of our small activities in any way. It always exists. There are great beings and energies constantly participating in and nourishing the field of intimacy. What we do by our activity is to build our own sensitivity, alignment, and vulnerability to that field so that we can finally, at least in moments, become aware of it and consciously participate. By doing so we nourish that field with a unique substance that can be drawn only from the conscious human. Those large energies—those deities if we want to call them that—are hungry for this human contribution, as we are hungry for the substance, the nectar, that we experience when we open to the realm in which they live.

Sometimes, when that field of intimacy opens a door or the slightest crack of a window through which its current touches or flows through me, I experience it as a physical taste that is sweeter and richer than any taste of earthly food. Then the moment is gone, and I fall back into the human condition, specifically the attitude of desperate aggrandizement. This most real moment becomes itself the object of acquisitive greed. I want to seize it by the throat and force it to return to me. What utter disrespect to the divine Beloved! What an inability to wait! The Lover, the Beloved, can only be known through enduring the moments when it seems there is nothing and no one to know. Only through penetrating the veil of absence as well as the veil of presence can we begin to know.

I asked Lee how to let go of this energy of aggrandizement, this greed for the real. He answered, "Letting go does not take energy. It's holding on that takes energy."

I said to Lee that I seemed to be feeling my way in the dark toward something that was right in front of me, but I couldn't quite yet touch it—something about the immense possibility locked in intimacy.

"You're going in the right direction," he said. "You just have to walk the next block."

❧

Later, thinking about Lee's statement that it takes energy to hold on, not to let go, I was reminded of a discussion at a Sunday teaching meeting. We were talking about the story of Krishna's play with the *gopis* as described in the *Bhagavata Purana* and elaborated in Vallabhacarya's *Commentaries on the Love Games of Krshna*. This story suggests that God creates the human simply for the purpose of joy, to share with him in his Play. Someone asked, if we are here to play with God, to participate in a joyous dance, why should we make effort? Aren't we being too serious about all this—about all these conditions and practices in spiritual life?

It seems to me that it is our effort and our engagement of responsibility that ultimately sets us free to play. When we are entangled in emotional recoil and mental illusion, we are unable even to recognize God's Play, and we are even more unable to respond wholly, to participate creatively and joyously. We are so busy holding onto our defenses that we can't even hear the joke half the time. We are overly serious not because we commit ourselves to action but because we do not make effort.

Commitment and effort are essentially joyous. They bring us in touch with the passionate life force within us that is longing to express and grow. That essential passion, the passion of the divine, is inherently joyous, playful, and responsive. That is why teachers from vastly different traditions, if they are real teachers, consistently display an inveterate sense of humor and a relaxed ability to play concomitant to the level of effort and responsibility they have engaged. They have stopped spending energy to hold onto defenses and grasp for self-aggrandizement, and as a result they have energy free to play. If we want to have real freedom to play, they show us the way, which is the shouldering of the greatest responsibility that we can engage. "Take my yoke upon you . . . For my yoke is easy, and my burden is light." (Matthew 11:29-30) When we step into the stream of reality, we step into a domain in which our preconceptions are shattered, and the heaviest responsibility opens into the lightest play.

~

One winter morning we were discussing plans for Lee's summer in France, which would include small and intimate teaching spaces with his students at the French ashram, La Ferme de Jutreau; weekend seminars which he offers all over Europe; and a tour with Shri, the community blues band, to music festivals and clubs. Some of us who would be traveling with Lee were asking about the specific schedule so that we could make plans for handling our personal "needs" in the various seminar houses and circumstances of the summer.

Lee's response was vehement. "You don't need a schedule," he said. "Wanting a schedule is just refusal to surrender. It's a refusal to accept the gift I'm offering. People want to think they're in control. They think if they look at a schedule it means they have control over their lives. We don't have control over our lives. We never need a schedule. We should be able to hear that we're going somewhere this afternoon and just throw some things in a suitcase and go."

Lee's view appears so totally demanding, a demand that we release all effort not just to control aspects of a trip or circumstance, but even to know what those circumstances might be. Yet I remembered hearing of another spiritual teacher, Mata Amritanandamayi, whose demand on her students is even greater. She tells her students simply, "We are leaving now on a trip. You have five minutes to get your things." If they want to go on the trip, her students must be able to respond instantaneously. As a result, they keep basic items always packed for traveling so that they can leave literally at a moment's notice. Occasionally, she has left on a trip without even giving people time to collect these small, prepacked bags. Those who wanted to go simply climbed on the bus without anything but what they were wearing.

If we want to live as beggars, we would do well to embrace this kind of flexibility and renunciation of the need for possessions. It is so easy to want theoretically to throw ourselves into a radical living of the teaching, yet in many practical daily moments to cling to habits of comfort and demands for predictability—of our physical circumstances, the emotions we will feel, the thoughts we will engage. Often the teacher uses unexpected and unusual physical circumstances to help open us to new domains of feeling and thought and subtler possibilities that we have not imagined.

~

One day in early 2000 I found myself remembering the morning thirteen years earlier when I had met some of Lee's close students the day after I first met Lee. At the time these students had no idea of the radiance that emanated from them or how it impacted and inspired me. Perhaps it was best that they did not know; our attention is not meant to be focused on our own radiance, but on the radiance of the divine which then imbues us and spills through us. There was a level of unconsciousness that was allowed them then that is no longer allowed as we grow in this work. They were not yet asked to be consciously responsible for themselves as artifacts of the divine being shaped through their working companionship with their master.

As we mature on this path we become increasingly responsible for these artifacts which we become. In our early work with our teacher, the reverberating jewel that is our essence is buried under so many shells and buffers that it is often practically invisible. As we pass through the fire of refinement, that jewel begins gradually to radiate more and more reliably. At first we ourselves may remain quite ignorant of this fact. Others may draw from this radiance in their own work, while we are conscious mainly of the struggles and obstacles that we face. Yet gradually we become responsible not only for the work of refinement, but for the radiance of the jewel as well. We can no longer choose to indulge unnecessary struggle with entanglement in illusory emotions. When we know the reality of the jewel, we are responsible to give our attention to that rather than to experiences we know to be false. For example, we can no longer excuse wallowing in reactive pain at the spiritual master's feedback concerning our dynamics when we are capable simply of using this infusion of energy for our work. Similarly, to allow ourselves to believe our own denigrating self-criticism and lose ourselves in its pain is a derailing of work energy for which we are responsible.

Our choice of attention determines which will grow: the radiance and the reliability to which we are called, or the rejection of ourselves, of others, and of our work. We are responsible for this choice moment by moment as we build a matrix either of practice or reaction. To use the real pain of our human imperfection is to feed remorse that can actually strengthen the radiance and work of essence. To indulge critical anger at the master or self-rejecting despair is to waste the energy he has given us and which we have built through our efforts with him.

⌣

One day I told Lee I had a small growth on my shoulder that had appeared a few months before and was gradually growing. I had showed it to our community nurse and she had said it should be checked out by a doctor, since a new growth on the skin signaled the possibility of skin cancer.

When I told Lee about it and asked what he thought about my seeing a doctor, he said, "Sure. You should see a doctor so that you're at ease about it."

Although his tone was accepting, his smile was enigmatic, and I sensed that his energetic communication contained more than one message. Beneath the direct instruction of his words he was suggesting that I should see a doctor because I had not reached a point where my relationship to health was unshakably founded in commitment to work rather than on sentimental fears and attachments based in a conventional human view of life and death.

He was suggesting that whether this small growth could be cancerous was totally irrelevant to my work. There was a sense that he himself did not believe it to be anything that needed investigation, but even if it were in fact the "cancerous growth" most humans so deeply dread, it was a totally irrelevant development. The way to handle it was to continue to work. While this point of view may seem inexplicably callous and irresponsible to a conventional view of human life, it did not surprise me. In the past months I had had similar unconventional visions about the relationship of life, death, and the temporary use of a body for work. I simply did not find myself ready at the time to freely choose to handle my health and body in total alignment with these visions.

Subsequent to a doctor's reassurance that the mole, although still growing, was benign, I began to work with it using simple natural methods and visualization. Within a few weeks it had entirely disappeared. It was a graphic confirmation of Lee's instruction that I did not need to spend emotional energy, particularly my habitual fear, on the welfare of my physical body.

We used to have discussions about whether Lee is teaching all the time or whether he can be "off-duty." Are there times when he makes a comment, tells a joke, or watches a movie when he isn't teaching—when he's just relaxing and being just a guy? If that's true, then we could take the comment or the activity at face value without having to read meanings into his every statement and action.

It seems to me now that this question defeats itself because it creates a dichotomy that doesn't exist. The teacher is always teaching, not because of what he says or does but because of his location. He is standing at a level higher than ours on the path, and as a result his point of view is founded in a context, a living vision, more encompassing than ours. To say Lee is teaching or not teaching when he laughs at a movie is to assume that his instruction is based in his conscious intention to make a point with us. But the deepest instruction that he offers us is the living transmission of the context of that higher point of view. The question is not whether the teacher is teaching or not teaching; the teacher is teaching through his living presence. The question is whether we are observing and responding; whether we are choosing in each moment to learn.

There are certain states that I experience as a kind of flow of higher feeling. It is not *my* feeling. It is the objective existence of some emotional current that is flowing through a being or beings much higher than myself. For some reason that I don't understand, it is useful for me to be willing to stand in the current of that higher feeling and let it flow through me. The quality of the emotional current may be at one time a kind of universal sorrow;

at another time an overwhelming, all-encompassing joy; at another time some union of both in which pleasure and pain cease to have distinction.

The flow of this current, whatever its particular quality, can be so strong that all ordinary thought dissolves, and ordinary attention dissolves also. I can only allow this flooding current; I cannot control or direct it, and the attempt to do so either shuts it out or, worse, leaves me tumbling and drowning in a frightening and chaotic overload. What allows me to receive and stand in this current is the matrix of practice that has been built through innumerable ordinary moments. It is the structure developed through practice that enables me to let go of conscious structures and surrender to this flow of energy. I have a sense that when we do this, when we allow the structures we have intentionally developed from our own level of consciousness to be used by a higher level of consciousness, we become a kind of human transformer. We become that which enables a higher force and voltage of energy and consciousness to enter the human planes in which we live. We do not have to understand this energy; we have only to be willing to feel it and to have developed the structures that enable us to receive it without burning up or disintegrating in its intensity.

In light of this possibility, one of the most dangerous developments in Western spiritual exploration is the easy availability and popularity of approaches which offer to stimulate higher energies such as kundalini and to open participants to expanded experiences of consciousness. It is not difficult to open these doors with a limited technical skill stolen from ancient practices rather than paid for with dedicated commitment. What is difficult is to maintain the ordinary and often austere life of practice over a period of time that is long enough to stabilize the inner matrices necessary to handle these inflows of higher energy in a useful way.

Much of the spiritual exploration in the West today appears to me to be like children playing with electrical sockets or building small fires at the edge of autumn grass fields. We have no idea what we are playing with. To engage this unsupervised exploration or to follow seductive leaders who offer a quick experience but do not have the matrix of lineage or the foundation of their own committed practice as a basis for offering real guidance is to risk possible spiritual destruction. Whatever energies wish to block our spiritual progress as a race play on our fear of false authority so that we run from real, recognizable spiritual authority. Instead, we end up dominated by our own petty emotions and desires and find ourselves, as a culture, vulnerable to seduction by the worst parodies of a true spiritual path.

One day I was sitting at lunch with Lee and some other students, and I found myself being washed by unending waves of bliss. Lee was sitting there, having just finished his gigantic lunch of an apple or two, burping in the Turkish style of expressing great appreciation for the meal. I knew in a moment he would say, as usual, "That was a *massive* lunch! Boy, am I stuffed!"

The only way I can see that someone can be stuffed on two apples is if that person is eating pure light or some other invisible substance in great quantities in addition to the apples. In any case, here was the generative source from or through which emanated the blissful state of unitive consciousness that I was experiencing, and that source was demonstrating no hint of such a state himself. In fact, he was behaving in a most ordinary and even crude manner, calculated to prick a hole in the balloon of any self-centered pretense of devotional ecstasy. Perhaps in homage to the movie "Austin Powers," which we had just seen (and at which Lee had laughed uproariously), I had this image that our ecstasies are just the farts of God. The whole scene, the paradoxical humor of the relationship between the human and the divine, sent me into paroxysms of laughter.

~

The human being is born in a state of exquisite sensitivity and vulnerability. In this delicate state, at least in the Western world, we, as infants, are met with a crude and unresponsive treatment that bludgeons us into numbness or reactive defensiveness. As adults, we are faced not with *developing* sensitivity but with *retrieving* an original state of sensitivity and responsiveness.

I asked Lee if it is possible to retrieve this original state. Has it been destroyed or killed, or is it only buried and distorted, and is it still possible to rediscover it? How can we move through the scarred territory to the underlying innocence? Lee answered simply that it is possible.

~

Another day I asked Lee about the purposeful use of language. I told him that I felt less and less interest in speaking, in using words except in writing, if it can help to communicate the teaching. I said I'd often found that in social situations, and even in gatherings to consider the teaching, I had nothing to say. It felt categorically different from my old silence, which was a despairing withdrawal. This wordless state of being actually felt as if it were an arising of my true voice. Occasionally this true voice had a few purposeful things to say, and in between it rested in silence. Yet I wondered at times whether this silence was a refusal of relationship; whether it was important to use words to be in communication and interaction with others. Specifically, I wondered whether the growth of love should naturally lead to a flow of words, of relationship through language.

Lee responded that the movement toward increasing silence seemed to be a positive movement. He said it is actually natural that we might find ourselves less and less interested in social chatter. As for expressing love, that expression is not bound or limited by words.

"Love should be based in bonding and communion, not in needing to talk," he observed, with that tone of truth that penetrates through all the superficial layers of our lives and relationships to name the deepest verities.

Language is not the foundation of love. Language may express love, yet the deepest expression lies far below the spoken forms. In listening to the current that lies beneath spoken language, we may hear the vibrant language of the heart, which is often eclipsed by our indiscriminate and unnecessary conversation.

～

Lee has enjoyed going to the movies ever since I have known him. In general he does not choose to see videos, which we could see on the ashram or at households. He does not want videos to be shown on the ashram except on rare occasions, and he would like to see households run as extensions of the field of practice maintained on the ashram. He goes to the movie theater in town if he wants to see a movie—often once or twice a week. There has been a lot of discussion among his students over the years about whether Lee is working and teaching when he goes to the movies, or whether it is a way for him to relax from the weight of his responsibilities. Exactly what is it that he's doing when he attends these Hollywood productions of romantic comedy or the adventures of superhuman heroes? Personally, I think the best explanation is Lee's own restatement of what Gurdjieff said about his own going to movies: that it is one way he can briefly "go to sleep"; that is, a way he can rest from the responsibilities he is carrying. As far as I can tell, Lee no longer gets this kind of rest, even when he physically sleeps, as he is constantly attuned to Yogi Ramsuratkumar even in his dreams or dreamless states. Of course, this attunement continues even during the movies, yet it is almost as if movies are the only kind of sleeping dream that he can experience anymore. In any case, for whatever reasons, Lee goes to the movies and takes students with him.

~

One of the places Lee has laid out a map of the relationships between disciple and teacher, and between teacher and God, is in the rock musical, "John T.," for which Lee wrote the lyrics and one of his students composed the music. When I first saw it, I was amazed at the power of the considerations of the teaching that Lee has encapsulated into a modern rock opera. Through this Biblically-based presentation he has portrayed many of the essential questions and challenges that arise for students engaging discipleship—or apprenticeship to discipleship—with a teacher.

The play abounds with illustrations of both the weaknesses disciples must face in themselves and the potential of the relationship between disciple and guru. At the same time, it offers insight into the struggles of the teacher as he turns more and more deeply toward the divine. In a passionate scene just before his death, John the Baptist cries to God from his cell in Herod's dungeon, "Could you, would you, make my next life normal?" Yet he ends with profound surrender to the will of His Father. Finally, with his attention wholly turned to the messiah for whom he is the messenger, he pleads, "Take care of your beloved Son."

The play vividly portrays the essential discrepancy between the temporal, materialistic view of the world, which Herod demonstrates, and the view of the world from the perspective of spiritual commitment, which is the ultimate basis for the actions of both John and Jesus. Faced with Herod's seductive offers to release him if he will only make some small compromises, John refuses absolutely. Even in the last moments of his life, as he chooses the death of a martyr, John offers Herod the chance to hear the teaching. Herod declares with empty bravado, "*I'm* the ruler," and John states with the simple power of truth, "Herod, you are just a pawn."

At one of our After Dinner Talks, Lee spoke about the existence of magic—the magic of divine Influence in our world—and about our difficulty in believing in the reality of this magic and allowing ourselves to receive and nourish its action in our lives. We cling to our limited, supposedly practical and rational modes of action and, by our lack of faith and receptivity, we actually block the action of magic in our lives.

It seems to me that the repetition of truth through language, song, and drama, as in the community presentations of "John T.," is one method of aligning to this possibility of magic and of inviting its action into the planes of our ordinary lives. As a child I loved a story of an early Quaker who felt the inner Voice calling him to go to a wilderness area and preach the gospel. The area to which he was directed was frequented by armed robbers, yet he was directed to go alone, without weapons or defense of any kind. The man obeyed this inner instruction. Reaching the wilderness camp of the robbers and finding it empty, he preached, amid the silence of the great trees, a passionate discourse on forgiveness and the ways of God.

Years later, the man was standing on a bridge in London when a somewhat rough-looking character approached him. It crossed the Quaker's mind that the stranger might be about to try to steal his wallet. Instead, the stranger held out his hand and began to thank this early Friend for transforming his life. The stranger explained that he had been one of the robbers. Returning alone to the camp for a knife he had forgotten, he heard the Quaker preaching into the empty silence. Almost against his will, the robber stopped and listened. The courage of this lone man speaking truth to the empty camp and the message he had preached of God's eternal forgiveness penetrated the robber's heart. He resolved to give up robbery and return to an honest life. He had kept his resolution, and from that moment of decision, his life had been transformed. This story has always communicated to me both the power of obedience and the power of truth spoken into what may seem to be an unreceptive void.

～

The children on the ashram had been learning about various tribal cultures from a young woman in the community who earned her college degree in anthropology and who had spent several months living with an indigenous tribe in Costa Rica. Most recently she had been teaching the children about the Jewish tradition in which she grew up, and after three days of preparation, they served the community a traditional Seder feast accompanied by the ritual of remembrance of the Exodus and the enduring presence of God through all circumstances of human life. We participated in the ritual in both Hebrew and English, hearing the repetition of the four questions that have been asked each year for thousands of years by those of the Jewish faith. We ate of the bitter herbs and the unleavened bread and drank the wine of remembrance.

Lee sat at the head of the table, dressed in a formal tuxedo shirt and suit coat, his dreadlocks pulled back into a ponytail. Rarely does he dress up in Western attire. I had seen him in a suit coat only once before, in preparation for the wedding of one of his children. At this ritual meal he appeared as the classic Jewish patriarch, gazing down the table with a benevolent power that encompassed both stern and tender compassion along with relaxed humor and an ever-present alertness of attention. Looking at him, I felt the richness of the tradition that has infused him even though he no longer draws upon it in any linear way—the tradition of the mysteries of the *Kabbalah* and of the radical commitment to classic forms of the Hassidim, the cradle from which Christianity itself was born.

How mysterious are the ways of God, whose divine purposes have drawn the grandson of a Jewish holy man into the function of the guru in the classic Eastern tradition—a tradition carried out, in this school, in a renegade manner closely parallel to an unknown Eastern sect called the Bauls of Bengal. The intricate mysteries by which East and West are being woven together in this and other spiritual schools on the planet at this time were palpably present as we carried out these ancient rituals. The forms in which the divine seeks to embody itself within our human world are so myriad and yet, at the source, so unitive. In that moment it seemed to me that Lee stood revealed as the carrier of two ancient and powerful seeds: a seed of the West and a seed of the East.

Two nights after Lee had sat like a traditional Jewish patriarch at the head of the table for the Seder feast, he sat on his chair at the front of the *darshan* hall dressed in the classic Indian *kirta* and pyjama, ritually fulfilling the role of the guru. He looked like a transplant from India. His head was wrapped in a turban like his Father Yogi Ramsuratkumar—a turban given to him by his Father during one of Lee's pilgrimages to Tiruvannamalai. A shawl from the same source was draped over his shoulders. We bowed and offered *prasad* and received *prasad* as blessing from him in the traditional exchange between devotee and master.

One night later, Lee was bellowing into the microphone on the stage of a local casino, wearing the same formal dress shirt that he wore to the Seder meal, this time paired with a silk lounge jacket. His attire that night also included a baseball cap reading "Rolling Stones" and a pair of sunglasses. He was surrounded by the entire ensemble of Shri, belting out the blues.

What a chameleon! Lee demonstrates the ability to "shapeshift"—to change forms—not in response to some random creative impulse but in resonance to the movement of divine purpose to which he is both responsive and responsible.

~

One cold winter evening we were seated at our usual Tuesday night dinner in "the greenhouse," which is no longer a greenhouse but in fact a long room fronting the main building of the ashram, with walls made mostly of glass. There were remnants of snow on the ground, yet we ate seated along extended tablecloths spread on a barely covered cement floor in a space that is totally unheated. People were shivering in shawls—some even huddled inside coats— but no one complained. This is the only space on the ashram large enough for us to gather together to eat the meals Lee ritually prepares for us on Tuesday and Thursday evenings. The company was warm, even if the air was cold.

Susanne, the woman who was serving the meal that night, has been assisting Lee with preparing and serving meals on Tuesdays and Thursdays for years. The fact that she is his first choice as his assistant speaks for itself in terms of the reliability and responsiveness to his direction that she consistently demonstrates in the kitchen. She has been a student for many years, entrusted with the care of the children and other jobs that are essential to Lee's work and in which he demands the most stellar attentiveness and grounded practice. She has a natural gentleness and surrender to service such that she rarely evokes from him direct input. She has even complained and questioned him over the years about the fact that he rarely gives her instruction or confronts her with demands for facing her dynamics. Lee's answer has repeatedly been that she did not need that kind of input from him at the time and that he would provide it if and when she did.

That night Susanne brought Lee a hot chutney specifically made for him, and he set the bowl in front of his plate. A few moments later two people arrived late for dinner. Susanne brought them salad and then approached Lee.

"Should I offer them the chutney?" she asked.

"No!" Lee replied, with an abruptness that is commonplace in his responses to some students, but is quite uncharacteristic in his interactions with Susanne.

Someone sitting near Lee commented, "Very few people can say 'no' the way that you do, with such clarity and without apology."

"That's because other people have compassion, whereas I have none," Lee responded. He gave Susanne no direct feedback. If she had missed a cue, she received only the subtle hint of his tone to give her another clue to the precision of action that he expected.

In many cases it is a lack of responsiveness to subtle cues that elicits that particular abrupt tone from Lee. Instead of reacting to the tone, we can use it as a hint to help us recognize the cue we missed and find our way to a more exact responsiveness to his direction. This is the kind of subtle responsiveness that he offers to Yogi Ramsuratkumar. He is offering us the chance to build this same kind of responsive matrix for ourselves.

For several days in the early part of the new century there had been a mood of sorrow emanating from Lee, as if his heart were vibrating with a sorrow or pain that set my heart vibrating as well. It was as if a tuning fork had been struck sounding a specific note, and that note echoed in reverberation. I wanted, as I have so often before, to somehow fix the situation so that this sorrow would dissolve. I did not want to watch Lee feel it, and I did not want to have to feel it myself. I sensed that Lee's mood had to do with his response to our imperfections, especially to the ways in which we hurt each other, and I wanted to find a way to deepen my own practice, to correct others' practice, or to change Lee's response to our humanness. Yet I knew that I could not fix or rescue or correct the situation. All I could do was be willing to feel, and go on.

I realized that in the willingness to feel lies a key—a key to nourishing the possibility of longing. The willingness to feel "what is" holds implicit within itself the willingness to feel what can be, and to feel the gap between these realities. To feel that gap is to open oneself to remorse, such as remorse for our failure to live wholly in truth with our children, friends, mate, and teacher. Yet beyond the experience of remorse lies the experience of longing, which is the opening of the heart to the infinite possibilities of love.

As I opened myself to Lee's mood and this possibility, I recalled a performance by Shri at a fair in the German town of Bremen one summer. The evening had begun with enthusiastic consumption of sausages and lamb stew at booths selling local specialties. It was Shri's last gig on the tour. The next day they would fly home to Arizona. As they played, the dusk deepened into night, and stars winked above the booths selling German beer. The mood began to soften even as the music intensified with the raw, hammering rhythms of the blues. A woman confined to a wheelchair sat at the edge of the stage, watching intently. She could not move almost any part of her body except her eyes, which drank in the music like a draught of holy wine.

Another woman, filthy and dressed in the ragged attire of a street dweller, danced wildly directly in front of the band. She appeared to have lost touch with the realities in which most of us live and survive, responding to the band with passionate directness. Every once in a while she would dance over to the woman in the wheelchair and most gently, tenderly, touch her cheek. It was obvious that the women did not know one another and had no prior relationship; they simply met on the grounds of tenderness that lay accessible in each because normality had been stripped away, revealing the unguarded heart. The sorrow these two women carried and the gift they gave to the space created a field in which the rhythms of the human heart became as tangible as the notes rippling out of the instruments on stage and the guttural cries pouring from the throats of the singers.

Finally, in the last moments of the gig, in response to the ravenous call for an encore, the band shifted from the wild renditions of "Voodoo Child" and "Take Another Little Piece of My Heart" into the sweet surrender of "Can't Find My Way Home." As Deborah's voice seduced the gathered field of humanity away from their beers and conversations into total attention, the space itself broke open. In that moment it seemed that Deborah became the heart of Lee, made visible and manifest in the midst of the silent cries of humanity pressed against the stage and each other. In that moment there was longing not just for what could be, but for what is, for the unfathomable dimensions of the divine met in this most ordinary of circumstances.

CHAPTER 9

"MAKE NO ASSUMPTIONS"

❧

A few years ago I asked Lee a question I can't remember. Whatever it was, I have never forgotten his answer. We were driving to the movies. I was sitting in the back seat, and he looked at me intently in the rear view mirror.

"Make no assumptions," he said.

Since then I have been repeatedly surprised or shocked or softened by seeing the myriad assumptions out of which we live and from which we choose our actions.

One of the most deeply rooted assumptions of Western culture is that we can handle situations best ourselves, without help. This is the attitude that underlies the bumper sticker motto, "Question Authority." It proclaims that *I* am the best authority. It is blind to the fact that real authority is based in wisdom; real authority stems from knowledge of the self. Real authority provides a mirror in which we can see in our humanity the undistorted reflection of the divine.

Ours is a culture steeped in self-hatred. A story I heard about the Dalai Lama creates a strong contrast to this. As I remember it, when the Dalai Lama met with a group of Westerners some years ago, they spoke to him about their self-hatred, asking how to work with this tendency in their spiritual development. For some minutes the dialogue came to a standstill as the translator searched for a way to convey the concept of self-hatred to the Dalai Lama. There was no word for "self-hatred" in the Tibetan language. Apparently, the Tibetan experience of such a relationship to the world is so foreign to that culture that the translator struggled even to communicate the idea.

Paradoxically, we in the West believe that this hated self is the best authority for our actions. We even project this hatred onto the teachers—the authorities—who could offer us help and lead us out of the black hole into which we have been sucked. To question authority that is based in abusive and violent power is to use our powers of discrimination. But to question *all* authority, as if the position of having reached greater wisdom makes a person by nature suspect, is to shut ourselves into a tiny world of human limitation, isolated from the divine which is the ultimate Authority, and cut off from the teachers who could guide us toward the realization of the divine Reality within ourselves, within all things, and beyond all things.

The assumption that underlay much of the political organizing in which I was involved was that we could fix the structure of human relationships through our own better idea of how to live compassionately and peacefully. This is an admirable ideal. Yet the history of human civilization demonstrates the fallacy of humans relying solely on human ideals to make a better society. These ideals quickly degenerate into violent revolution and counterrevolution. The new rulers who begin with such idealism are predictably overwhelmed by the unrecognized greed, cruelty, and lust for power that lurks in the human soul unless routed out by clear self-observation under the guidance of those who have penetrated these weaknesses in themselves—under the guidance of spiritual authorities.

The fall from idealism to enactment of the lower aspects of the human condition can be seen in both secular and religious movements: in the French Revolution, which degenerated into mass murder at the guillotine; in the Christian Crusades, which distorted spiritual teachings into an excuse for fanatical brutality; in the Russian Revolution, which degenerated into violent abuse of power by the new rulers, the bureaucrats; in the history of the United States, in which the great ideals of the Declaration of Independence—ideals based at their core in the concept of freedom to engage spiritual growth—have degenerated into the freedom to consume at a rate that is destroying the planet, to bear arms which are murdering our children, and to refuse the most basic elements of human existence—food and shelter—to a growing percentage of the citizens of the richest country on earth.

Parallel to the assumption that we can handle things best ourselves, without the intervention of wiser authority, is the assumption that some higher authority can handle it all, and we have no responsibility. This is the fundamentalist view that all we have to do is let Jesus save us. It is a childish reliance on the savior.

To enter spiritual work is to let go of both of these assumptions. It is to accept the responsibility of discrimination, trust, faith, and obligation to work. The avenues of this work may take us far from the linear directions we would have chosen on our own. They may take us to hawking basketball throws at a county fair, or to spending years cooking and cleaning in a community kitchen, or to speeding past the exit that seems to offer the assurance of salvation, demanding instead that we head directly into the emptiness (and possibility) of the wholly unknown. This is the possibility of life with a teacher; life that neither blindly follows nor rejects demonstrated authority; life that discriminates and trusts in the teaching as expressed in a living authority offering us guidance toward the deepest reality of human existence, the life of the divine seeded at its core.

When asked why a person would need a spiritual teacher, Lee has used the analogy of someone trying to cross a minefield. Certainly one can try to cross without a map and guidance, but the chances of crossing safely are highly increased by following a guide who has already negotiated the field and mapped the locations of the mines. The mines in spiritual work range from being sabotaged by pride, spiritual materialism, greed, vanity, or territorialism within the spiritual culture to prematurely or suddenly releasing the explosive force of kundalini energy without training or guidance in how to work with it.

With guidance, we have the opportunity to learn how to handle and use energies far beyond those that most humans ever encounter, energies that become available to us to the degree that we prove ourselves reliable and responsible to use them in the service not of our own small purposes but in the larger purposes of the divine.

The demand for questioning assumptions increases rather than decreases as a student's years with the teacher increase. The effects of what may seem to be tiny dissonances—minor filters or distortions of view—become proportionately greater as we move into greater responsibility and the teacher relies more heavily on our work. For senior students in any school, this demand to penetrate our assumptions and to see anew is a central obligation. The assumption that because we are senior students we do not have to work so hard at seeing clearly—that we already know who the teacher is, what he wants, and what is in consonance with him—is the very assumption that can feed the tendency for us to become like the dead outer bark of a tree. The newer cells in the tree carry the life force, the nourishment that flows through the entire system.

Senior students who become crystallized in their belief that they are the holders of the tradition, when in fact they have become the deadwood, offer a warning and reminder to all of us of the crucial importance of "beginner's mind." We face the challenge of a constant rededication to learning and growing, a process that can feel at times like a repeated confrontation with death itself. Yet this process, when truly engaged, opens into life.

The teaching continues daily in many small schools and hidden or public efforts around the world. Some schools have the responsibility of working in the streets, correcting the social structures in which humans live. Bernie Glassman's Peacemakers offer a prime example of this way. Others have a different and more esoteric direction. Although our school appears in many ways ordinary to the point of being casual or even crass, nevertheless our focus is in this esoteric direction, which eventually demands both inner and outer elegance (in the mathematical sense of being the most simple and beautiful expression). Paradoxically, we pursue this essentially inner direction through the physical body, through the world of incarnate matter, discovering and meeting the divine within the outer world of form. This is a hard path, demanding the ability to use the substances of ordinary human life with an uncommon intent and with a highly refined sense of discrimination and purpose. Many of the specific practices we use in this process can usefully be given only in direct transmission from a teacher with whom the student has a mutually committed relationship.

The responsibilities of this school meet and blend with the responsibilities of other spiritual schools with similar, contrasting, and complementary paths of work. Together the interplay of real spiritual schools on this planet is building a matrix for a level of work beyond our imagination.

"No Top End"

I began this story with the view of myself as one strand being woven into the larger matrix of this community, the lineage of this particular school and its work. The more deeply I am interwoven, the more my attention turns to the larger pattern of which I am only a small part: to the work of the teachers and the infinite field they serve.

Contemporary Western culture spends a great deal of energy in its concern about whether the teachers are true teachers, whether they can be trusted. Obviously discrimination about the quality of a teacher is a foundational consideration before making a commitment of one's life to that teacher and that path. Yet that is only the preliminary consideration. Once we have approached a teacher and been accepted, we come face to face with the question of our own trustworthiness. This question can only be answered through our own life commitment to practice and responsibility. To the degree that we as students become reliable and trustworthy, we become able to participate in the awesome responsibility which the teachers shoulder; we become able to wait with our teacher, to listen and obey, to act in creative resonance, and to contribute the offering of our lives into this great Work.

That is the possibility to which the teacher stands as a doorway; how far we walk into the world beyond that doorway is up to us. To walk deeply into that world requires our penetrating self-observation, our courage, our truthful relationship to our fears and emotions, our flexible consideration of our most cherished assumptions, and our practical willingness to persevere, to learn, to serve, to work and, finally, to love.

In our school, we say there is "no top end" to the Work. Likewise, there is not an end to this story of work with a teacher. No written account can do more than awaken the taste for this ancient wine. One must then go in search of the winemaker. Having found the teacher, the student begins to work in a living tradition of apprenticeship to a spiritual master. Then we begin to be pressed into wine that can be drunk by the divine even as we ourselves drink.

GLOSSARY

~

Acharya(s): An honorific title designating a teacher or master.

Advaita (Advaita Vedanta): The metaphysical tradition of nondualism based on the Upanishads.

After-Dinner Talk: Specific to the author's spiritual community, a bi-weekly gathering of students with the teacher for questions and *dharmic* considerations; takes place on Tuesday and Thursday nights following a simple dinner prepared by the teacher.

Alchemy: In the Middle Ages, the form of chemistry and speculative philosophy that attempted to discover an elixir of life and a method of transmuting base metals into gold. Any seemingly magical process of transforming ordinary materials into something of true merit, a fitting description of spiritual practice/spiritual work.

Amrit: The nectar of immortality.

Arati: The traditional Hindu ceremony of "waving lights" or waving a burning flame, usually ghee or camphor, before a shrine, sacred relics or artifacts, or the guru's seat or chair. It is intended to invoke the living spiritual power of the relics or artifacts, or to invoke the Presence of the spiritual master.

Ashram: The Eastern equivalent of a monastery, which in the Eastern traditions may include both men and women and their families. The sanctuary for the master and his or her family, and residence for a group of students who attend the master or support the master's work; often with facilities for retreat and housing for visitors and guests.

Beloved: In the Sufi tradition, the Divine as an objective love (who may or may not be personified), as regarded by one who has been submitted to the Will of God. Also called the Guest, or Friend. In Baul terms, the Beloved is a *Maner Manush*, "the Man of the Heart."

Bodhisattva: In Buddhism, a being or deity who is the embodiment of compassion.

Bodhisattva vow: A vow to save all sentient beings from the illusion of existence before he himself is saved.

Burning ghats: Hindu. The place at the river's edge at which open-air cremation ceremonies are held. *Also see: ghats*

Darshan: The sighting or glimpse of the embodiment of the Divinity within the person of the guru. In some traditions, a formal ritual which may include additional elements such as the guru

347

dispensing teaching communication, chanting the name of God (*kirtan*) and the exchange of gifts (*prasad*) symbolic of the devotee's surrender to the guru and the guru's surrender to the devotee.

Dewali: Holiday in the Indian tradition. For the business community in India, this is the time for the worship of Lakshmi, the goddess of wealth. Includes the lighting of tiny earthenware oil lamps, not only to re-kindle the spirit of jubilation but also to symbolize the time described in the *Ramayana* when Lord Rama returned to the Kingdom of Ayodhya, after fourteen years in exile.

Dharma (dharmic): A Buddhist term; the defined and formally-propagated spiritually-lawful and right way to live. In English it can be translated as "the Teaching" and "the Dharma." These terms are used interchangeably to refer to the perennial Teaching that abides as objective truth or reality as it is.

Ego (egoic), separative ego: The distinction-making function of any person, whereby the individual distinguishes itself from others; the function of self-preservation. Often used pejoratively to mean self-importance, or that which denies the unity of all things, choosing rather to keep the being under the illusion of separation from God.

Enquiry (inquiry): Traditionally, a form of spiritual practice in which the question "Who am I?" is used. In the teaching of Lee Lozowick, that question becomes: "Who am I kidding?" It is used randomly in response to any feeling, thought or experience that arises. It is used to gain insight into one's true nature.

Ghats: Hindu. A wide set of steps descending to a river, used for bathing. *Also see:* burning *ghats.*

Ghee: Clarified butter, used in Indian cooking and in lamps for ceremonial worship.

Hanuman: A typically Vaishnava deity in the form of a monkey who represents the archetypal and quintessential devotee and helper of Prince Rama in the Hindu epic, the *Ramayana.* Hanuman is an example of the perfect servant or devotee. His impeccable warriorship, courage, strength and unfailing devotion serving Lord Rama is considered the expression of complete surrender to the Will of God.

Influence (Divine Influence): Literally, the Influence of the Divine. A transformative power fully embodied by the spiritual master, and an agent of our alignment to the will of God.

Jayanti: Day of birth. In the Hindu tradition, the guru's birthday is a day of high celebration.

Kali: Aspect of the divine feminine (or Shakti) as Shiva's consort, usually depicted in her "terrible" form, with a necklace of human skulls and a skirt of human arms, eyes bulging and tongue outstretched indicating Shakti force. Kali is an aspect of Shiva's consort Durga, or Parvati, and represents that feminine force which destroys illusion and ego.

Kirta: In India, a long shirt worn by many men; worn over loose fitting pants called pajamas.

Kirtan: Devotional chanting intended to be the expression of adoration, joy, gratitude, awe or the ecstatic surrender to God through music and/or song.

Kundalini: The divine force or power that sleeps "coiled" at the base of the spine (from the root verb, *kund*, "to burn"). In the traditional Indian system of kundalini yoga, this divine power or Shakti (feminine) force must be raised through the six (or seven, depending on the system) spiritual centers of the body, mind, and soul complex to unite with the (masculine) power of Shiva, which resides at the crown of the head. This union of Shiva and Shakti is an inner, esoteric marriage that results in the activation of all divine potencies latent in human beings (wisdom, enlightenment, supreme joy, etc.). The process of awakening kundalini also involves the unraveling of all psychological knots, and can result in intense psychological and physiological phenomena. It is generally considered a powerful and unpredictable force of nature or Shakti, which should only be awakened slowly with the guidance of the spiritual master or guru.

Mela(s): Bengali. Traditional Baul gatherings or fairs where large numbers of *sadikas* or *sadakas* (male and female practitioners) gather to share their practices, songs and dances.

Middleworld: In the shamanistic view of three worlds (upper-, middle- and underworld), it is the domain of ordinary life experience of the human being, in which the body must be protected, fed, clothed if it is to survive, and in which relationships must be established with others. Life lived on earth.

Mudra: A sacred posture, gesture or symbol, usually formed with the hand and fingers but also with the entire body, which represents and communicates subtle dimensions of the Divine. Mudras are used in yogic systems to stimulate the awakening of the kundalini, and are used in both Buddhism and Hinduism.

Namaste: Sanskrit, "honor unto." A greeting phrase used in India, referring to both internal and external obeisance and reverence. Commonly, "The light within me honors the light within you."

Pranam: To bow. The ceremonial bowing by the devotee as a sign of respect toward the deity or the deity embodied in the spiritual master; symbolic of the devotee's vulnerability, gratitude and expression of honor.

Prasad: The ceremonial gift exchanged between devotee and master (guru), symbolic of the reciprocal relationship between the devotee and the master. Usually fruit or flowers from the student and candy, sweets or other gifts from the master. The exchange is symbolic of the devotee's surrender of illusion and egoic will, and the master's transforming of that gross substance and returning it pure and Blessed.

Puja: Worship, specifically religious ceremony. *Puja* is traditionally a specific, formal ritual offered as a prayer to a divine person, object or shrine. The ritual often includes using substances such as ghee, incense, fire, water, flowers, etc. The *puja* ceremony is traditionally conducted by a trained priest, or as in the Western Baul tradition, a *pujari* who is appointed by the spiritual master.

Punjabi: Casual women's garment worn in India. It consists of a pair of loose-fitting pants and a long blouse.

Pushti: Sanskrit, literally means "grace," specifically in the grace freely dispensed by Krishna whether or not scriptural norms have been fulfilled. The "fat" path or path in which the devotee experiences the Divine's extraordinary abundance.

Samsara: Buddhist, from *sam*, "together," and *sri*, "*to flow*"; hence, to flow together. The beginningless cycle of birth, death and rebirth in which all beings are trapped, the results of which entail suffering.

Sangha: One of the three jewels (Buddha, *dharma, sangha*), in which one may take refuge as an aid to liberation, in the Buddhist cosmology. The *sangha* is the community of practitioners.

Tabla: Indian percussion instrument.

Tantra (tantric): Literally "continuum, or thread." A type of spiritual practice in both Hinduism and Buddhism. Some scholars trace the beginnings of tantrism back to the ancient cults of the *Vedas*, while others find elements of tantrism in even more ancient, indigenous and tribal, earth-based Indus culture that existed in India prior to the invasion of the Aryans, originators of the *Vedas*. Tantric or Vajrayana Buddhism is often characterized by its view of all facets of life as natural, but needing to be transformed and subsumed through spiritual practice. Much of tantric practice focuses around rituals and practices related to the Divine Feminine and the basic orientation of kundalini yoga.

Underworld: In the shamanistic worldview, the underworld is the domain of the demons, the residence of life-negative forces, pain, suffering, the darkness. The underworld, however, must be passed through to gain entry to the upperworld.

Upperworld: In the shamanistic cosmology of three worlds (upper-, middle- and underworld) it is the domain of the gods and spirits; the heavenly realm.

Vajrajana Buddhism: The third vehicle or path in Buddhism, which is equated with tantra, or the fast path to realization. *See also: tantra*.

Veda (vedic): The Vedas are a vast set of spiritual teachings dating from the dawn of history. The Vedas are the origin of Hindu religion and culture and have influenced religions and philosophies all over the world. They are centered in the deepest spiritual and self-knowledge, the unity of the individual soul with the Divine. They teach that there is only One Self in the universe, in which is bliss and liberation from the cycle of karma and rebirth. Vedic knowledge expands from this central point to help in understanding the meaning of existence on all levels, including the physical body and the world of nature.

RECOMMENDED READING

—

Desjardins, A. *The Jump into Life: Moving Beyond Fear.* Prescott, Ariz.: Hohm Press, 1994.

Fedorshak, VJ. *The Shadow on the Path: Clearing Psychological Blocks to Spiritual Development.* Prescott, Ariz.: Hohm Press, 1999.

Gopi Krishna. *Kundalini, The Evolutionary Energy in Man.* Shambhala: Distributed in the U.S. by Random House, 1997.

Hulme, K. *The Undiscovered Country: The Search for Gurdjieff.* Revised edition. Lexington, Kentucky: Natural Bridge Editions, 1997. Original copyright, 1966, published by Little, Brown and Company.

Lozowick, L. *Conscious Parenting.* Prescott, Ariz.: Hohm Press, 1997.

Lozowick, L. *The Alchemy of Love and Sex.* Prescott, Ariz.: Hohm Press, 1996.

Mann, J. *Rudi: Fourteen Years with My Teacher.* Portland, Ore.: Rudra Press, 1987.

Miller, A. *The Drama of the Gifted Child.* New York: Basic Books, 1981.

Ouspensky, P.D. *In Search of the Miraculous.* New York: Harcourt, Brace and World, 1949.

Ryan, R. *The Woman Awake: Feminine Wisdom for Spiritual Life.* Prescott, Ariz.: Hohm Press, 1998.

Trungpa Rinpoche, C. *Cutting Through Spiritual Materialism.* Boston and London: Shambhala, 1987.

Tweedie, I. *Daughter of Fire: A Diary of a Spiritual Training with a Sufi Master.* Nevada City, Calif.: Blue Dolphin Publishing, 1986.

Yogananda, P. *Autobiography of a Yogi.* Los Angeles, Calif.: Self-Realization Fellowship, original copyright 1946.

ADDITIONAL TITLES FROM HOHM PRESS

AS IT IS
A Year on the Road with a Tantric Teacher
by M. Young

A first-hand account of a one-year journey around the world in the company of a *tantric* teacher. This book catalogues the trials and wonders of day-to-day interactions between a teacher and his students, and presents a broad range of his teachings given in seminars from San Francisco, California to Rishikesh, India. *As It Is* considers the core principles of *tantra,* including non-duality, compassion (the Bodhisattva ideal), service to others, and transformation within daily life. Written as a narrative, this captivating book will appeal to practitioners of *any* spiritual path. Readers interested in a life of clarity, genuine creativity, wisdom and harmony will find this an invaluable resource.

Paper, 840 pages, 24 b&w photos, $29.95   ISBN: 0-934252-99-8

. . .

THE SHADOW ON THE PATH
Clearing the Psychological Blocks to Spiritual Development
by VJ Fedorschak
Foreword by Claudio Naranjo, M.D.

Tracing the development of the human psychological shadow from Freud to the present, this readable analysis presents five contemporary approaches to spiritual psychotherapy for those who find themselves needing help on the spiritual path. Offers insight into the phenomenon of denial and projection. Topics include: the shadow in the work notable therapists; the principles of inner spiritual development in the major world religions; examples of the disowned shadow in contemporary religious movements; and case studies of clients in spiritual groups who have worked with their shadow issues.

Paper, 304 pages, 6 x 9, $16.95   ISBN: 0-934252-81-5

**TO ORDER PLEASE SEE ACCOMPANYING ORDER FORM
OR CALL 1-800-381-2700 TO PLACE YOUR ORDER NOW.**

ADDITIONAL TITLES FROM HOHM PRESS

HALFWAY UP THE MOUNTAIN
The Error of Premature Claims to Enlightenment
by Mariana Caplan
Foreword by Fleet Maull

Dozens of first-hand interviews with students, respected spiritual teachers and masters, together with broad research are synthesized here to assist readers in avoiding the pitfalls of the spiritual path. Topics include: mistaking mystical experience for enlightenment; ego inflation, power and corruption among spiritual leaders; the question of the need for a teacher; disillusionment on the path . . . and much more.

"Caplan's illuminating book . . . urges seekers to pay the price of traveling the hard road to true enlightenment." —Publisher's Weekly

Paper, 600 pages, $21.95   ISBN: 0-934252-91-2

. . .

CONSCIOUS PARENTING
by Lee Lozowick

Any individual who cares for children needs to attend to the essential message of this book: that the first two years are the most crucial time in a child's education and development, and that children learn to be healthy and "whole" by living with healthy, whole adults. Offers practical guidance and help for anyone who wishes to bring greater consciousness to every aspect of childraising, including: • conception, pregnancy and birth • emotional development • language usage • role modeling: the mother's role, the father's role • the exposure to various influences • establishing workable boundaries • the choices we make on behalf of our children's education ... and much more.

Paper, 384 pages, $17.95   ISBN: 0-934252-67-X

TO ORDER PLEASE SEE ACCOMPANYING ORDER FORM OR CALL 1-800-381-2700 TO PLACE YOUR ORDER NOW.

ADDITIONAL TITLES FROM HOHM PRESS

TOWARD THE FULLNESS OF LIFE:
The Fullness of Love
by Arnaud Desjardins

Renowned French spiritual teacher, Arnaud Desjardins, offers elegant and wise counsel, arguing that a successful love relationship requires the heart of a child joined with the maturity of an adult. This book points the way to realize that blessed union.

Paper, 182 pages, $12.95   ISBN:0-934252-55-6

. . .

THE JUMP INTO LIFE
Moving Beyond Fear
by Arnaud Desjardins
Foreword by Richard Moss, M.D.

"Say *Yes* to life," the author continually invites in this welcome guidebook to the spiritual path. For anyone who has ever felt oppressed by the life-negative seriousness of religion, this book is a timely antidote. In language that translates the complex to the obvious, Desjardins applies his simple teaching of happiness and gratitude to a broad range of weighty topics, including sexuality and intimate relationships, structuring an "inner life," the relief of suffering, and overcoming fear.

Paper, 278 pages, $12.95   ISBN: 0-934252-42-4

TO ORDER PLEASE SEE ACCOMPANYING ORDER FORM
OR CALL 1-800-381-2700 TO PLACE YOUR ORDER NOW.

ADDITIONAL TITLES FROM HOHM PRESS

SIT
Zen Teachings of Master Taisen Deshimaru
edited by Philippe Coupey

 Like spending a month in retreat with a great Zen Master, SIT will "tell it like it is . . ." to both beginners and long-time students of Zen, particularly those who desire an experience of the rigorous Soto tradition in a form that is accessible to Westerners. The primary subject of this series of talks was a comparison between the two schools of Zen: Soto Zen, of which Deshimaru was a teacher and practitioner, and Rinzai Zen. Using the *Rinzai Roku (The Record of Rinzai)* and other traditional texts, the Zen Master made critical commentary and analysis, told stories, and answered the questions of the several hundred participants in attendance. The book derives its name from Deshimaru's strong emphasis on the necessity of sitting practice (zazen) as the living exemplification of all that is taught in the Soto system.

Paper, 420 pages, $19.95, Photographs   ISBN: 0-934252-61-0

• • •

LIVING GOD BLUES
by Lee Lozowick

This book is the first exposition of a twenty-year experiment in both intentional community-living and spiritual practice that has been going on in the United States and Europe. Focused around the author's teaching work, the Hohm Community has grown from a handful of friends and students to a culture of several hundred men, women and children. Drawing from its roots among the Bauls—or Bards of Bengal—a rag-tag bunch of musicians, ecstatic poets and lovers of God, this community of Western Bauls share an eclectic approach to spiritual life, drawing from all the great religious traditions—Sahajia Buddhism, Vaishnava Hinduism, esoteric Christianity, and others. Introductory sections, written by senior students, describe the spiritual practices of the community and spell out principal tenets of the Master's teaching—such as the idea that "God does not live in the sky."

Paper, 168 pages, $9.95   ISBN:0-934252-09-2

**TO ORDER PLEASE SEE ACCOMPANYING ORDER FORM
OR CALL 1-800-381-2700 TO PLACE YOUR ORDER NOW.**

ADDITIONAL TITLES FROM HOHM PRESS

THE ONLY GRACE IS LOVING GOD
by Lee Lozowick

Love, God, Loving God, Grace, Divine Will—these subjects have engaged the minds and hearts of theologians throughout the ages, and even caused radical schisms within organized religions. Lee Lozowick dares to address them again, and in a way entirely original. He challenges all conventional definitions of love, and all superficial assumptions about the nature of loving God, and introduces a radical distinction which he calls the "whim of God" to explain why the random and beneficent Grace of loving God is humanity's ultimate possibility. More than just esoteric musings, *The Only Grace is Loving God* is an urgent and practical appeal to every hungry heart.

Paper, 108 pages, $5.95   ISBN: 0-934252-07-6

...

THE YOGA OF ENLIGHTENMENT/ THE BOOK OF UNENLIGHTENMENT
by Lee Lozowick

Enlightenment, contrary to popular misconceptions, is much more than the experience of the "heaven-realm" of bliss and light. To fully grasp the reality of enlightenment is only possible when one is willing to embrace the other side—the not-knowing, the ignorance, and the darkness. The balance and interdependence of paradoxes is the basis of this book.

Paper, 240 pages, $9.95   ISBN:0-934252-06-8

TO ORDER PLEASE SEE ACCOMPANYING ORDER FORM OR CALL 1-800-381-2700 TO PLACE YOUR ORDER NOW.

ADDITIONAL TITLES FROM HOHM PRESS

THE ALCHEMY OF TRANSFORMATION

by Lee Lozowick

Foreword by: Claudio Naranjo, M.D.

A concise and straightforward overview of the principles of spiritual life as developed and taught by Lee Lozowick for the past twenty years. Subjects of use to seekers and serious students of any spiritual tradition include: A radical, elegant and irreverent approach to the possibility of change from ego-centeredness to God-centeredness—the ultimate human transformation.

Paper, $14.95, 192 pages   ISBN: 0-934252-62-9

. . .

THE ALCHEMY OF LOVE AND SEX

by Lee Lozowick

Foreword by Georg Feuerstein, Ph.D.

Reveals 70 "secrets" about love, sex and relationships. Lozowick recognizes the immense conflict and confusion surrounding love, sex, and tantric spiritual practice. Advocating neither asceticism nor hedonism, he presents a middle path—one grounded in the appreciation of simple human relatedness. Topics include:* what men want from women in sex, and what women want from men * the development of a passionate love affair with life * how to balance the essential masculine and essential feminine * the dangers and possibilities of sexual Tantra * the reality of a genuine, sacred marriage. . .and much more. " ... attacks Western sexuality with a vengeance." —*Library Journal.*

Paper, 312 pages, $16.95   ISBN: 0-934252-58-0

TO ORDER PLEASE SEE ACCOMPANYING ORDER FORM
OR CALL 1-800-381-2700 TO PLACE YOUR ORDER NOW.

ADDITIONAL TITLES FROM HOHM PRESS

PLAYING WITH FIRE
A Search for the Hidden Heart of Rock & Roll
by Steve Ball
Foreword by Felix Cavaliere

As a long-term student of Lee Lozowick's, Steve Ball was organist with Lee's rock and roll band *liars, gods and beggars,* from the very beginning of this grand experiment in alchemy, entertainment and exploration of the underworld. This book tells that story, and many others. From Atlanta, Georgia 1967 ... to Bombay, India 1986 ... to Berlin, 1989 and '90 ... Steve explores the "hidden heart of Rock & Roll" as he traces his own journey —that of a Southern-born, starry-eyed young churchgoer turned rock musician and then D.J. who finds his spiritual master and a whole new context for the music that has always moved his life. He offers invaluable insight into the esoteric implications of Lee's work with this band.

Paper, 304 pages, $16.95, photos   ISBN: 0-934252-72-6

. . .

THE BLUES ALIVE
The Timeless Tradition
by Ed Flaherty of Shri

As a Blues guitar-player, a composer and an avid student of world music, Ed Flaherty traces the history of the Blues from its roots in the American South to the present day. Along the way he points out parallels to the Blues in other cultures, including the flamenco music of the Spanish gypsies, and the soulful laments of the Bauls of Bengal, India. Ed takes the reader on tour and onstage with Shri, the Blues band established in the early '90s. The book is a testimony to the unconquerable human spirit and the African-American music that celebrates it!

Paper, 220 pages, $16.95   ISBN: 0-934252-86-6

**TO ORDER PLEASE SEE ACCOMPANYING ORDER FORM
OR CALL 1-800-381-2700 TO PLACE YOUR ORDER NOW.**

ADDITIONAL TITLES FROM HOHM PRESS

WESTERN SADHUS AND SANNYASINS IN INDIA
by Marcus Allsop

This book contains interviews and stories about a unique group of Western-ers who have lived in India for twenty years or more. Now known as *sadhus* and *sannyasins* (traditional Indian holy men or women), they have renounced the materialistic values of their native culture in favor of a life of austerity and spiritual practice. Their exact numbers are unknown—since many of them have chosen a life of anonymity. Marcus Allsop's pilgrimage takes him from Mt. Arunachala in southern India to the source of the Ganges in the foothills of the Himalayas. He stops at age-old shrines and majestic temples, and shares the powerful insights into Indian spiritual culture that he gains along the way.

Paper, 232 pages, 24 photographs, $14.95   ISBN: 0-934252-50-5

• • •

THE PERFECTION OF NOTHING
Reflections on Spiritual Practice
by Rick Lewis

With remarkable clarity, reminiscent of the early writing of J. Krishnamurti or Alan Watts, Rick Lewis weaves practical considerations about spiritual life with profound mystical understanding. Whether describing the "illusion of unworthiness" that most of us suffer, the challenges of spiritual practice, or his own awe in discovering the majesty of the present moment, this book is full of laser-sharp analogies that make complex philosophical/religious ideas attractive and easy to understand. His nonsectarian approach will be appreci-ated by seekers and practitioners of any religious tradition—whether they are actively engaged in spiritual work, or approaching it for the first time. His words provide guidance and inspiration for revealing the spiritual in every-day life.

Paper, 180 pages, $14.95   ISBN: 1-890772-02-X

**TO ORDER PLEASE SEE ACCOMPANYING ORDER FORM
OR CALL 1-800-381-2700 TO PLACE YOUR ORDER NOW.**

ADDITIONAL TITLES FROM HOHM PRESS

FACETS OF THE DIAMOND
Wisdom of India
By James Capellini

A book of rare and moving photographs, brief biographies, and evocative quotes from contemporary spiritual teachers in the Eastern tradition, including Ramana Maharshi, Swami Papa Ramdas, Sri Yogi Ramsuratkumar, Swami Prajnanpad, Chandra Swami, Nityananda, Shirdi Sai Baba, and Sanatan Das Baul. This mood-altering book richly captures the texture and flavor of the Eastern spiritual path and the teacher-disciple relationship, and offers penetrating insight into the lives of those who carry the flame of wisdom for the good of all humanity.

Cloth , 240 pages, $39.95, 45 b&w photographs   ISBN: 0-934252-53-X

. . .

FOR LOVE OF THE DARK ONE
Songs of Mirabai
Revised edition
Translations and Introduction by Andrew Schelling

Mirabai is probably the best known poet in India today, even though she lived 400 years ago (1498-1593). Her poems are ecstatic declarations of surrender to and praise to Krishna, whom she lovingly calls "The Dark One." Mira's poetry is as alive today as if was in the sixteenth century—a poetry of freedom, of breaking with traditional stereotypes, of trusting completely in the benediction of God. It is also some of the most exalted mystical poetry in all of world literature, expressing her complete surrender to the Divine, her longing, and her madness in love. This revised edition contains the original 80 poems, a completely revised Introduction, updated glossary, bibliography and discography, and additional Sanskrit notations.

Paper, 128 pages, $12.00   ISBN: 0-934252-84-X

**TO ORDER PLEASE SEE ACCOMPANYING ORDER FORM
OR CALL 1-800-381-2700 TO PLACE YOUR ORDER NOW.**

ADDITIONAL TITLES FROM HOHM PRESS

THE WOMAN AWAKE
Feminine Wisdom for Spiritual Life
By Regina Sara Ryan

Though the stories and insights of great women of spirit whom the author has met or been guided by in her own journey, this book highlights many faces of the Divine Feminine: the silence, the solitude, the service, the power, the compassion, the art, the darkness, the sexuality. Read about: the Sufi poetess Rabia (8th century) and contemporary Sufi master Irina Tweedie; Hildegard of Bingen, Mechtild of Magdeburg, and Hadewijch of Brabant: the Beguines of medieval Europe; author Kathryn Hulme *(The Nun's Story)* who worked with Gurdjieff; German healer and mystic Dina Rees ... and many others.

Paper, 35 b&w photos, 520 pages, $19.95   ISBN: 0-934252-79-3

• • •

WOMEN CALLED TO THE PATH OF RUMI
The Way of the Whirling Dervish
by Shakina Reinhertz

This is the first English-language book to share the experience of Turning practice by women of the Mevlevi Order of Whirling Dervishes. The beauty and mystery of the Whirling Dervishes have captured the mythic imagination of the Western world for centuries. Rumi, the great Sufi saint of 13th-century Turkey, taught both male and female students this whirling dance, but in the centuries after his death women were excluded from participation. Not until the late 1970s, when Shaikh Suleyman Dede brought the turn ritual to America, was this practice again opened to women. The heart of the book is the personal experience of contemporary women—interviews with over two dozen American initiates (from adolescents to wise elders), many of whom have practiced on this path for twenty years or more.

"I love the wisdom and fire of this book. It's full of the light of longing and people trying to experience the mystery of that truth." —Coleman Barks, translator of Rumi's poetry.

Paper, 300 pages, $23.95   ISBN: 1-890772-04-6
200 black and white photos and illustrations

**TO ORDER PLEASE SEE ACCOMPANYING ORDER FORM
OR CALL 1-800-381-2700 TO PLACE YOUR ORDER NOW.**

ADDITIONAL TITLES FROM HOHM PRESS

THE YOGA TRADITION
History, Literature, Philosophy and Practice
by Georg Feuerstein, Ph.D.
Foreword by Ken Wilber

A complete overview of the great Yogic traditions of: Raja-Yoga, Hatha-Yoga, Jnana-Yoga, Bhakti-Yoga, Karma-Yoga, Tantra-Yoga, Kundalini-Yoga, Mantra-Yoga and many other lesser known forms. Includes translations of over twenty famous Yoga treatises, like the *Yoga-Sutra* of Patanjali, and a first-time translation of the *Goraksha Paddhati,* an ancient Hatha Yoga text. Covers all aspects of Hindu, Buddhist, Jaina and Sikh Yoga. A necessary resource for all students and scholars of Yoga.

"Without a doubt the finest overall explanation of Yoga ... Destined to become a classic." —Ken Wilber, author of *A Brief History of Everything*

Paper, 520 pages, Over 200 illustrations, $29.95 ISBN: 1-8990772-18-6

. . .

JOURNEY
From Political Activism to the Work
by Janet Rose

This book recounts the story of a spiritual journey that led the author from a life of political and social activism to a life of spiritual transformation. Having worked as a newspaper reporter, a manager of a food cooperative, a coordinator of a rural health service and a VISTA volunteer, Janet Rose thought her next step was to build her practice as a psychotherapist in a large southeastern city. In the summer of 1986, however, almost overnight her life took a radical turn. Following inner mystical guidance, she turned west, to the mountains of Colorado, to "find God more deeply." In her quest for genuine wisdom, compassion and service, she left behind the vestiges of her previous life to pursue a path of renunciation and to apprentice herself to a spiritual teacher. How that choice was made, what that commitment entailed, and how it has changed every aspect of her life is what this book is about.

Paper, 384 pages, $19.95   ISBN: 1-890772-04-6

**TO ORDER PLEASE SEE ACCOMPANYING ORDER FORM
OR CALL 1-800-381-2700 TO PLACE YOUR ORDER NOW.**

RETAIL ORDER FORM FOR HOHM PRESS BOOKS

Name _____ Phone (   ) _____

Street Address or P.O. Box _____

City _____ State _____ Zip Code _____

	QTY	TITLE	ITEM PRICE	TOTAL PRICE	
1		AS IT IS	$29.95		
2		THE SHADOW ON THE PATH	$16.95		
3		HALFWAY UP THE MOUNTAIN	$21.95		
4		CONSCIOUS PARENTING	$17.95		
5		TOWARD THE FULLNESS OF LIFE	$12.95		
6		THE JUMP INTO LIFE	$12.95		
7		SIT	$19.95		
8		LIVING GOD BLUES	$9.95		
9		THE ONLY GRACE IS LOVING GOD	$5.95		
10		YOGA OF ENLIGHTENMENT	$9.95		
11		THE ALCHEMY OF TRANSFORMATION	$14.95		
12		THE ALCHEMY OF LOVE AND SEX	$16.95		
13		PLAYING WITH FIRE	$16.95		
14		THE BLUES ALIVE	$16.95		
15		WESTERN SADHUS AND SANNYASINS	$14.95		
16		THE PERFECTION OF NOTHING	$14.95		
17		FACETS OF THE DIAMOND	$39.95		
18		FOR LOVE OF THE DARK ONE	$12.00		
19		THE WOMAN AWAKE	$19.95		
20		WOMEN CALLED TO THE PATH OF RUMI	$23.95		
21		THE YOGA TRADITION	$29.95		
22		JOURNEY	$19.95		
			SUBTOTAL:		
			*SHIPPING:		
			TOTAL:		

*Please see following page for
shipping charges.

RETAIL ORDER FORM FOR HOHM PRESS BOOKS

SURFACE SHIPPING CHARGES

1st book $5.00

Each additional item $1.00

SHIP MY ORDER

☐ Surface U.S. Mail—Priority   ☐ FEDEX Ground (Mail + $2.00)

☐ 2nd-Day Air (Mail + $5.00)   ☐ Next-Day Air (Mail + $15.00)

METHOD OF PAYMENT:

☐ Check or M.O. Payable to Hohm Press, P.O. Box 2501,

Prescott, AZ 86302

☐ Call 1-800-381-2700 to place your credit card order

☐ Or call 1-520-717-1779 to fax your credit card order

☐ Information for Visa/MasterCard/American Express order only:

Card #_____–_____–_____–_____

Expiration Date_____

Visit our Website to view our complete catalog: www.hohmpress.com

ORDER NOW! Call 1-800-381-2700

or fax your order to 1-520-717-1779.

(Remember to include your credit card information.)

www.hohmpress.com